THE PEARL-POET

The Pearl.

HIS

Translated, with an Introduction, by

POET

COMPLETE WORKS

MARGARET WILLIAMS, R.S.C.J.

VINTAGE BOOKS

A Division of Random House, New York

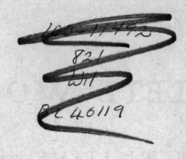

FIRST VINTAGE BOOKS EDITION, February 1970

Copyright © 1967 by Margaret Williams, R.S.C.J.

All rights reserved under International and Pan-American Copyright
Conventions. Published in the United States by Random House, Inc., New York
and simultaneously in Canada by Random House of Canada Limited, Toronto.

Library of Congress Catalog Card Number: 67-12739

Manufactured in the United States of America

PREFACE

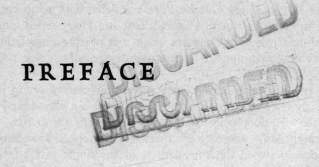

Until recently, knowledge of the Middle English poems attributed to the Pearl-Poet (or the Gawain-Poet) was restricted to scholars, and to specialists at that. *Patience, Cleanness, Sir Gawain and the Green Knight,* and *Pearl* lay concealed in a unique manuscript in the British Museum, all but unread until 1839 when *Sir Gawain* was published for the Bannantyne Club. The other three works appeared in 1867 as *Early English Alliterative Poems,* number 1 of the Early English Text Society. By 1926 separate editions of each, and one of *Saint Erkenwald* (a poem in another manuscript attributed to the same author) had been published. All but *Cleanness* and *Patience* were sporadically translated. Beginning in 1904 a tide of critical work, devoted almost exclusively to *Sir Gawain* and to *Pearl,* has been steadily rising and is now at its height. To follow in chronological order the editions, translations, and articles listed in the bibliography at the end of this book offers an enlightening study in the development of twentieth-century scholarship and criticism. This intense academic interest, this recognition of the artistic worth of poems that all the specialists admit to be masterpieces, points in one direction: to the readers of literature who do not know an obscure dialect of fourteenth-century Middle English.

At last, in 1965, the five poems were placed in the hands of such readers when they appeared for the first time in one volume, *The Complete Works of the Gawain-Poet,* translated with a full commentary by John Gardner. This excellent and long-needed work was published just as the present book was nearing completion, too late to be drawn upon; it is here most appreciatively acknowledged.

Thus two translations have been made simultaneously and independently. Divergences are inevitable. They are also desirable in the case of a poet whose language and content are so rich. A bewilderingly wide range of interpretation lies open. Translators must choose between the emendations of the single text offered by its various editors. Any rendition of the complex metrical patterns into modern English must necessarily fall far short of the original; each translator must follow his own ear and use his own devices. Mr. Gardner's spirited rendition—according to his own statement of purpose—inclines toward freedom in the use of idiom and technique, especially in *Pearl.* The present version follows the structure of the original somewhat more closely. Both methods have their advantages and their hazards. It is good that a variety of renditions should be offered. May there be still more! The desire of all admirers of these inexhaustible poems is that they should be read by more and more lovers of literature.

The present book has grown out of the happy experience of exploring this poetry with students of Manhattanville College, whose response has been the translator's constant encouragement. The work owes more than can be expressed to the strong, enlightening and devoted guidance of Dr. William Alfred of Harvard University. It owes most to the privilege of sharing—through years of pondering study—the vision of a poet distant in time but near in thought, the Pearl-Poet himself.

M. W.

Manhattanville College
Easter, 1966 °

CONTENTS

CONTENTS

INTRODUCTION

THE BOOK AND
ITS MAKER

The Past in the Present

> Seasons shall not cease for you, nor seed nor harvest,
> nor heat nor hard frost, nor rain nor drought,
> nor the sweetness of summer, nor the sober winter,
> nor night nor day, nor the new years,
> but all run on, restless; you shall reign over them.
>
> (*Cleanness*, 523–27)

What the Pearl-Poet wrote in the fourteenth century, T.S. Eliot has echoed in the twentieth: "Time past and time present/Are both perhaps present in time future." [1] Eliot was once asked why he drew so much from the thinkers of the past since "we know so much more than they did." He answered: "Precisely. They are what we know." He claimed that every poet should have the historical sense that "involves a perception not only of the pastness of the past but of its presence." What Eliot asks of every poet, poetry itself asks of every reader, a consciousness "not of what is dead but of what is living." This simultaneity of experience can be gained by reading, for in literature "the existing monuments form an ideal order among themselves." To read the poetry of the past is, for the modern reader, "to become most acutely conscious of his place in time, of his own contemporaneity." [2]

The work of the Pearl-Poet belongs in this "ideal order," but it has hardly been recognized as part of the *continuum* of English literature. He is as great a poet as his famous contemporaries, Chaucer and Langland, but he has not yet made the past present to us as they have done. He has no name, in his medieval diffidence, and will here be called the Pearl-Poet, or simply the Poet. His difficult dialect is one excuse for this loss. A translation of the poems attributed to him, placed against the background of their own traditions, will allow his living voice to reach us. He promises:

> If you will listen to this lay but a little while,
> I will tell it straight off, as I heard it in town
>   by tongue,
>   as it is set, well-stocked,
>   in a story brave and strong,
>   with true letters interlocked,
>   told in this land for long.
>   (*Sir Gawain and the*
>   *Green Knight,* 30–36)

The Manuscript

> Thanne mote we to bokes that we fynde,
> Thurgh whiche that olde thinges be in mynde,
> And to the doctrine of these olde wyse
> Yeve credence in every skilful wise
> That tellen of these olde approved stories.
>
> . . . .
>
> And if that olde bokes were aweye,
> Yloren were of remembraunce the keye.
>   (*Legend of Good Women,*
>   Prologue, F, 17–22)

Unlike Chaucer, the Pearl-Poet has left us only one "key of remembrance," which was nearly lost more than once. Each manuscript is literally unique, and in the Middle Ages each was valued accordingly. As early as the ninth century an Anglo-Saxon poet had sung:

> Books are glorious; they give in earnest
> a wise will to him who wonders.
>
> . . . .
>
> Strong is he who tastes of book-lore.[1]

Richard de Bury, the fourteenth-century bibliophile, would give any price asked for a book, "because if wisdom alone, which is an infinite treasure to men, determines the price of books, and if the value of books is ineffable, as the premises suppose, how can a bargain be proved dear which purchases an infinite benefit?" Then, with perverse realism, he insists that any borrower of one of his books must leave a surety "in excess of its value" with at least three librarians! He lamented the ravages that come to books, by fire and by "war, more injurious to books than all other plagues," [2] and by readers who set wet beer mugs on the patient script. There were also the original bookworms to be reckoned with, for whenever "a moth ate words,/a worm swallowed the songs of a man." [3]

The priceless book holding the works of the Pearl-Poet is in the British Museum, MS Cotton Nero A.X. It is a thick quarto volume, measuring only seven by five inches. Folios 37 through 126 contain the only existing copies of *Pearl, Cleanness, Patience,* and *Sir Gawain and the Green Knight,* in that order. (The only other poem attributed to the same author is *Saint Erkenwald,* found in a separate manuscript.) The scribe is nameless; his sharp script, crowded but evenly spaced, is not found elsewhere; it dates the manuscript c. 1400. He was probably a speaker of the same dialect as the author, though from an area slightly further north. He neatly followed the ruled lines that reach from margin to margin, but he had a bad habit of turning the page before the ink was dry, and was careless in other ways. The poems have no titles. Capital letters, varying from two to sixteen lines in height, are done in red and blue, with long spidery flourishes; from some letters peep the comic faces that few rubricators could resist. An illustrator—crude and bold, with vivid insight—did twelve pictures in red, blue, green, and yellow. All the figures have faces too large for their bodies, round-eyed and lopsided; the hands are enormous and energetic. The costumes show the styles of Richard II, whereas the text describes those of Edward III. The manuscript is unsigned, but scribbled on the first page of *Sir Gawain,* in a different hand, is the baffling name "Hugo de." [4]

The book was finished in the early fifteenth century, then it disappeared from history. It probably lay in the library of some northern monastery or baronial manor until the middle of the sixteenth century, becoming unreadable as the English language underwent drastic changes. By then the Middle Ages had been submerged in the high tide of the Renaissance, followed by that of the Reformation. When the monasteries were despoiled under

Henry VIII, manuscripts were destroyed or used for their parchment value. Some became the inner lining of the new printed volumes, where their colors can be seen today, bright through the crumbling leather. The Pearl-Poet's book escaped and made its way into the library of Sir Henry Savile (1568–1617) of Bank, Yorkshire. His cataloguer described it as "an owld booke in English verse beginning 'Perle pleasant to princes pay' in 4⁰ limned."

Scholars then realized that a whole culture was being lost, and retrieved as many as possible of the scattered manuscripts. The newly founded Society of Antiquaries first met in Cotton House, London, where Robert Bruce Cotton stored his remarkable collection. He acquired the Pearl-Poet's book. Richard James, his librarian, managed to read the opening lines and wrote a sweeping description of the whole volume: "Vetus Poema Anglicanum, in quo, sub insomnii figmento, multa ad religionem et mores spectantia explicantur." He bound it, without regard to its contents, between two Latin works: a panegyric by Justin de Jury on John Chadworth, Bishop of Lincoln, dated July 16, 1416, and some theological excerpts in a thirteenth-century hand, ending with the words: "Epitaphium de Ranulpho, Abbate Ramesiensi" (1231–53). In Cotton's library, books were catalogued according to their places in one or other of fourteen presses, surmounted by busts of Cleopatra, Faustina, and twelve Roman Emperors. The Pearl-Poet's book became Cotton Nero A.X.

Robert Cotton's collection, enlarged by his son Thomas, was given to the British nation in 1700, and the 958 volumes were transferred to Ashburnham House where, in 1731, a fire broke out among those manuscripts, each "worth wisdom itself," the worst of the disasters lamented by Richard de Bury! The "greedy ghost" (as an Old English *scop* would have called it) consumed 114 books and injured 98. The Pearl-poems once more escaped. In 1753 the collection was taken to the British Museum. Very slowly, interest in their author, a "Master Anonymous," [5] awoke.

The Language

The first clue to the identity of this nameless poet is the language in which he wrote. There were three main linguistic areas in Middle English: Northern, above the Humber; Southern, below the Thames; and between them Midlands, divided into East and West. Of these dialects Southeast Midlands is the one most easily read today, the language of London and of Chaucer, the "King's English" which became the medium of modern English literature. The most difficult is Northwest Midlands. In this part of England, remoter than others from the violent changes of history, the Norman domination was less strong. Old English traditions were tenacious, and archaic words and constructions lingered on. Danes and Norwegians had settled here between 876 and 950, more peaceably than on the eastern coast; many Norse words had become part of the English vocabulary. Thus literature from this area drew upon four sources: the poetic vocabulary common to Middle English everywhere; the French vocabulary, drawn from Anglo-Norman and built up by constant reading in French literature; Anglo-Saxon heroic language, archaic but kept alive by oral tradition; and local Norse words.

Tests of phonology, syntax, accidence, and rhyme, as well as of vocabulary, place the Pearl-Poet in this Northwest Midlands area. Verb endings, plural forms, the treatment of vowels and consonants, local expressions and place names, narrow the locality of his probable home to North Cheshire, North Derby, the West Riding of York, or Lancashire. The most conclusive scholarship favors south Lancashire, in the neighborhood of the Ribble and Aire valleys.[1]

Did the poet, a well-educated and presumably traveled man to whom the more standard dialect of London would have been familiar, deliberately choose his native speech of a remote shire, in the same spirit in which Dante chose his Tuscan speech for a great poem? In the *Convivio* Dante had said: "A man's vernacular is closest to him . . . to body forth excellently the idea."[2] In any case, other poets around him were doing the same thing.

The Alliterative Movement

The poetic techniques of Anglo-Saxon England had also clung to this region. Old English poetry, indefinitely old in its heroic spirit and form, had been written down under Christian auspices between the eighth and eleventh centuries in the characteristic Teutonic prosody, the alliterative line. This was accentual rather than quantitative as in languages derived from Latin; it was formed of clustering patterns of lifts and drops, feet of five different types which could be used interchangeably. The drops could contain more than one syllable. Each half-line or hemistich held two feet, linked together by alliteration. Rhyme was rarely used. These patterns have become familiar to the modern ear in the cadences of free verse.[1]

After the Norman Conquest, as French and English blended into Middle English, the rhymed syllabic meters of French poetry derived from the classic system took hold of English poetry. But the old prosody, first chanted by a *scop* to the harp, never lost its hold in the western shires. Between 1000 and 1250 it was perpetuated in many forms. In the monastery it was used in pieces like the Worcester Fragment which lamented the passing of the Old English writers:

> Their light was not dark, but it glowed fair;
> Now their lore is lost and their folk forlorn.

It was heard in castle halls where knights were warned by the "Lament of the Soul to the Body," and in village huts where the peasants chanted "Rats Away!" In church it was kept familiar by vernacular sermons in the style of Aelfric. The *Ancren Riwle* and the saints' lives of the Katharine Group used alliterative prose artistically. The popular *Proverbs of Alfred* shows the hemistich struggling with the new couplet form:

> Alfred was in England
> A king very strong.
> He was king and he was clerk,
> Well he loved God's work.

And the *Bestiary* used both French and Anglo-Saxon meters deliberately.

About 1205 a priest named Layamon, near the Severn River in the west, "lovingly took a feather in his fingers/And wrote on book-skin." His epic-length *Brut*, echoing the phrasing and the spirit of *Beowulf*, was English, not Norman, in inspiration. It shaped the Old English line to the character of Middle English speech. Teutonic though it was, King Arthur and his Celtic magic appeared in it. For many years after *Brut* only a few religious lyrics like "The Wooing of Our Lord" were written down in the alliterative meter; the French forms held sway.

But the old poetic way had not died. About 1350, when the Pearl-Poet was young, it surged up in the Northwest Midlands. Its users formed a "school," now known as the Alliterative Movement, which lasted for about fifty years. Its causes are unknown. Perhaps it was connected with baronial resistance to the court; it was composed for an aristocratic audience in a style and vocabulary different from those of London. It was possibly patriotic, expressing English pride in its heroic past. From Glousterchire to Cumberland it had patrons in the castles of the great magnates: the Mortimers, the Bohuns, the Beauchamps. It was not a consciously "learned revival," but was the flowering of a continuous tradition that had been running parallel, in oral form, to the French tradition that culminated in these same years in the poetry of Chaucer. By 1400 the movement had spent itself in England, though it continued for another fifty years in Scotland.[2]

This poetry was not popular but highly artistic, appealing to cultivated listeners—for it was still recited orally for entertainment, even at a time when literature had as many readers as listeners. In vocabulary as well as prosody it was archaic; it used formulaic phrases, rich poetic diction with endless synonyms, traditional patterns and figures of speech like the kenning. But the poets were educated and up to date; they blended this ancient matter with new forms such as the dream convention. They could combine the alliterative lines with stanza grouping and linking. At their worst they were loose, verbose, repetitious, formlessly episodic, formulaic. But even the worst were full of energy, exuberance, and zest, writing with strength and purpose.

Only one name can be connected with the movement, that of William Langland, author of *Piers Plowman*, who wrote in the Southwest Midlands dialect and lived in London. Other satires and political or religious allegories were grouped around his name: *Richard the Redeless, Wynner and Waster, The Parlement of the Three Ages*, and *Death and Life*. But further north, poetry dealt not with the "field full of folk" of contemporary England, but with the borderless world of heroic romance where the Nine

Worthies met their adventures. It stretched from Britain into France, then into the Holy Land and on to India, with fairy-land overlapping at every point. There were chronicles in epic form: *The Wars of Alexander, Alexander A and B*, the *Destruction of Troy*, and the *Morte Arthure*. There were out-and-out romances: *William of Palerne*, full of shape-shifting, *Chevelre Assigne* (Godfrey of Bouillon) bent on the Crusades, *Golagrus and Gawain*, and the *Awntyrs of Arthur*. The core of the grail legend was found in *Joseph of Arimathie*. There were a few religious poems, The *Pistyl of Susan* and *John the Evangelist*.[3]

These poems (anonymous but for Langland's) have much in common. The alliterative meter lent itself to a tone of high moral earnestness, lit with a vivid sense of beauty and abounding high spirits, which marks the whole group. These poets are serious, religious, moral, and cultured men, masters of description and of a rich and distinctive vocabulary. In the Pearl-Poet alone there is a distinctive style that raises his works to greatness.

The Author

Clues to the identity of the Pearl-Poet must be drawn from his works; no contemporary document mentions him. His life covered the same years as those of Chaucer and Langland, c. 1335 to c. 1400. For a poet who knew castle life there is surprisingly little echo of current events in his work, which must have been done between c. 1360 and 1390. Edward III and Richard II had exciting reigns. The Poet was born into warfare. The wars for Scottish independence kept the countryside near his home on the alert. In the Hundred Years' War, fought out in France, gunpowder was heard on the battlefield for the first time, sounding doom to the armored knight. The struggle of the Barons against the Crown and of the Crown against Parliament kept the whole of England in unrest. As a boy the Poet lived through the Black Death. As a man he felt the shocks of the Peasants' Revolt, of the political and economic upheavals that marked the end of feudalism, and of the intellectual ferment in the universities raised by thinkers like William of Occam. In his old age he may have seen the deposition of a king.

In the broader field of Christendom he saw the Babylonian Captivity of the Popes at Avignon, and the woes within the Church at which Dante had cried out in the *Divine Comedy*. In 1377 Gregory XI returned the Papacy to Rome. Under Urban VI the Great Western Schism broke out, and by 1400 Boniface IX was facing the anti-Popes. Corruption in the Church and in the religious orders was both cause and effect of these troubles. Langland caught the scene at the close of *Piers Plowman*, where Anti-Christ storms the Barn of Unity and not even Conscience knows where Piers has gone. Chaucer rode to Canterbury by the side of the worldly monk and the sacrilegious pardoner. One writer stormed angrily, the other smiled shrewdly. Did the Pearl-Poet, their equal in vision and in poetic power, find an ivory tower in his North Country? Or did he see the scene from another angle, with an insight all his own, and comment in a different style? His poems must be searched for an answer. In the meantime, who could he have been?

Attempts have been made to find him in other writers. Huchown of the *Awle Ryale* was first proposed. This Scottish poet is known only by a reference made by Wyntown in *The Orygynale Cronikel of Scotland*, c. 1390:

> Men of gud dyscretyowne
> Salt excuse and love Huchown;
> . . . .
> he cunnand was in literature.
> He made the gret geste of Arthure
> And the Awntyre of Gawane,
> The Pystel als of Swete Susane.
> (254, 273)

The name "Hugo de" scribbled on the opening page of *Sir Gawain and the Green Knight* could be Huchown's. Nielson urged, unconvincingly, that Huchown was the author of *The Awntyrs of Arthure*, *Pearl*, and *Saint Erkenwald* on the ground of common indebtedness to Gregory's *Trentals*, a work in which Gregory's mother appears first as a hideous ghost to ask prayers for her sins, and then as a bright soul crowned in heaven. But the possibilities of Huchown's identity with the Pearl-Poet have been dismissed on philological grounds.[1]

Gollancz claimed as author of *Pearl* and *Saint Erkenwald* one of the friends to whom Chaucer dedicated *Troilus and Criseyde*:

> O moral Gower, this book I directe
> To the and to the, philosophical Strode.
> (V, 1856–57)

Ralph Strode was a logician at Oxford, and may be the poet of the same name who was at Merton College in 1360. He may also be the Sergeant of London named Strode who lived near Chaucer and died in 1387. The Merton College catalogue states that "Ralph Strode was a noble poet who wrote a book in elegiac poetry called the Dream (or vision, *phantasma*) of Ralph." Gollancz considers this a description of *Pearl*, and adds that a Sergeant of London would have been interested in a legend of Saint Erkenwald. But it is not likely that the two (or three) are the same man.[2]

Two other names proposed are connected with the Pearl-Poet's North Country. The first is that of John d'Erghome, an Augustinian Canon at York, who died in 1390. He wrote a Latin poem, *The Prophecy of John of Briddlington*, in which parallels to *Sir Gawain* and to *Cleanness* have been found. The library in his monastery had many of the books which the Pearl-Poet used as sources, but the similarities end there.[3]

The second name is hypothetical: Hugh de Mascy. This starts from "Hugo de" again. Then, in the manuscript containing *Saint Erkenwald*, two names are written in the margins: "Thomas Masse, Esquier," and "Easybyt Bothe at Dunham in the Comytye of Chester." Thomas Mascy was a trustee in 1495 for Elizabeth Mascy's marriage to George Booth. The names Hugh and Marjorie had been common in that aristocratic Norman family for generations. Now the Pearl-Poet seems to have had a strong interest in numerology (witness his patterns of threes and twelves), and the numerical significance of the letters in the name Hugh de Mascy adds up to 101, the number of stanzas in both *Pearl* and *Sir Gawain*. Is this an ingenious acrostic by way of signature? A study of the numerical significance of the coat of arms of the Mascy family adds further evidence, as does a well-concealed pun in line 730 of *Pearl*, "a perle wat3 mascelle3," which can be translated as "a Marjory that was a Mascy."[4]

Another clue leads to the court of Edward III, a pearl-fancier who gave 2,000 of these popular gems to his daughter Margaret at her marriage to John Hastings, Earl of Pembroke. Their infant daughter, also named Margaret, died at the age of two: "Thou didst not live two years in our land" (482). An elegy in honor of so royal a Pearl would be called for. Her father, no poet, was not the type of man to see a vision of heavenly glory. But he had many friends who were poets, of the school that delighted in the French cult of the marguerite. Among his connections at the court of Edward one has been found by the name of John Donne! [5]

Another connection with a great name has been made through *Sir Gawain*. Savage would like to find the Pearl-Poet (still nameless) in a member of the household of Enguerrand de Courcy, a French nobleman sent to England in 1363 as a hostage by John II. He was so favorably received that two years later he married Isabella, daughter of Edward III, was given estates in Lancashire, and was made Earl of Bedford. In 1377 he returned to France, leaving his wife and all his possessions. The romance might have been written to commemorate his wedding, or his reception into the Order of the Garter that had been founded in 1348, the motto of which was added in the manuscript: "Hony soyt qui mal pence." The poem says that on the night of Gawain's arrival at Bercilak's castle he dons a robe emblazoned with heraldic *vair*, like the coat of arms of the de Courcy family; on his last night there he wears a blue mantle with surcoat and hood lined with white, the ceremonial robes of the Order of the Garter. Perhaps a devoted clerk in de Courcy's household wrote the poem to console and honor his patron at the time of his disgrace.[6]

After these attempts to place the Poet in history, one can only turn back to his poetry itself. In the West Derby section of Lancashire, or the neighboring counties where his language places him, is the landscape of his poems; here are the weather, the trees and shrubs and flowers that formed his pictorial imagination as a boy. Here are the moorlands rising into hills that wear "mist-hats" in threatening weather; here are the woods good for hunting with their copses and crags; here are the streams, wells, falls, and pools that have given the recurrent imagery of running water to his poems. A land of austere and lovable beauty, with strong seasonal changes, with winds, clouds, and brilliant flowers, stirred his keen perceptions of color, sound, scent, and touch.

It was a land of castles and manors. Whether of noble blood or not, the Poet knew court life from within: feasts where courses

were announced by trumpets; small talk around the fire after
dinner; etiquette and dancing; the grooming of horses and the
lowering of drawbridges. These were bred into him, and formed
the basis of his *cortayse*. But he was more than a courtier; he knew
books outside the reading habits of knights and squires. He must
have been some kind of "clerk." He himself says:

> I have listened and heard from many learned clerics,
> and also, as is right, I have read it myself.
>
> (*Cleanness*, 193–94)

Where did he find the education that gave intellectual and artistic
dimensions to his work? He may have attended, as a boy, one of
the choir schools attached to churches at a time when "all good
Englishmen were singers" and accompanied themselves on the
small, vibrant musical instruments which Fra Angelico placed in
angel hands. The poet knew them well: the guitars and "royal
ringing viols" of courtly "glee" heard around Our Lady in *Cleanness;* the trumpets and hunting horns in *Sir Gawain;* the organ and
the "bright bursts of singing from the church choir" in *Saint
Erkenwald,* fit to become the "new song" heard in *Pearl.* Such
training in tone and rhythm would have made him the excellent
versifier that he was.[7]

After that he may have studied law. There are many legalisms in
Cleanness; the Judge in *Saint Erkenwald* describes his practice
clearly; the Green Knight and his other self, Bercilak, form legally
binding covenants with Sir Gawain; the maiden in *Pearl* argues like
any lawyer in dealing with valid requirements for entering heaven,
"the court where all causes must be tried" (700).[8] Legal training
would have developed that sense of the order required by divine
law which is the very pattern of each poem.[9]

His knowledge in wider fields, his informal and unpedantic
command of learned sources, smack more of browsing in the
library of some West Midland monastery, such as Whalley or
Furney, than of lectures in a university classroom. This natural
storyteller shows his wide range of reading unobtrusively. A listing
of the books suggested by scholars as sources or analogues of his
poetry reveals surprising breadth in his trilingual curriculum:

The Vulgate, both Old and New Testaments
Guillaume de Lorris and Jean de Meun, *The Romance of the Rose*

Alliterative romances and chronicles, e.g., *Wars of Alexander* and *Morte Arthure*

Alliterative allegories, e.g., *Wynnere and Wastour, Parliament of the Three Ages*

The Book of the Travels of John Mandeville

Langland, *Piers Plowman*

Religious lyrics of the Northwest, e.g., *Pety Job*

Dante, *Divine Comedy, Vita Nuova, Convivio*

Boccaccio, *Olympia*

Boethius, *Consolations of Philosophy*

Virgil, *Aeneid*

Chaucer, *Book of the Duchess, Legend of Good Women*

Tertullian, *De Patientia, De Jona et Nineve*

Marco Polo, *Travels* (French version)

Peter of Comestor, *Historia Scholastica*

Cursor Mundi

Andreas Capellanus, *De Arte Honesti Amandi*

The Book of the Knight of the Tour Landry

The Book of Vices and Virtues

Ayenbit of Inwit

Lapidaries

Legends of the Jews

Bishop Bradwardine, *De Causa Dei Contra Pelagium*

Saints' legendaries, e.g., *Legenda Aurea*

Encyclopedic works, e.g., *Speculum Christiani*, Vincent of Beauvais, *Speculum Morale*

Exegetical commentaries, e.g., Rupert of Deutz, *Commentarium in Jonam Prophetam*, Haymo of Halberstad, *Enerratio in Jonam*, Bede, *Explanatio Apocalypsis*, Rabanus Maurus, *Allegoriae in Sacram Scripturam*

Albertus Magnus, *De Laudibus Beatae Mariae*

St. Augustine, e.g., *Sermones, Enerratio in Psalmos*

Richard Rolle, *Form of Perfect Living, Prick of Conscience*

Matthew of Vendome, *Ars Versificatoria*

Geoffrey of Vinsauf, *Poetria Nova*

Chrétien de Troyes, *Livre de Caradoc*

Other French romances, e.g., *Parlevaus*, and the Vulgate Cycle

Celtic and Welsh romances (indirectly?)

Middle English sermons and catechisms

Manuals on penance

At this point conjecture takes over. Was he an ecclesiastic, in priestly or in minor orders? In the latter case, he could have been married, as was Langland. Or was he a devout, well-educated layman, either noble or a member of some nobleman's suite, perhaps his secretary? If he married, did he lose an infant daughter at the age of two, as *Pearl* implies? Did he go through poverty and trial, as *Patience* implies? Did he travel and know London well, as *Saint Erkenwald* implies? Experienced in more than one way of life, did he write homilies and a saint's story for edification, a romance for entertainment, and an elegiac dream-allegory to express his own spiritual life?

It is possible to combine the evidence into a temptingly facile pattern, rearranging the order of the poems to suit it. A romantic young aristocratic, well read and devout, marries; he loses his wife and daughter, enters a monastery, and becomes a contemplative. If so, *Pearl* may be biographical. Or a young clerical student receives orders and then, under the patronage of a nobleman, develops his talents and expresses his wide human interests in a variety of poems. If so, *Pearl* may be fictional. The events of his life may be arranged to every student's taste.

But no matter who he was or what he did, he was born to write poetry. He had vision, a rich poetic inheritance, and finely trained craftsmanship. His artistry holds the five poems together as the work of a single man. Scholars have accepted as relatively certain the common authorship of the four poems in the Cotton MS and, with less assurance, of *Saint Erkenwald*.[10] This agreement rests upon tests of language, vocabulary, and prosody, but more convincing are the similarities in imagery, tone, insight, ideas, and cultural background found throughout. Most convincing is the distinctive personal stamp of genius, hardly to be found in more than one man in the same place and at the same time.

Thus, despite diversity in subject matter, the poems share dominant characteristics. The first is the Poet's manner of handling his own resonant dialect. He wrote "as a man who loved words and sat down to his vocabulary as a musician to his instrument." [11] It was a three-handed instrument; he drew out the Anglo-Saxon, Norse, or French stops at will, with onomatopoetic power. The words released become alive; they gesture; they give in sound the sensations of bodily movement, of touch, and of sight. The overtones change from poem to poem, as scenes and speakers change or the musician shifts his key with his theme. But some words appear like tonic notes in all; such is *wyrd*, the ancient Nordic name for fate, which became, in Anglo-Saxon poetry, man's destiny freely accepted, and finally divine Providence, as Christ took charge of His thanes. Some words of obscure origin are unique to this poet: *nurne* (to speak or make known) and *runisch* (mysterious). He uses a wide sweep of technical terms drawn from up-to-date life in the fourteenth century with the accuracy of experience: hunting and musical terms, scholastic and liturgical terms, and the unclassifiable words of daily conversation. These are blended with formulaic phrases older than any written poetry, the alliterative words linked by unbreakable sound patterns, the archaic, ornate, and elevated diction of the heroic stock, with its untranslatable wealth of synonyms for the simplest realities: ten for the notion of a man! He uses *kay* (left) and *misy* (swamp) with some seventy-six other words that survive today in the Lancashire dialect, and he uses (or coins) Latinate theological terms like *pertermynable*. His is a consecrated poetic diction used with originality.[12]

In controlling this lavish vocabulary, the Poet had command of two metrical forms: the Anglo-Saxon made current by the Alliterative Movement, and the French used in all other Middle English poetry.[13] He could combine them, in sharp contrast in *Sir Gawain* or with elusive subtlety in *Pearl*. He gives the verse-movement in both systems a buoyant, athletic rapidity; he gives clean-cut contours to the lavish outpouring of words. And within each shapely line is found the essence of poetry, the heightening of sound to "articulate music," words "raised to their highest intensity"—Eliot's idea of poetry. Like the miller in the ballad of "The Two Sisters," this poet "Set his harp upon a stone/ And straight it began to sing along." All the poems:

> evince their writer's knowledge of vowel and consonantal quality, his awareness of that elusive but very real nexus between sound and sense, the quickness of his imaginative powers. . . . These exalt our author above his less gifted brethren of the school. Nor need he dread comparison with Chaucer as metrist, for he seldom wrote a line lacking in zest or imagination or rhythm, and Chaucer sometimes did. To say so much is simply to say that he was past master of his medium.[14]

Each poem is structured with architectonic skill according to its own design; the story-lines and the thought-lines unfold together, reach a climax together, and end in unison. These same lines, curved or tapering, flower as do the lines of Gothic structure into repeating images supplied by his "ain contree," images of wind and water, beast and bird, flower and mountain, all sharply experienced. His life at court gave his work the texture of rich fabric. His hours in the library let it speak with the voices of old books. From his hours of prayer came the loved Scripture texts that link the poems by their haunting echo in one after the other. In each poem the voice of the narrator-commentator is heard in the fashion of the oral storyteller: "Listen, while I tell"; "So it seems to me"; "This would be too tiresome to describe." And like a cryptic signature is the Poet's way of echoing the first line of a poem at its close, before he says "Amen."

Thus paradoxical traits of the same rare personality appear in all poems: earnestness and humor, realism and fantasy, exuberance and discipline, bright color and firmly delicate line. All this adds up to style:

> For every man who creates great poems there is an infinite truth, of grandeur and terror, in the adage: "Style is the man himself," that there must be in him and in those who would read him, all of the human possibilities which can be realized in his works.[15]

To pass through style to the inner life of the "Master Anonymous," each poem must first be considered in its genesis and in its artistic totality.

BACKGROUND OF
THE POEMS

Critical Approach

A medieval poem does not now speak easily. Not only its language but also its aesthetic principles need translating. It must be approached through the *milieu* of its author. Only study can make possible a free response to it as a work of art. A poetry reader today expects to make such a response, trained as he has been by the New Criticism and by "close reading." Modern criticism aims at a direct apperception of form, of that which actualizes the matter of a poem into the organic unit that is the poem itself. A work of art is a significant structure alive with its own being, its own beauty. And "the degree of beauty, that is, of aesthetic fulfillment, will be determined by the degree to which the formal actualization has been harmonious and complete." [1] Since medieval poems were produced in accord with medieval aesthetics, it may be best to approach them as their first readers (or listeners) would have done. This method may show the Pearl-Poet's work to be surprisingly modern.

The medieval poetic came from two sources: the study of the literature of Greece and Rome as it filtered through the post-classical Schools of Rhetoric into the compositions of monastery, chancery, and university, and the application of the exegetical methods of the Fathers of the Church. The resulting literary criticism theorized about poetry, laid down rules for writing it, then related it to the other disciplines of education and—most importantly—to man's ultimate end: salvation.

Classical studies began as soon as the Church outgrew the catacombs; it took hold of its pagan inheritance as something to be treasured and put to work. The grammatical models of Quintilian, the rhetorical models of Cicero's *De Inventione* and the anonymous *Rhetorica ad Herennium*, and the *Ars Poetica* of Horace were amplified and allegorized into the massive works of Macrobius and Martiana Capella. Virgil and Horace were imitated and "moralized." As the Seven Liberal Arts became the bases of education under Boethius and Cassiodorus, poetry was drawn into the Trivium as a division of Rhetoric. From the schools of Chartres and Orleans came teachers like Bernard of Sylvester, and humanists like John of Salisbury and Alanus de Insulis. The twelfth-century Renaissance broke out. The wandering scholars sang their way into all the vernaculars. Europe was flooded with poetry; it was time for handbooks of the poetic craft to appear, with a new name for it: *poetria.*

The *Ars Versificatoria* of Matthew of Vendome (1175) was followed by the *Poetria Nova* of Geoffrey of Vinsauf (1210) and the *Poetria* of John of Garland (c. 1250). They applied the rules of rhetoric to poetry, and schematized them for classroom use. Matthew defined verse as:

> metrical speech proceeding in a succinct and controlled manner, by a happy marriage of words, and adorned by little flowers of fine sayings; it contains nothing too little and nothing too much. It is formed not of a mere collection of words, but of words in tasteful combination, and by the exactly right descriptive epithet for everything. (I, 1)

The subject matter was to be drawn from tradition, and could be treated, according to its nature, "in a high, low or middle style."

The work of Geoffrey of Vinsauf (written in hexameters) was the best known of these treatises in England; it is he upon whom Chanticleer mock-heroically calls in Chaucer's *Nun's Priest's Tale:*

> O Gaufred, deere maister soverayn,
>
> . . . .
>
> Why ne hadde I now thy sentence and thy loore?
> (VII, 3347–50)

Poetria Nova insists on the seriousness of the poet's craft:

> If you must build a house, run not to the act
> With impetuous hands; deep in your inner heart
> The work must be long pondered, as to form,

> With the heart's hand rather the body's.
> This form is the archetype.
>
> (43–47)

In building the poetic artifact, certain methods will ensure attractiveness, and will make it "a piece of rhetoric set to music, to move the heart's of men," as has been said of *Troilus and Criseyde*.[2] In brief: 1) To begin a poem, be either natural (begin at the beginning), or artificial (begin in the middle). 2) End it with an aphorism, or something memorable or instructive. 3) Develop the narrative by the skillful use of *amplificatio* (there are seven types) and *abbrevatio* (there are seven types) of the source. 4) Add beauty by the use of the Ornaments of Style, known as "Colors of Rhetoric," of which there are:

- a) ten difficult devices, or Tropes, such as onomatopoeia, metaphor, transposition of words, expressions with hidden meanings;
- b) thirty-four easy devices, or Figures of Speech, such as repetition, reversal, antithesis, balance, exclamation;
- c) nineteen Figures of Thought, such as description, comparison, suggestion, example, simile, personification, dilemma, inuendo.

Vincent of Beauvais summed up the matter in his *Speculum Doctrinale*:

> Alphorabius puts *poetria* last among the parts of *logica;* in his book on the origin of the *scientiae* he describes it thus: "*Poetica* is the lore of ordering meters according to the proportion of words and the times of feet and of their rhythms." Again he says: "It belongs to *poetica* to make the hearer, through its locutions, image something as fair or foul which is not so in truth, nevertheless, the minds of hearers are roused to shun or desire what they imagine. . . . The function, then, of the poet is this: that with a certain beauty he converts actual events into other species by his slanting figures.[3]

All this applied primarily to Latin poetry, but it affected the vernaculars as well. Dante, in *De Vulgari Eloquentia* that put native poetry on a level with Latin, claimed that a poem was "a rhetorical composition set to music." Deschamps wrote a manual for French verse, *L'Art de Dictier et de Fere les Chançons*. English writers knew that poetry must persuade through style, and they knew which "flowers of rhetoric" to use. Chaucer artfully discussed his own art even as he wrote it. The Pearl-Poet did not. His command of the techniques is such as to make his use of them seem spontaneous: his portrait of Pearl, his description of the seasons, his antitheses and turns of language are all according to rule—and handled originally. And in his case another tradition gave him a set of techniques older and more basic than the classical ones: oral recitation, with its own intricate forms, to the sound of a harp in the days before schoolbooks. All the poets of the Alliterative Movement had the "sounds" rather than the "colors" of a very distant "rhetoric," the song of a *scop* chanting before a king. Understatement, story within story, allusions to famous names, words to the audience, all these were used in combination with the classical devices that were "in style." The work of the Pearl-Poet is sophisticated in the best sense.

But the medieval critic did not stop with evaluating versified rhetoric. As Vincent de Beauvais hints, the hearer of poetry must be led to shun evil and seek good, and in this he was guided by a conception of poetry drawn from patristic writers. Literature gives to life "a certain beauty" which transforms it into *species aeternitatis*. The reader must seek for substance under the form, "crack the shell" of poetic figures with delight, to find the sweet kernel of truth within. In this aesthetic code the literary, philosophical, and theological canons were inseparable.

Patristic times faced the problem of reconciling pagan writings with Christianity, of absorbing the beauty of classical art without harm to revealed truth or to virtue according to the gospel. One school looked upon the poetry of Virgil as a beautiful vase filled with vipers. Not so St. Augustine. He formulated Christian humanism when he said: "Every good and true Christian should understand that wherever he may find truth, it is his Lord's," and "Those things which can be learned from men should be learned without pride." [4] His *De Doctrina Christiana* shaped the thought of poets for the next thousand years, till human wisdom was to divine wisdom what Virgil was to Beatrice. Aesthetic pleasure comes from the charm of style with which truth is presented; it is sharpened by the excitement of finding truth through figures of speech and allegory. But pleasure is not the final end of poetry. God alone is to be enjoyed for His own sake, and the end of literature is the promotion of the charity that leads to Him.

> Therefore in the consideration of figurative expression a rule such as this will serve, that what is read should be subject to diligent scrutiny until an interpretation contributing to the reign of charity is produced.[5]

Such interpretations were generally found in biblical exegesis, for the Bible is the exemplar of all literature, and "a man speaks more or less wisely as he is more or less skilled in Holy Scriptures." [6] The works of the Pearl-Poet could be used as exemplars of this patristic outlook on literature, as will be seen in the analyses of each poem. The delight found in their stylistic expression is at the service of charity, the basis of all virtue; they all point to heaven. As for the Bible, the Poet quotes directly from it more than eighty times, in addition to the lengthy paraphrases of whole chapters and the innumerable indirect echoes. Even in the romance, Sir Gawain, at the moment of his greatest humiliation, finds comfort in biblical precedents—in the tricky women of the Old Testament who got greater heroes than himself into trouble!

Biblical exegesis led straight into allegory. St. Augustine gave an archetypal example of scriptural accommodation in allegorical form when he showed how the Christian writer is to approach his classical sources:

> If those who are called philosophers, especially the Platonists, have said things that are indeed true and are well accommodated to our faith, they should not be feared; rather what they have said should be taken from them as from unjust possessors and converted to our use. Just as the Egyptians had not only idols and grave burdens of unnecessary labor which the people of Israel detested and avoided, so also they had vases and ornaments of gold and silver and clothing which the Israelites took with them, as if to put them to a better use. In the same way some of the teachings of the pagans contain . . . liberal disciplines more suited to the uses of truth, and some most useful precepts concerning morals.[7]

This same example was used by Dante to explain to Can Grande the use of allegory, a notion basic to medieval literature. The Greek work *allegoria*, meaning to speak otherwise than one seems to speak, had been taken into the Vulgate by St. Paul when he told the story of the two wives of Abraham and used them as types of the Old and New Testaments, "quae sunt per allegoriam dicta"

(Gal. IV:24). Wycliffe rendered this: "The which thinges ben seid by allegorie or ghoostly undirstonding." And so the word came into English use at the time when the Pearl-Poet was writing. If allegory can be loosely described as "expanded metaphor," then Aristotle had shown its relation to poetry long before: "By far the greatest thing for the poet is the use of metaphor. It alone cannot be learned; it is the token of genius. For the right use of metaphor shows the power to see similarities in dissimilars." [8] This natural unity in variety, these harmonies in the Chain of Being, had been sublimated by the Christian sacramental system till the medieval mind lived in a climate of allegory.

St. Augustine's principle that figurative interpretation of Scripture could reveal truths that otherwise would remain hidden soon became applied more widely. Macrobius, in his *Commentary on the Dream of Scipio*, used the phrase *narratio fabulosa* for any story which, even though not true in itself, could convey truth, especially moral truth, thus giving "a decent and dignified conception of holy truths presented beneath the modest veil of allegory." [9] Soon the stories were drawn not only from Scripture and the classics but from romance and folklore. The more *fabulosa* the *narratio* the better! Behind the Pearl-Poet, influencing both his outlook and his techniques, were many lengthy allegories, religious and secular, derived from classical and Christian sources, didactic and satirical, romantic and mystic. Any figure that he chose to deal with was already charged with symbolic significance in such works as the *Psychomachia* of Prudentius, *The Marriage of Philology and Mercury* of Martianus Capella, the *Romance of the Rose* of Guillaume de Lorris and Jean de Meun, and Langland's *Piers Plowman*.

A method of allegorical interpretation evolved from scriptural exegesis. To the question as to whether Holy Scripture should use metaphor, St. Thomas answered: "Yes, for God provides everything according to the capacity of its nature. It is natural to man to attain to intellectual truths through sensible objects because all knowledge originates in the senses." [10] Following the Alexandrian School, he then gave the "four-level method" of interpretation that was soon carried beyond Scripture into literature:

A. 1) The literal (historical) meaning, whereby words signify things.

B.   The spiritual (allegorical in general) meaning, whereby
the things signified by words have themselves a significa-
tion. This meaning contains the next three levels:

2) The typical or analogical or transferred meaning (allegory
proper), whereby a given reality is expressed in terms of
another reality.

3) The tropological (moral) meaning, whereby a given reality is related to what is right or wrong for man as a free
but responsible agent.

4) The anagogical (final) meaning, whereby a given reality
is placed in relation to the life of the world to come, men
in glory.

All four meanings may be present in almost any work, since even a
lyric, a satire, or a romance can be symbolic and point to man's last
end through moral reflections. Any work could be enjoyed on the
literal level, and the tropological was close to the anagogical. The
second level, allegory proper, is the most complex; here meanings
may be multiple and elusive. Personification allegories, such as
Everyman, use fixed symbols and are unambiguous. Others are free,
subtle, and suggestive, and even employ the "floating symbols"
familiar to the twentieth century, in which the values represented
may be subjective and ambivalent. Here the Pearl-Poet is remarka-
bly modern; most of the critical studies of *Sir Gawain* and of *Pearl*
are concerned with some aspect or other of "speaking otherwise."

So, in dealing with poems shaped by medieval aesthetic practice,
it may be well to follow a medieval prescription for intelligent
reading, given by Hugh of St. Victor. His key words will be kept
in Latin, as too rich to translate save by his own comments on them:

> Explication [or literary analysis] consists of three things: *littera*,
> *sensus* and *sententia*. *Littera* is the harmonious patterning of
> language which we call structure [or form]. *Sensus* is that open,
> easily graspable meaning which *littera* offers at first sight. *Senten-
> tia* is that deeper significance [or intelligibility] which can only
> be found by analysis [or interpretation]. This order should be
> followed: first *littera*, then *sensus*, finally *sententia* should be
> examined. When this is done the literary analysis is complete! [11]

This suggestion will be followed in discussing the five poems.
Under *littera* comes all that belongs to language, style prosody, and
structure; under *sensus* comes the subject, the story told in each

poem, in the light of the sources from which it is drawn and the traditions that shaped it; under *sententia* come the varying interpretations. At the end, each poem must speak for itself.

The works will be treated not in their manuscript order, but in their chronological order—a highly debated matter. On the basis of the development in style and in thought, of interlinking references, of the use of sources, and of hypothetical events in the Poet's life, the following arrangement is proposed: *Patience* followed closely by *Cleanness*, between 1365 and 1375; *Sir Gawain* between 1376 and 1380; *Pearl* between 1381 and 1385; and *Saint Erkenwald*, 1386.

The Homilies

Patience and *Cleanness* are companion poems in form and purpose, drawn from the same traditional sources. Sermon poems of such length would hardly have been delivered from the pulpit, but they would never have been written but for a lively pulpit tradition.

Preaching in the vernacular became an art in the eleventh century when Aelfric, "monk and mass-priest" of the monastery of Cernel, wrote his sermons in English because: "It grieved me that men did not have the gospel lore, except those men who knew Latin." [1] His patterns, including a highly alliterative prose style, were followed by generations of preachers, and because this art was oral it was very tenacious. By it English sermon forms crossed the cultural gaps caused by the Norman Conquest and the Renaissance and were still influential when Bunyan wrote *Pilgrim's Progress*. Materials for sermons were collected in manuals for the use of priests; instructions for laymen, sometimes in poetic form, brought home moral instruction. Among such treatises that would have been known to the Pearl-Poet were *Handlyng Synne, The Prick of Conscience*, and, most importantly, the popular book of *Vices and Virtues*. These earnest and attractively presented moral works, with their homely *exempla*, or little stories, combatted the all-too-real laxity of the times, and emphasized the right use of the sacrament of penance. Sermon poems were written for edification in the highest sense:

Together *Patience* and *Cleanness* outline in detail the standard way that the Christian soul was instructed to follow toward its goal of happiness in heaven; and thus together the two poems participate themselves in the fourteenth-century movement for religious education that undoubtedly provided the fundamental stimulus for their composition. For they put into action some of the most vital elements of the Christian ethic, as defined in contemporary moral treatises, and thereby illustrate vividly a crucial series of doctrinal principles which the Church has taught throughout its history but particularly sought to strengthen and reanimate among the faithful in the period following the Fourth Lateran Council.[2]

Listeners to medieval sermons relished the *exempla* that drove home the point. In *Patience* and *Cleanness* these form the body of the sermon, for both poems are biblical paraphrases. The Bible, in the form of St. Jerome's Latin Vulgate, was "the Book" of the Middle Ages, the taproot of their culture. It influenced vernacular literature through racy poetic paraphrases that turned the inspired texts into "good stories," and made the "heroes" of the Old and New Testaments as familiar as knights in armor. Dress and customs were made contemporary; Moses straps on his helmet when he leaps on his steed to lead the Israelites over the Red Sea. But human nature is never anachronistic, nor are "the ways of God to man" that these poems justified by their imaginative honesty long before Milton undertook to do so.

The practice of turning the word of God "into sweetest song" began in 680 at Whitby where, as Bede relates:

In the monastery of this Abbess [Saint Hilda] was a certain brother wonderfully gifted and honored with God's grace because he was in the habit of putting into song those things that tended to piety and virtue, so that whatever he learned through scribes of holy lore, that he adorned after a little while with song-speech, with the greatest sweetness and zeal; and he always put it into the English tongue. (*Ecclesiastical History*, IV, 24)

Caedmon, this unlettered goatherd who slipped away from a social gathering because he could not sing, received his gift that same night, when in a dream a voice bade him "Sing me the First-Shaping." He sang:

> Now must we praise heaven's Keeper,
> the might of His hands and His heart's thought.

This was, it seems, the first Christian poem in English. Caedmon then put the whole Bible story, from Creation to Doomsday, into alliterative verse. Poems in this vein by his followers are in the Junius Manuscript: *Genesis, Exodus, Daniel, Christ and Satan*. The tenth-century *Judith* glorifies a heroic woman. Around 1200 an earnest but profuse Augustinian canon named Orm showed the purpose of biblical storytelling in the prologue to his *Ormulum:*

> Into English have I turned the gospel's holy lore,
> According to the little wit the Lord has given me.
> It was thy thought that it might well into great profit turn
> If English folk, for love of Christ, would learn it earnestly,
> And follow it, fulfilling it in thought, in work, in deed.
>
> (19-23)

Orm's Middle English followers used more than the Vulgate text; they called on such works as the *Historia Scholastica* of Peter of Comestor, while legends and apocryphal tales sprinkled salt through their holy stories.

Patience and *Cleanness* are similar in their *littera*. The vocabulary, while properly respectful to the Bible, is vividly colloquial, especially in dialogue, and runs the full gamut of the Poet's imagination. The alliterative line responds to the rapid story-movement, and rises to its traditional sonorous power in descriptions of terror or grandeur. Its free flow is shaped into quatrains, sometimes blurred or defective. Unrhymed poems often used the quatrain form, sometimes in strophic groups of multiples of four, perhaps to make oral recitation easier to follow. Since these poems are sermons they suppose a preacher who works out his text in a structure approved by homiletic manuals on the *ars praedicandi*. In *Patience* he presents: *protheme* (1-8), *dilatio* (9-60), *exemplum* (61-523), *peroratio* (524-30), and return to theme (531-34). In *Cleanness*, which is four times as long, the same structure is present, but complicated by the fact that there are three main *exempla*, with elaborate interlinking commentaries, forming three sermons on the same theme held within one framework. In both the preacher, who is the poet-narrator, speaks out in his own voice, amused, piquant, wise.[3]

Patience

The *sensus* of the poem is delightfully easy to follow. This preacher speaks from personal experience. "Once on a holyday at high mass" (probably the feast of All Saints) he was struck by the gospel of the eight Beatitudes (Matt. V:3–12). He develops these in his prologue, stressing the patience needed to endure a life of poverty, which he knows only too well! He paraphrases the eighth Beatitude so as to suggest the patient control that gives strength in suffering and persecution:

> And happy are they who can steer their own hearts,
> for theirs is heaven's kingdom, as I said before.
> (27–28)

But now see what happened to someone who could not endure! The entire Book of Jonah is then related, with fidelity and vigorous freedom. Verbal echoes are close: "sloumbe-slepe" for "sapore gravi," "passe to no pasture" for "nec pascantur." Not one verse or phrase in the original is omitted, but almost every verse is expanded, a sentence to a quatrain. Swift, pungent improvisations play in and out of the spare Latin. A word of God is answered in an all-too-human tone; motives and emotions are searched; stark action becomes dramatic. A sudden simile brings the story into a medieval setting: Jonah goes through the whale's jaws "like a mote through a church-door" (268). At times the text loops into a long imaginative amplification: the storm; Jonah's discomfort in the whale and his comfort under his woodbine; his gasping, lyrical prayers. Psalm 94 is invoked to warn the foolish Prophet: "Do you think that He hears not who made ears for all?" (123). This warning will be repeated in *Cleanness* (583–86), linking the two poems.

Other possible Latin sources give a classical flavor to some very Anglo-Saxon descriptions; the heroic sea-vocabulary was traditional in the Northwest poetry, but the Poet could hardly have read *Andreas* or *The Wanderer*.
He could have read in Virgil:

Talia jactanti stridens Aquilone procella
Velum adversa feret; fluctusque ad sidera tollit,
Fraguntur remi, rum prora avertit et undis
Dat latus, insequitur cumulo praeruptus aquae mons.
(*Aeneid*, I, 102–5)

In *Patience*, God rather than Juno bids:

Eurus and Aquilo who live in the east,
blow, both of you, at my will, on the blue-black waters.
(133–34)

A Virgilian poem entitled *De Jona et Nineve*, a fragment of 103 hexameters attributed to Tertullian, offers even closer parallels: some inversions in the biblical story found also in *Patience;* the scene in which the elements rush together over the reeling boat and the sailors cry aloud. The snoring Jonah is raised by a kick; the shipmaster asks questions not in the Vulgate; the inner regions of the whale are unsavory: "Sisara velificans, anima inspirata ferina" (98). In other works Tertullian deals with Jonah; in *De Fuga Persecutione* the prophet behaves as a servant of God should not; in *De Pudicitia* he suffers as an example of the Lord's Passion to redeem the heathen; *De Patientia*, without mentioning the Prophet, links patience with the Beatitudes.

The Poet does not make direct use of exegetical commentaries on the Bible story, but his presentation is shaped by such works as *Enerrationem in Jonam Prophetam* by Haymo of Halberstadt and the *Commentariorum in Jonam Prophetam* by Rupert of Deutz, both based on a work of St. Jerome. These treat Jonah both as a figure of Christ in His redeeming death and resurrection, and as an example of sin and repentance. The liturgy kept these truths before the faithful. The Book of Jonah was read in the Divine Office during Passion Week. The dark interior of the whale suggested Sheol, the Hebrew land of death: "Therefore Sheol hath enlarged its appetite and opened its mouth beyond measure" (Isa. V:14). Sheol further corresponded to the Limbo of the Patriarchs. The descent and return of Jonah had been given its significance by Christ Himself: "For as Jonah was three nights and three days in the whale's belly, so will the Son of Man be three days and three nights in the heart of the earth" (Matt. XII:40).

Although the Poet generally keeps free of apocrypha, there are flashes of legend and folklore in his story. His whale is "Warlow," a popular name for a monster, especially the devil, from the Anglo-Saxon *waerloga*, or breaker of oaths. It resembles "Cathegrande," the big fish of the *Bestiary* who symbolizes the devil, and it echoes classical accounts such as Lucian's *Vera Historia*. The subject was popular in art; Jonah and his whale enliven many manuscripts. The Raguel (or Ragnel) invoked by the sailors may be either the angel of chastisement in the apocryphal *Book of Enoch* or a demon in the Chester plays. The sailors call on a medley of pseudo-gods: the Muslim Mahomet (a heathen deity to the medieval imagination), the Roman Neptune, the Asiatic (not Greek) Diana, and Mergot, a Saracen sun-god. The strangest is Vernagu, a black giant of French romances killed by the epic hero, Roland. He appears in *Roland and Vernagu*, a version written in the West Midlands dialect (165–68). One name of ancient dignity is the Anglo-Saxon "Wyrd" (247); it translates *Dominus* when it summons the whale in the nick of time. Gollancz remarked:

> It is a pity that at least one eastern fable was unknown to our poet, to wit, the Rabbinic legend that taught how a wondrous pearl illuminated the darkness of the vast hall within the monster. The Poet of *Pearl* would have prized a fancy so near his own spirit.[4]

Patience has links with two better-known contemporary works. *Piers Plowman* is also, in its own way, a homiletic poem, a literary commentary on the social gospel. The Pearl-Poet, after personifying the eight Beatitudes, says:

> Since I am brought to that pinch that is called Poverty,
> I shall provide Patience too, and play with both of them.
> (35–36)

Langland, who knew the pinch of actual poverty, meets these same playfellows together in many passages. No less a personage than Scripture tells the dreamer:

> Patriarchs and prophets and poets both
> write to teach us not to wish for riches,
> and praise Poverty with Patience; these apostles bear witness
> that these will inherit heaven by true right.
> (B., X, 34–37)

Through the whole of Passus XIV Patience explains to Hawkyn the Active Man what true poverty is:

> Where there are perfect truth, a poor heart and patient tongue, there is Charity, chief chamberlain of God Himself.
>
> (B., XIV, 99–100)

He ends with the assurance that "Patience is bread for Poverty itself" (B., XIV, 313). If one poem influenced the other, it is hard to say which way the influence worked.

The second parallel is found in Chaucer's *Pardoner's Tale*. It too is an exciting story forming the body of a sermon in a homiletic frame that encloses the whole company of Canterbury pilgrims. But the character of the preacher is quite different, and so too his text: "Radix malorum cupiditas." The pilgrims call on the scoundrel Pardoner for "some moral thing." But he must drink while he thinks, and leads them into a tavern where he gives his text and a preamble on vice. The *exemplum* is the grim tale of finding death under an oak that brings home the evil of cupidity as the adventures of Jonah bring home the value of patience. But while the mock sermon ends with a farcical kiss, the Bible story ends with a good resolution: "Softly, with long suffering, I must settle down" (529).

The *sententia* of a sermon should not be hard to find; otherwise, the work would fail. The story of Jonah is no allegory in the usual sense; in the mind of the Poet it was a fact of Old Testament history. Yet its interpretation as a sign of Christ was confirmed by Christ Himself: "An evil and adulterous generation seeks for a sign, but no sign shall be given it except the sign of Jonah" (Matt. XVI:4). As a type of New Testament truth it was allegory on the exegetical "second level."

But sermons must also be effective on the tropological level, or again they fail. The moral of the poem is in its title, its opening word: "Patience has its good points." The word "patience" in a medieval context meant more than sitting still and waiting. It was cognate with "passion," the act of suffering, undergoing, submitting as patient to agent, being passive under action. It involved humility and obedience, an acceptance of the right order of things, especially the right order between creature and Creator, servant and overlord, messenger and sender. The Prophet's adventurous mission was carried out because he was forcibly taught this complex virtue. This is the special theme of *Patience*, which shares with *Cleanness* the broader theme of sinners brought through repentance and penance to salvation. Jonah is a sinner; he is proud and stubborn. He learns the hard way, gives in, and does his duty by preaching in Nineveh. Then his troubles begin again. He is again proud and stubborn, arguing with God petulantly. The story ends without telling of a second and final conversion. Yet saved he must be! The tone of the poem, so sympathetic, affectionate, and amused, is assurance enough. Jonah was sinful, but he was more foolish than bad, and the theme of the poem is sharpened (or softened) into this: a silly man runs from trouble; he becomes wise when he accepts it as God's will. Surely Jonah could not resist God's final plea:

> Be not so gruff, good man, but go forth on thy way;
> be steadfast, be patient in pain and in joy.
> For he who is too ready to rend his clothes
> must sit down in worse ones and sew them together.
>
> (524–27)

The artistic pattern in *Patience* is tightly woven into its message. As a preacher:

> The poet's primary purpose was to make the Jonah story appeal vividly to the English folk of the fourteenth century. . . . His artistry depends upon his ability to present vivid detail and to understand the workings of men's minds—the mind of Jonah and the mind of the individual in his audience.[5]

And so, "the purple patches are not digressions, however artistic, from the progress of the sermon, but firm and necessary parts of the *exemplum*."[6] The imagery balances all the elements of a delightfully told "cautionary tale." The major image-complex is that of "traps, tricks and games," as the hunted eludes the divine Hunter who finally takes him. The two parts of the hunt, Jonah in flight and Jonah in Nineveh, become images of one another through contrasting parallels: the violent and the gentle winds, the uncomfortable and comfortable "bowers," alternations of sleep and waking, the echo of key words like "unsounde" (58 and 527). God's obedient servants, animate or inanimate, are personified as each teaches a lesson to the disobedient Prophet.[7]

All this is told in a colloquial tone, ironic and shrewd, with hilarious realism. The combination (so frequent in medieval writing) of reverence and humor is brilliantly effected, and made plausible by the author's understanding of the feelings of God's faulty, lovable messenger. The readiness to laugh at human nature while admonishing it is authentic Christian humility. Virtue is no somber matter; there is zest in being good, especially after being bad! The Pearl-Poet's shortest, simplest, and probably earliest work holds the seeds of his more fully developed art: "It may well be that future study will reveal that the author of *Patience* has in this poem manifested a more subtle power and beauty than that which so obviously illuminates his other poems." [8]

Cleanness

The *sensus* of this curiously compelling poem is found in the illustrative unfolding of the sixth Beatitude: "Blessed are the clean of heart for they shall see God" (Matt. V:8), a text that unites a whole series of sermons. The prologue relates the parable of the wedding feast (Matt. XX:7-14, Luke XIV: 16-20). A pithy, personalized epilogue resolves a complex interweaving of themes. Within this framework are set the major *exempla* warning against God's punishment of uncleanness, or defilement incurred by sin: the flood, the destruction of Sodom and Gomorrah, and Belshazzar's feast. Six shorter episodes, each showing a failure in "trawthe" or loyalty, set off the three main ones: the revolts of Lucifer and of Adam preface the story of the flood; the incredulity of Sarah and of Lot's wife leads to the destruction of the cities; the faithlessness of Zedechiah and of "Nabugo" offsets the fall of Belshazzar. A seventh short tale, the repentance of Nebuchadnezzar, is woven into Belshazzar's feast. Transitional passages of homiletic exhortation link the four main sections and set each in its own frame. The apparently rambling poem falls into a clear pattern.

The Poet handled the Vulgate as he had done in *Patience*, paraphrasing closely, often quatrain for verse. But he weaves back and forth through his sources. The story of the wedding feast places the subsequent Old Testament stories squarely in the light of the gospel. The *exempla*, both major and minor, draw freely upon the books of Genesis, Exodus, II Chronicles, Jeremiah, and Daniel. But behind these direct sources are three others which, taken together, not only unite all the stories, but point to the theological bases of the poem, its unity of theme, and its artistic shaping. The first source is from the Book of Wisdom:

> Wisdom protected the first-formed father of the world; when he alone had been created, she delivered him from his transgressions and gave him strength to rule all things.
>
> But when an unrighteous man departed from her in his anger he perished because in wrath he slew his brother. When the earth was flooded because of him, wisdom again saved it, steering the righteous man by a paltry piece of wood. . . .
>
> Wisdom rescued a righteous man when the ungodly were perishing; he escaped the fire that descended on the Five Cities. Evidence of their wickedness still remains—a continually smoking wasteland, plants bearing fruit that does not ripen, and a pillar of salt standing as a monument to the unbelieving soul. (X:1–7)

The other passage is from the Second Epistle of St. Peter, a Christian reflection upon the lessons of Jewish history:

> For if God did not spare the angels when they sinned, but cast them into hell and committed them to pits of nether gloom to be kept until the judgment; if he did not spare the ancient world, but preserved Noah, a herald of righteousness, with seven other persons, when he brought a flood upon the world of the ungodly; if by turning the cities of Sodom and Gomorrah to ashes he condemned them to extinction and made them an example to those who were to be ungodly; and if he rescued Lot, greatly distressed by the licentiousness of the wicked, for by what the righteous man saw and heard as he lived among them, he was vexed in his righteous soul day after day with their lawless deeds; then the Lord knows how to rescue the godly from trial, and to keep the unrighteous under punishment until the day of judgement, and especially those who indulge in the lust of defiling passion and despise authority. . . .
>
> If, after having escaped the defilements of the world, through the knowledge of our Lord and Savior Jesus Christ, they are again entangled in them and overpowered, the last state has become worse for them than the first. (II:4–13)

The last passage, too lengthy to quote, comes from the end of the Bible, the culmination of the plan of salvation in the Apocalypse, a book with which the author of *Pearl* was very familiar. The second and third chapters warn the Seven Churches against falling into sin, specifically the sin of impurity; they use imagery of "cleanness," white raiment, the white stone which was interpreted in the Commentaries to be a pearl, symbol of purity and of Christ Himself. (The same chapters also suggest the themes of *Patience*.) Each of the seven messages ends with the homiletic warning: "He that hath an ear let him hear what the Spirit saith unto the Churches."

In expanding the sacred text the Poet turned to three books which were the best sellers of his day; through them much legendary matter drifted into his work. *The Book of the Travels of John Mandeville* had reached England by 1371. Mandeville (alias John de Bourgoyne) claimed to have set sail in 1332 on a pilgrimage to Jerusalem and beyond, into India, China, and the Eastern Isles. Oriental glamor had appealed to English writers from the ninth century on: *The Phoenix* and *The Wonders of the East* prepared Englishmen to accept any marvel from the lands of spices and jewels—commodities of which the Pearl-Poet was fond. Crusaders, pilgrims, and merchants went to the lands that Mandeville seems only to have visited by wishful thinking and by reading Josephus' *De Bello Judaeorum* and Itineraries. His extravaganza was convincing, and he ended by saying: "My book is affirmed and approved by our Holy Father." The Pearl-Poet drew on it for some of his most fearsome and most glittering scenes. Here he found the horrors of the Dead Sea:

> The water of that sea is still bitter and salt; and if the earth were made moist and wet with that water it would never bear fruit. And the earth and the land often change their color. And it casteth out of the water a thing that men call asphalt. . . . And neither man or beast, nor anything that beareth life in itself can die in that sea. And that has been proved many times by men who have deserved death and have been cast therein and left therein three days or four, and they could never die therein, for it receiveth nothing therein that beareth life. And no man can drink of that water, for its bitterness. And if a man cast iron therein, it will float above, and if a man cast a feather therein it will sink to

the bottom. And these things are against nature. And also the cities therein were lost for sins. And beside it there grow trees that bear full fair apples, and fair of color to behold, but whoso breaketh them or cutteth them in two shall find within them coals and cinders, in token that by the wrath of God the cities and the land were burnt and sank into hell.[9]

The poet visited, with Mandeville, the palace of the Great Khan:

In this city [Cathay] is the seat of the Great Khan in a full great palace, the most passing fair of the world. The walls are in circuit more than two miles. And in the garden of the great palace is a great hill upon which is another palace. And it is the most fair and the most rich that any man can devise. And all about the palace and the hill are many trees bearing diverse fruits. . . . And the hall of the palace is full nobly arrayed and full marvelously attired on all sides with all the things with which men may adorn any hall. And first, at the head of the hall, is the Emperor's throne, very high, where he sits at meat, and it is of fine precious stones set about with refined gold and more precious stones and great pearls. And the steps by which he goeth up to the table are of precious stones mingled with gold. . . . And at great solemn feasts before the Emperor's table men bring great tables of gold and thereon are peacocks of gold and many other birds all of gold and richly enamelled, and men make them dance and sing, clapping their wings together to make great noise, and whether it be by craft or necromancy I know not.[10]

The same lavish use of jewels is seen in the description of the palace of Prester John.

Another French manuscript crossed the channel at about this time: *The Book of the Knight of the Tour Landry*. The author had lost his wife. Sitting in his garden in April of 1371, "all heavy and full of thought, I saw coming towards me my three daughters, at which I was joyful and had great desire that they should turn to good and worship above all earthly things." He resolved to make "a book of examples, to teach my daughters how they should govern themselves and know good from ill." [11] This book would have appealed to the Pearl-Poet's gay and affectionate nature, his moral earnestness, and his love of cleanness and courtesy. One passage, drawn from real life, recalls the scene in *Clean-*

ness (133–48) where "one not very handsomely arrayed for a holiday" enters the marriage feast:

> I have heard the lord my father say that once he came into a great feast where there was a gathering of lords and ladies. He arrived as they were sitting at table, and was clothed in a coat-hardy of the German style. He came to greet the ladies and the lords and while he was making his reverence Messire Goeffrey called out before everyone and asked him where was his viol or other instrument, and what he did for his living. "Sire," he said, "I have nothing to do with such things." "Sire," said he, "I cannot believe it, for you are disguised and dressed up like a minstrel." . . . Then he called to a minstrel and gave him his coat and made him put it on, and he came back into the hall. (Chap. XVII)

The principal virtue that the Knight wishes to see in his daughters is the "cleanness" of a pure life, and for this he tells them startlingly pointed tales. In three different ones this virtue is associated with pearls, as it is in *Cleanness*. The Knight exalts chastity in the married state, in a passage echoed in *Pearl:*

> Thus must every good wife and woman do, and so must she think, and thus she will earn the love of God and of her lord and of her friends and of the world, and will save her soul, which is the most precious thing of all, for God calls it the precious marguerite, which is a fine stone, white and round and clear with no spot seen in it. (Chap. CXVI)

Another story illustrates the part of *Cleanness* (1140–48) in which a soul who is "reconciled and made sacred to the Lord" sins again, is compared to a bowl, clean and sanctified, which is afterward defiled. A woman had a vision in which she drew from a dunghill a silver vessel, and was told to scrape it until it became clean and white, for:

> The vessel of silver drawn from the dunghill signified the soul which is in the body. . . . And for this, fair daughter, the voice in the vision told you to scour and clean the spots on that vessel, which were the spots of your sins . . . and that you should keep from sinning further. For it is good to confess, but better it is, after confession, to keep from falling back, for the second fall is worse than the first. (Chap. VIII)

The Pearl-Poet used his third contemporary source more directly. *Cursor Mundi* was a popular biblical paraphrase written in a northern dialect in the early fourteenth century; its four-beat couplets race for 25,000 lines over the Seven Ages of the World, for the benefit of those who, ignorant of French, "yearn to hear rhymes" in the English tongue. The thread of Bible history, spun from the Vulgate and the *Historia Scholastica*, winds excitingly through less authentic matter: apocryphal gospels, saints' legends, popular lore, both eastern and western. Its energy, warmth, and rapid style would have been congenial to the Pearl-Poet, who echoed many lines from his northern neighbor. The theme of *Cleanness* is touched on in the *Cursor*'s account of the fall of Lucifer; he could not remain in heaven because:

> In that court that is so clean
> No filth may dwell nor yet be seen.
> (476–78)

In both, in the story of the flood, birds and animals are pictured in flight as wells overflow and banks break down. The "cursed crow" finds a dead beast and:

> Of that flesh he was so fain
> That he came not to the ship again.
>
> (1887–88)

And when Lot's wicked wife is licked away by beasts:

> Then was she found in the morn
> As whole as she was heretofor.
> (2856–60)

This last point was drawn from Jewish lore. *The Legends of the Jews* states: "The pillar exists even to this day; the cattle lick it all day long, and in the evening it seems to have disappeared, but when morning comes it stands as large as before." Another Jewish tale said that the angels visited Lot on the Passover, when unleavened bread should contain no salt. Rabbi Isaac adds:

It was because she sinned in the matter of salt on that day on which the angels came to Lot. What did she do? She went to all her neighbors and said: "Give me salt, for we have strangers." Word of that presence was thus spread throughout the city.[12]

This last version is not found in any secondary source, and suggests that the Poet may have known Hebrew. When he said that "Lot's good-looking wife" had "glanced over her left shoulder," he expressed what seems to have been already an old superstition.

Legend had also played with the episode of the raven who, in the Vulgate, simply flies from the ark and never comes back. A Jewish Midrash makes Noah tell the treacherous bird that because it is unclean it can serve neither as food nor as sacrifice. No wonder that in both Jewish and Arabic stories it stops to feed on carrion and earns Noah's curse! Latin commentators treated the episode allegorically, and the Old English poem, *Adrian and Ritheus,* made the raven's "untrueness" the cause of its being changed from white to black, the bad-luck bird of the ballads. Another apocryphal strain running through the popular versions of Genesis was the notion that giants were among the wicked descendants of Cain. In *Cleanness* the "fiends" who saw that "the daughters of noblemen were delightfully fair" (270) are clearly Cain's progeny, though his name is not mentioned; they "engendered giants by their evil jesting" (272). The story of the fall of Satan, which had reached great length in the Old English *Genesis,* had followed the dramatic lines implicit in the words of Isaiah:

> How are you fallen from heaven, O Daystar, Son of Dawn! How are you cut down to the ground, you who had laid the nations low! You said in your heart: "I will ascend to heaven; above the stars of God I will set my throne on high. I will sit on the mount of the assembly in the far north; I will ascend above the heights of the clouds, I will make myself like the most High! But you are brought down to Sheol, to the depths of the pit! (XIV: 12–16)

In *Cleanness* the rebel angel cries:

> I will place my throne near the pole-star,
> and be like the Lord, Maker of heaven aloft.
>
> (211)

His word for pole-star is *tramountayne;* the *transmontana stella* gleamed in the north, and this location for the throne of Lucifer is still found in Milton:

> At length unto the limits of the North
> They came, and Satan to his royal seat
> High on a hill far blazing.
> (*Paradise Lost,* V, 755–57)

Touches from New Testament Apocrypha color the narrative. Christ as the King of courtesy who alone could break bread with his fingers without bad manners (1101–8) is found also in the Coventry and Townley plays, where "He broke bread as evenly as though it had been cut." The exquisite passage on the joy of Mary when:

> All charming things that make hearts chastely glad
> were gathered round my Lady when she was delivered
> (1083–84)

is reflected in many medieval lyrics on "The Five Joys of Mary." These so delighted the Pearl-Poet that he named them among the causes of Gawain's strength as he rides to battle (644–47).

Other bits of folklore or heroic legend are evoked by swift allusions. When the rabble blunder around Lot's house they are struck "as blind as Bayard" (886), a magic bay horse given by Charlemagne to Renaud, which became a type of blind reckless-ness. When Sodom and Gomorrah sink into the ground, hell itself hears "the hounds of heaven" (961). These are the "Gabriel-hounds," a spectral pack whose cries warn the folk in Lancashire of disaster. Belshazzar, pouring wine into the sacred cups, cries "Waissal"; long ago Hengist and Rowena had pledged each other with "wes hal" as they drank. And twice the Nordic "Wyrd" appears (122, 1605) where it renders the old notion of destiny, but in this context it is in the impersonal plural and must be rendered "fate."

But while he evokes the dim past, the Poet sets his Bible tale in the vivid present of his own world. All fighters, even Medes and Persians, must be dukes and knights, clothed accordingly; their dwellings have "bantels;" their banquets are served like those in Camelot or in some hall in the Northwest shires. The meat platters have "arbors over them, cut at the edges, / pared out of paper" (1407–8). These were the elaborate paper cutouts set over dishes of food in Chaucer's *Parson's Tale*. Sir Gawain thought of them when he saw the twinkling parapets of Bercilak's castle that "seemed to be pared out of paper only" (802). Paper was a luxury in the fourteenth century. When the King in the parable told his guests that his "bulls and boars are baited," he meant that, in the fashion of the day, they had been worried by dogs "to the intent that violent heat and motion might attenuate their blood, resolve their hardness, and make their flesh softer for digestion." [13] And at the height of the ominous action during the last catastrophe when "the merry weather darkens," an exquisite little picture of medieval home life is flashed against the clouds:

> Each man hurries fast to his own home,
> sits down to supper and sings after it.
>
> (1762–63)

A reference to the *Romance of the Rose* (the only place in the Pearl-Poet's work where he mentions any other source than Holy Writ) brings *Cleanness* into the current romantic tradition:

> Clopinel, in the course of his "Clean Rose,"
> gives advice to one who would have good-speed
> with a lady he loves.
>
> (1057–59)

The advice given is a paraphrase of that given to the Lover by a Friend on how to please Fair Welcome who can gain him access to his Rose:

> Observe Fair Welcome through and through,
> And see just how he looks at you,
> With what expression on his face;
> For his whole manner you must trace.
> If he moves with age and dignity,
> Then keep your own solemnity;
> If like a fool he carries on,
> Then a fool's manner you must don.
> Take care to follow every way:
> If he is bright, then be you gay;
> If he is angry, let wrath fly,
> If he laughs, laugh; if he cries, cry!
> If he loves someone, love him too,
> If he blames something, so must you.
> If you do everything I say
> Things will turn out in your own way.
>
> (7719–33, 7792–93)

The situation gives a strange touch of *amour courtois* to a Bible tale. Clopinel, better known as Jean de Meun, had played over the sophisticated surface of love. The Pearl-Poet, in his seriousness (or perhaps his light irony), turns the romantic meaning to his own purposes by the epithet "clean," which lifts his reference out of the none-too-pure atmosphere of the original. He then places the whole scene on another symbolic plane, when he reveals that the Loved One is Christ Himself:

> If thou wilt make love to thy leader then,
> loving thy Lord loyally and loved by Him,
> conform thee to Christ and make thyself clean;
> He is polished as smooth as the pearl itself.
>
> (1065–68)

In this recurrent image of the pearl the *sententia* of *Cleanness* may be sought. "The clean of heart shall see God" as He is in heaven, for:

> In those shining houses
> a man must be as bright as a burnished beryl
> that is round on all sides, with no blemish seen,
> unmarred, unstained, like a marjorie-pearl.
>
> (554–56)

Does "cleanness," the title and first word of the poem, mean freedom from the stain of sin in general, or from fleshly impurity in particular? A study of the passages that connect the main stories and form the logical backbone of the poem reveals the broad meaning as the dominant one. Many sins besides impurity are named. Each will prevent a man from coming into God's court where he must be clothed in clean garments, that is, good works of every sort. This is a homiletic poem urging the soul to turn by means of penance from anything that will prevent the ultimate vision promised to the clean of heart. To bring home his point the Poet chooses a series of warnings against God's wrath incurred by uncleanness, and as no sin (as proved by Bible history) so rouses Him to swift punishment as sins of the flesh, the stories of the flood and of the destruction of the Five Cities are cited. The third story of Belshazzar's feast sees the same sin on another level. The defilement of the sacred vessels is a sacrilege; impurity in a member of Christ is also a sacrilege, in the light of St. Paul's words: "If a man will defile the temple of God, him God will destroy, for the temple of God is holy, which temples you are" (II Cor. III:17). In Chaucer's *Parson's Tale* adultery is said to be: "a fouler thefte than for to breke a chirche and stele the chalice; for thise avoutiers breken the temple of God spiritually and stele the vessel of grace, that is the body and the soule" (X, 878). A recognition of the revulsion of God from fleshly defilement, shown anthropomorphically in His special chastisement of it, will lead to the gift of understanding, which sees the true nature of sin in general as a defilement of the soul. Thus the two meanings of "cleanness" are "counterpointed against each other." [14]

The theology of the Middle Ages saw impurity as a less serious sin than pride; it was, in fact, the lightest of sins. Dante made this clear in his descent through hell from lust to pride—the most malignant of sins—and his reverse ascent through purgatory. The Pearl-Poet does not negate this view in *Cleanness*. He does emphasize the particularly hasty and severe earthly chastisement which God inflicts for fleshly sins, but his structure and imagery place these tales in a larger ethical framework. Impurity is a socially harmful sin, and its effects upon society are brought out with grimly unpleasant realism. Behind mere lust is the deeper failure in the "courtesy" of loyal and humble obedience. The right order of the universe as well as of feudal society demands mutual respect, of which clean and proper clothing is a sign. And at the climax of the poem pride stands out as the worst of sins. Nebuchadnezzar "was touched with pride" and "had so deep an insight into his own deeds / that he plain forgot the power of the High Prince" (1559–60). With his punishment "his wits came back to him," and he knew both himself and God. But Belshazzar, who held his empire in *olipraunce*, was cut down in his sin. He is linked with "Satan, the black one" who would not repent; Babylon was a symbol of damnation, the city of pride.

The effectiveness of such a long homily, repeating its lesson three times over, depends again upon poetic power. Its very massiveness is impressive; the thought-laden movement of story into story gives it a tone of epic grandeur. The hero is the just man, be he Noah, Abraham, Lot, or Daniel; he learns the divine plan through familiar talk with God, the First Mover of the action which His friends carry out. The villain, be he Lucifer, Adam (who repents), Lot's wife, or one of the proud kings, precipitates the catastrophe which God then brings about and which leads to the ultimate happy end in His court. Behind these central figures are the multitudes of nameless people who are actually guilty of "uncleanness," the members of the fallen human race who refuse salvation and who—drowned, swallowed alive, or cut down with swords—must die. Their voices—carousing, blaspheming, then crying out for help—intensify the epic sense.

In tone the poem is somber, its humor mordant. Unpleasant sense images revolt: pots of boiling grease, smells of corruption, rotten fruits, ashes. It is crushingly serious. These sinners are not lovably naughty like Jonah. God cannot tease or coax them; they must perish. Yet this unsparing Poet is no Manichee in thus denouncing the sins of the flesh; he wrote the radiant passages on the joys of Mary's pure motherhood, and on the bliss of rightly ordered human love, "pure paradise, nearly, should prove no better" (704). Cleanness is not a negative virtue; it is intensely beautiful, as hot and pure as fire, as clear and white as a pearl. Beauty lifts the stories above their smoky setting by the sheer lyric power with which the horrors are described. They are relieved by the sparkle of jewels, the freshness of sunrise, the lithe loveliness of animals and birds, the charm of a picnic lunch, the womanly wisdom of a queen. The poem has the artistic unity of balance. Centered on the pearl image, it moves in widening circles that brush hell and heaven. It blends violence with serenity, dirt with dazzlement, God's wrath with His tenderness.

Sir Gawain and the Green Knight

This poem is a downright romance which somehow yields a spiritual experience. It points up the same values as the homiletic poems, all the more surely because the brilliant texture of its *littera* holds the imagination, inescapably, in the excitement of good narrative.

The vocabulary ranges far beyond that of the earlier poems: the connotative words of Anglo-Saxon fighting and fellowship, of French love-making, of Celtic spells, used by speakers equally at home in real and magic worlds. Its near-synonyms run the gamut of "high, middle, and low" words for the same entity, such as for a battle or a man. More than one hundred terms are rare or obscure, while those for heraldry, hunting, falconry, wine, and music are technically exact.

The word choice changes with the scene. Within the castle

knights and ladies talk in polished and playful words, with the "mandarin-like" courtesy of elaborate subjunctives, "if my liege-lady were not to dislike it!" (346). The alternations of the "thou" and "you" forms of address reflect elaborate social custom; Arthur is angry and retorts ironically "Sir! Courteous knight!" when the man in green dares to call a king "thou" (276). But outdoors more rugged words, not found in Chaucer, are needed, and:

> Of these words [such as *wysty*, desolate, *harled*, tangled] it can be said that they accord with Paget's gesture theory. They are onomatopoetic, or they reproduce in sound the shape or feel of rough or intractable objects, or they recreate in sound the sensa-tions of smart or pain, or they are mimetic of violent or laborious body-movements and action. . . . A knight is to undergo a rough journey in winter, and the experience is actualized in muscular images and rhythms, in a firm grasp of concrete particulars.[1]

The Anglo-Saxon and French meters are juxtaposed. The allitera-tive lines are molded into 101 firmly unified stanzas, from twelve to thirty-eight lines in length, each brought to a spinning close by a "bob and wheel," five short iambic lines rhyming crisply. Each is an artfully shaped poem in itself, in which the same metric moves lightly or ponderously, glows limpidly or opulently, with a shift of mood.

The Poet is true to the technical conventions of the manuals of rhetoric. The *Ars Versificatoria* had said that *descriptio* was "the supreme object of poetry"; it must be functional to the story and at the same time beautify it. Catalogues of appropriate phrases, given in the right order, were furnished, especially for descriptions of feminine beauty and of scenery. In *Sir Gawain* the poet's insight made him original within a traditional framework. He was describ-ing his own landscape in its various weather-moods; he made it a vital correlative of the mood and moral of his tale: the thick woods and clattering waterfall of the first journey, the lawns and glim-mering parks of the castle of ease, the snow-muffled valley of combat, all are pictured with a fusion of realism, rhetoric, and symbolism. The Poet's sense of nature in this land so near the Lake Country is more than Wordsworthian; it is psychological. The formula "he saw" gears Gawain's sense impression to his emotions, and the reader's emotions are manipulated by shifts in technique.[2] At both courts Gawain's figure dominates the crowded scene; when he is alone he shrinks against the landscape which magnifies progressively with his fear. Cinematographic close-ups are used, as when the focus narrows to the Green Knight's severed head on the floor (420–8), or to single features of a face, "with small lips laughing bright" (1207). The Poet had "an exceptionally fine sense of space distribution as well as unmatched talent in transferring a visual experience into poetic utterance." [3]

This poetic style "moves over an almost flawless structure as smoothly as supple skin over the bones of the hand." [4] The poem is a complex of literary forms. It opens and closes like a chronicle, a *Brut* throwing history back to the coming of Brutus, son of Aeneas, to eponymous Britain. The Poet calls it a "lay," and gives it the fairy-like precision that marks the Breton Lays, but he casts it in the light-hearted form of an Interlude fit for Christmastime. But it remains a romance in which the usual rambling episodes are controlled by the conscious art of a thinking artist. Movement is purposeful; the hunting and temptation scenes fold into each other within stanzas. Repetition becomes pattern, the folk-stylization of fairy tales such as *Goldilocks and the Three Bears*. There are triads of feasts, prayers, hunts, temptations, kisses, chapels, and journeys. There are pairs: sunrises and sunsets, two axes, two arming scenes, two symbols of protection: the shield with its pentangle of perfection and the fallacious green girdle. External details move in rhythms that reflect deeper currents within, and: "All life is shown as a kind of exquisite ballet subject to rhythmic laws." [5] Such craftsmanship has produced:

> an aristocratic romance, reflecting a many-faceted solidity which is both comic and serious. It is meant to entertain and to some extent to reach a sophisticated audience. Its style is probably mixed, and part of its humor lies in the juxtaposition of high and medium style. It is a combination of secularism and religion, of the marvelous and the real, of the decorative and the direct, of the vague and clear, of courtesy and horror, of the elevated and the plain. There is a solidity about *Sir Gawain* which encompasses a variegated world. [6]

The *sensus* is a Christmas story, done up in red and green and gold and easily unwrapped for sheer enjoyment. After a swift telescoping of the past, the present grips the tale. The year is perhaps 1371.

Its listeners recognized the dress, the architecture, the customs as contemporary; they too enjoyed "the shouting of the clerics" on the Feast of Fools, and the "hand-gifts" on New Year's. They could watch Gawain ride northwest from a vague Camelot at Winchester or in the hills of Somerset; as he reached North Wales the scenery leaped into focus. The land here was rich in Arthurian place-names, due to the long British rule in Strathclyde. But in the Wilderness of Wirral, "few men were there / who loved either God or man with good heart" (700); in 1377 Edward II issued a writ to "disafforest" the place because of marauders lurking there. Bercilak's castle may have been the one still standing at Clitheroe in the Ribble Valley, Lancashire. Or it may have stood in Stafford-shire near a place which today still looks like the Green Chapel, "nothing but an old cave / or a crevice of an old crag" (2182) named Thorsdale or the Fiend's house; it juts out, complete with rocky doors and windows, over the Hoo Brook. In any case, the Green Chapel is a barrow, or ancient burial mound, like the one at Bridestone. Gawain might well fear such a site; an archaic meaning of the word "chapel" is a "place of combat," or "place where a butcher kills animals."

The familiar was shadowed by the strange. If the first listeners knew fewer facts than do modern scholars about the mythology, folklore, and legendary history distilled into the poem, they were more responsive to the overtones and undertones that play through the spritely tale and give it an immense sense of distance, Eliot's "presentness of the past." The Poet's sources and analogues were part of "the Matter of Britain." He found them in "these old books, the key of memory," and used them in the manner of Shakespeare after him, of whom it was said that he used time and place only in as much as he couldn't get on without them. He selected three themes and blended them into one plot: the beheading challenge, the temptation test, and the exchange of winnings. They are Celtic in origin and French in form, but the Poet handled them like an Englishman.

The beheading game first appears in *Bricriu's Feast*, an Irish saga of the ninth century, when material for the Arthurian cycle was being shaped from the beautiful, strong, and grotesque elements of the Heroic Ages. The story there appears in two forms: the Terror version and "the Champion's Bargain," in both of which Cuchulainn meets a frightening challenge. It then passed into the courtly French romances of the twelfth and thirteenth centuries: the *Livre de Caradoc*, in the First Continuation of Chrétien de Troye's *Perceval* (so close to *Sir Gawain and the Green Knight* as to be possibly its primary source); the Grail episode in *Parlevaus* where Lancelot meets a similar trial in the Waste City; *La Mule sans Frain* where Gawain himself is the hero, as he is in *Humbaut*. The German *Diu Krone* repeats the story.

The theme of the testing of a guest by the host's wife at his instigation also goes back into Celtic myth. It too is found in *Bricriu's Feast*, in the episode of Curoi's Castle; an even more elemental version is *Pwyll*, one of the Welsh *Mabinogion*. It appears in the Anglo-Norman *Lanzelet;* in the French *Ider* and *Chevalier à l'Épée;* in the Vulgate *Lancelot;* in two Italian *Canzoni* which come from Latin *exempla*. After the Pearl-Poet's version, it reappears in the Middle English *Carl of Carlyle*. In some versions, such as *Humbaut* and the *märchen*-like *The Turk and Gawain*, both themes are present, but nowhere are they joined into one plot as in *Sir Gawain and the Green Knight*. Here the Poet united them by means of the third theme, the exchange of winnings, which emerges from folklore in the *fabliaux* of the thirteenth century.

The interrelation between *Sir Gawain and the Green Knight* and its sources is a complicated problem, opened by Kittredge in 1916. It can be followed by reading in chronological order the relevant articles in the bibliography. Here it will be more helpful to follow the main characters in their long life in the imaginations of storytellers, through myth, legend, and romance into the fourteenth century.

To begin with Arthur—he is the hub about whom revolves the noble brotherhood of the Round Table whose code shaped the story. The Arthuriad, not yet unified by Malory, was familiar in its endless ramifications to the Poet's listeners. This Arthur shows few traces of his earlier self: the Celtic divinity, combining battle-god, bear-man, and culture-hero, whose mythic qualities entered into the semihistoric Arthurius who rode out of Wales in 516 to fight the Saxons at Mount Badon. He carried Our Lady on his shield and felled 960 men, alone; Europe had found its ideal hero. He continued his fairy career in the *Mabinogion* and his military career in Geoffrey of Monmouth's *History of the Kings of Britain* (1136). From there he went to France to become king of courtly romance, to be drawn into the endless search for the Holy Grail, and to be carried off to Avalon where he is still waiting to come back. And here he is in *Sir Gawain* simply enjoying himself at Camelot, attractive, reckless, and "somewhat boyish." He starts the action when "his young blood and wild brain" meet an absurd challenge. At Gawain's departure the king is declared (in whispers) to be foolish; at the end he welcomes the hero home, still laughing but now wise. And Gawain loves him:

> Since you are my uncle I am worth praising,
> with nothing good but your blood, I own, in my body.
>
> (356–57)

Next comes the antagonist, the "aghlich mayster," the Green Knight. In the eighth century he was the carl who stormed into the high hall of Ulster in *Bricrui's Feast:*

> Terrible and hideous was his appearance. An old hide next to his skin, and a black tawny cloak about him, and upon his head the bushiness of a great tree, the size of a winter-fold in which thirty yearlings could find shelter. Fierce yellow eyes in his head, each of those two eyes standing out of his head big as a cauldron that would hold a large ox. . . . In his right hand was an ax into which had gone thrice fifty measures of glowing metal.[7]

He is a *blachlach*, a Celtic word for wild man, which can yield, in Anglo-Norman, the name Bercilak. After losing and restoring his own head and sparing Cuchulainn's because of his loyalty, he admits that he is Curoi himself. Curoi was remotely a sun-god with elements of a storm-god in his make-up. In the Terror version he is Uath, "a man of great strength who used to form himself into whatever shape he pleased," really Curoi playing a part. And in Curoi's castle Cuchulainn's loyalty is further tested by Blathnat, Curoi's wife, while the host, knowingly, is away from home—like Bercilak of the fire-red face, beaver-hewed beard, and tempestuous disposition. The carl had been dressed in gray, but the same word, *glas*, can also mean green.

The challenger's uncouth looks stay with him through many versions. In *La Mule sans Frain* he is a *vilein*, "bushy-haired, black and of frightful appearance, taller than St. Marcel, and he carries on his shoulder a great battle-ax."[8] In the *Earl of Carlisle* he has "a wide mouth, gray beard, long locks and a hooked nose." But in the French versions he has become refined. In *Parlevaus:*

> The knight came down into the middle of the hall, clad in a short red jerkin; and he was girt with a rich girdle of gold and had a rich clasp at his neck wherein were many rich stones, and on his head he had a great cap of gold, and he held a great ax. The knight was of great comeliness and young of age.[9]

In the *Livre de Caradoc* the grandnephew of Arthur has just been dubbed at a feast; while the king waits for some strange thing to happen:

> There rides in at the hall door a very tall knight on a tawny steed; he is dressed in a long ermine robe which reaches to the ground, and on his head a gold circlet clasps his headpiece. He wears a very long sword. Riding up to the dais he greets King Arthur courteously and asks a favor.[10]

These two aspects are combined in the Green Knight as he rides into Arthur's hall. He is dressed elegantly, gruesome but no *blachlach*. But the description of his fine clothes sounds another note. He must be straight out of fairyland; his green hair and skin come from folklore. Green is the color of the Irish *sidh*. It is also the color of death, for "death is greener than the grass," in balladry at least. Graves open at New Year's, and the same hollybob that the knight carries in token of peace will keep those graves open till the ghosts return. The Lord of Death in European folk tales is hideous and gigantic, and rides a demonic horse. So perhaps:

> The mysterious Green Knight is no other than the Lord of Hades who comes to challenge to a beheading game the heroes sitting round the fire. His challenge is taken up by Gawain who thereby proves himself the equal of Herakles.[11]

But perhaps the Green Knight is merely a fiend; diabolical hunters from the North Country wear green as in Chaucer's *Friar's Tale*. Still more basic is the nature of green itself; in folk art the vegetation-god is "the Green Man," shown on woodcarvings even in church, or he is the Jack-in-the-Green of winter festivals. A French miniature shows a knight decked in green branches for a May Day tournament. Is the Green Knight thus "an intruder from a pre-courtly and pre-Christian world? Something of the old untamed, unreclaimed north of Europe has come back here." [12] If so, the Green Knight (who as Bercilak loved to hunt) may be Arwen who, in the *Mabinogion*, is "a horseman coming after the pack on a big dapple-gray steed, with a hunting-horn round his neck and a garment of brownish-gray stuff about him," who submits Prince Pwyll to a chastity test. He is the mythical Wild Huntsman, the personification of winter's storms. In the mythical realm an even vaster story-exchange takes place between East and West. *La Mule sans Frain* has an analogue in the Indian tale of *Kathasaritsagara*, in which Indivarasna "frequently cut off the Rakshasa's head, but it grew again."

All this may account for the eerie effect of the Green Knight, but it neglects the fact that his other (and true) self, Sir Bercilak, is very much of a man, humorously bluff and shrewd, a lavish host, an expert hunter, a warm and righteous friend. Source-hunting in other directions has found his human counterparts. In the Poet's day there were two men known as "the Green Squire." Simon Newton, *scutifer viridis*, was a favorite of Edward III and had connections with the Northwest Midlands.[13] Froissart says that when King Pedro of Aragon was decapitated in 1369, "there was slain with him a man from England, Ralph Holmes, who had formerly the surname of the Green Squire, and another squire of the name of James Roland, because they had put themselves in postures of defence." [14] Holmes was a follower of the Black Prince. Color nicknames for knights were common, but none deserved his more than Amadeus VI, Count of Savoy, "il Conte Verde," for he and his court dressed in bright green for the spectacular tournaments at which this extravagant host entertained his friends. His most gorgeous feast was given in honor of the marriage of Lionel, Duke of Clarence. Is this why a Duke of Clarence is mentioned in the poem (552)? Amadeus also created a knightly Order of the Annunciation of Our Lady, the members of which wore green collars that could have suggested the green baldrics adopted by the Round Table.[15]

Bercilak's nameless and entrancing wife is only playing at her sinister game, but she does it so well that "her love will not let her sleep" (1134). She reflects the beautiful wife of Pwyll or the bejeweled daughter of the host in *Lanzelet*. Behind her lurks the hideous old lady who turns out to be Arthur's half-sister, Morgan le Fee. The Poet shows a knowledge of her primeval origin when he calls her "goddess"; she was once either the Irish battle-deity Morrigan or a Welsh *morgen,* a sea-born being. The mention of her dealings with Merlin long ago recalls her accomplished career in magic, which had involved many knights before Gawain. She could act as a beneficent fairy or a nasty witch. It is hard to tell which she is here. In manipulating the plot which drew Gawain to the Green Chapel and sent him home a moral victor, was her intention spiteful? Did she want to frighten the Queen, humiliate the King, and make Gawain fail the chastity test central to the theme? Or was it her lofty wish to purge the court by revealing its moral weakness and redeem it through Gawain's virtue? [16] The ambiguity is part of the delightful irony of the poem, which ends happily in spite of, or because of, Morgan's magic. She is seen only as an ugly human, but the shape-shifting upon which the story depends is all her work. Through her, the stream that always lies between reality and fairyland is crossed.[17]

Gawain himself is as old as his elvish challenger. He is a doublet of Cuchulainn, a sun-god; his Welsh name, Gwalltaduwyn, means golden-haired. He could not shake off his solar habits:

> But Sir Gawain, from nine of the clock, waxed ever stronger and stronger, so that when it came to the hour of noon his might had increased by three times. So when it was past noon, and drew towards evensong, Sir Gawain's strength grew feeble, and he waxed faint, so that he could scarcely go on longer.[18]

When the Arthuriad took form he entered it as Galvagin, the son of King Loth of Orkney, and of Anna, Arthur's half-sister. He is first mentioned historically by William of Malmesbury: "At that time (1087), in a province of Wales called Ros, was found the sepulchre of Walwin, the noble nephew of Arthur." [19] In the chronicle versions he is the first of knights, a warrior of untarnished repute, though impulsive and overready to boast:

> And now Gawain, still glowing with fire kindled by his former exploits, endeavored to cleave an opening whereby he might come at the Emperor himself and foregather with him. Like a right hardy knight as he was, he made a dash upon the enemy, bearing some to the ground and slaying them in the fall.[20]

In episodic French romances he is the center of interest, the much-talked-of favorite of maidens, amorous but not in the code of courtly love, being too simply passionate and light-of-love to engage in subtleties. His solar origin may account for his readiness to accept a draw in many a combat, as in *Ywain and Gawain* and the *Geste of Sir Gawayne;* he is sure that his wounds will heal again—until he dies of an old wound. He is dashing, likable, unpredictable, and (usually) honorable. He is, as in *Golagros:*

> Sir Gawain the gay, the good, the gracious,
> Secure in bliss and ever full of bounty,
> Handsome, gentle and right chivalrous,
> Who failed in no point of that which he should be,
> Eager and brave and most adventurous,
> Brilliantly loyal, always to be praised.
>
> (389–94)

But in the prose Vulgate versions his character degenerates; the blackest picture is in *Tristan*, where he is tricky, captious, treacherous, cruel, and cowardly.[21] Malory's fascinating picture of him reflects these inconsistent sources and shows a tragically lovable figure who starts the search for the Grail and fails to achieve it:

> "Alas," said King Arthur unto Sir Gawain, "you have nigh slain me with the avow and the promise that you have made. For through it you have bereft me of the fairest fellowship and the truest knighthood that ever were seen together in any realm of the world. . . . I have loved them as well as my life. Wherefore it shall grieve me right much, the parting of this fellowship. For I have an old custom to have them in my fellowship." And therewith the tears filled his eyes.[22]

Malory seems not to have known the Pearl-Poet's work, where Gawain is no less the perfect knight for being a fallible man. The human failure in one so brave, chaste, and true wins for him the wisdom lacking in the other versions of his literary life which, like that of his king, would seem to be without end. Here, he is supremely what he is in almost every tale, "the hende," the knight of courtesy. When Chaucer wrote his *Squire's Tale* (whose opening passage shows a possible knowledge of the Pearl-Poet) he paid tribute to the courtesy of his own hero by saying:

> That Gawain with olde curtesye
> Though he were come again out of Faerye,
> He could not him amende with a word.
>
> (F, 95–97)

And if proof is needed that his courtesy is real, it is given by all the minor figures in the story, the laughing lords and ladies, the eager, efficient, attentive retainers, from porter to stableboy, who swarm around him. They are very real people, and they simply love their handsome knight.

Answers to the question as to why the poem was written have swung through a wide arc. To say that it was composed for a wedding, or a Christmas dinner, or a celebration of the Order of the Garter, is to give the occasion but not the cause. Some claim that it was simply meant to entertain; laughter rings through it; let us enjoy it and be grateful. The whole adventure is a game that demands good players.[23] Others find it a profoundly symbolic version of the Quest that makes up the life of Everyman. No one denies that it is entertaining, yet no one denies that the glittering, swift-moving current of the tale runs deep, and the question becomes: What does the poem mean?

Its *sententia* is not simple, but the tropological level is the most easily explorable. Moral questions are bound up with the very adventures of the attractive hero; they are part of his character and of his role as the knight of courtesy. In one sense the whole poem is a homiletic *exemplum* of *cortayse*, a complex word that ranged from good manners to reverence before the divine Majesty. Gawain had all of its many qualities, but his "testing" involves a specialized meaning of "courtesy" derived from the code of courtly love.

This strange and ambiguous tradition had its roots in very differing soils. It began in the dry-rot of Augustan Rome, when Ovid wrote his flippant, satirical *Ars Amatoria*. His parody of love-making indicated that a man had best seek the love of another man's wife in secret, that love is a warfare and also a religion. Medieval chivalric society played with these ideas in the elegant, lonely life led in the great castles. Into them filtered the Platonic, exotic, and often mystic concept of love sung by Arabic poets like Ibn Hazim. This strange blend was sublimated by the Church's ideal of woman, inspired by the Mother of Christ. In Champagne it was given literary expression by Chrétien de Troyes, and in Provence by a host of troubadours; from there it was brought to England by Eleanore of Aquitaine. By the fourteenth century the poetry of courtly love was flowing in two streams which often crossed each other: the immoral or at least amoral found in many romances, and the Christian found in Dante's portrayal of Beatrice. In many lyrics and even homilies Christ is the knight who fights and dies for man's soul. In the *Ancren Riwle:* "This King is Jesus Christ, God's Son, who came to prove his love and show by knightship that He was loveworthy." The Pearl-Poet makes Sir Gawain "the best knight after Christ."

The code had its textbook, written c. 1185 by Andreas Capellanus, the chaplain of Marie of Champagne, a book which the Poet must have known. He presents its teaching "in reverse," with deft and light-hearted irony. Andreas had defined love as "a certain inborn suffering derived from the sight of and excessive meditation on the beauty of the opposite sex." It had many rules: "Love can deny nothing to love." Gawain is smitten by the beauty of Bercilak's wife and treats her courteously. But this is not the "cortayse" that the Lady expects; she is forced to take the initiative and play the game backwards. Her blunt offer is not in the code at all, but her suggestions and reprimands, her questions and his evasive answers are in it. The verbal fencing echoes Andreas' Fifth Dialogue, "Between a Lady and a Knight," where the latter says: "So much ability is apparent in you and you are distinguished by so much courtesy, that I believe that in the presence of your prudence I may without fear of censure say all those things that are lying in my heart." [24] When the Lady says this very thing to Gawain the change of roles would have been highly amusing to fourteenth-century eavesdroppers. The Poet handles the scenes so as:

> to establish a dichotomy between two conceptions of courtesy [the courtly and the Christian] and to express implicitly his preference. For courtesy is such a wide concept that it can embrace both the lady's request for a kiss and Gawain's refusal to grant it.[25]

The Christian ethic wins out, and the knight keeps intact "cleanness and courtesy that were never corrupted" (653). This method of refuting the code of courtly love is more effective than the right-about-face of Andreas when he warns in his conclusion: "For many reasons any wise man is bound to avoid all the deeds of love and avoid its mandates. . . . What good can be found in a thing in which nothing is done except what is contrary to the will of God?" [26] The Poet's *exemplum* is not negative as in *Cleanness* but delightfully positive; Gawain carries off his victory without failing in charm or in good manners. The lesson is easily learned when "the romance exists to show us what a splendid man Gawain is." [27]

This is all in the tone of high comedy, but we come close to tragedy when we come to the heart of Gawain's dilemma. He has no magical powers of his own to fall back on (despite the sun-god origin which folklore assigns him); he is bound by a knightly code with a high pattern of behavior, and the honor of his king is at stake. He is tested for many virtues, including courage and loyalty. He passes his tests only to be tripped up by a piece of green silk. He is tricked and confused, Andreas had said that a knight could offer a lady a ring or a girdle. When the lady offers the same, shall the knight refuse? He did refuse the ring, but took the girdle and, more seriously, failed to exchange this "winning" with his host. He confessed his faults aloud when he saw the truth of the plot and of his own conduct. Then Bercilak absolved him with a roar of laughter; he had done it "for the love of your life—the less I blame you" (2368). Gawain himself says, surprisingly, that he has failed in covetousness, the sin of the Pardoner whom he so little resembles. This marks the Poet as a theologian as well as a romancer; the current definition of covetousness in its deepest sense was "a sin against charity, inordinate love of anything other than God." [28] This points back to St. Augustine's dictum that all literature must lead to charity. And so this hero struggles, slips, admits defeat, gains self-knowledge, and ends up a hero still. His tragic flaw may be slightly comical, but the laughter that ends the poem puts all in the right perspective: Gawain is the ideal Christian knight.

But the Poet is extolling not only the virtues of an individual but a whole complex of virtues, those of feudal Christian society. A romance may be a piece of social criticism. It has been claimed that the Poet was satirizing the luxury, loose morals, and twisted romantic concepts connected with court life by a plot that turns on the need of cleansing the Round Table. If so, the warm and mellow tone make this poem an unusual piece of satire.[29] It has been claimed that the unusual characterization of Arthur as reckless and foolish is an indictment of fourteenth-century kingship in the light of the ideal set forth by John of Salisbury, and that "the Poet is a humanist who wanted to deliver a warning on a high intellectual and artistic level." [30] The poem may be "the most cunning and most perfect of the medieval celebrations of the chivalric ideal. That ideal is not celebrated; it is questioned, defined, criticized." [31] Roundly:

> In an age and a country which deliberately tried to keep the fading aristocratic ideals alive by tournaments and the founding of chivalric orders, we find a poet striving to present both the serious and the comic sides of this aspect of his times. *Sir Gawain* both praises and belittles the past and the ideal. It tries to come to terms with the political and ideological tensions of its age by the dissolving force of humor and clarity, and it definitely assumes the importance of loyalty and Christianity. Life is perhaps at bottom such a suspenseful and wondrous game! By means of an art so vivid and so rich that many have been tempted to regard it as life itself, the Gawain-poet has created a new world which both beckons to and laughs at our own. The great charm of the poem perhaps is due to this curious mystery which both amuses and sobers, delights and frightens us at the same time, as it teeters on the edge of tragedy and defeat but at last safely brings us back to the solid ground of a happy ending.[32]

The anagogical import of this poem so "fairly and squarely Christian" is obvious. It leaves its hero ready for heaven "as clean / as if doomsday were due the next morning" (1884). It asks the same grace for its readers in the spritely prayer at its close: "May He who wore crown of thorn / so bring us to his bliss."

Interpretation on the level of allegory proper is not as simple as this. The poem uses no personification, yet:

> The persons live in a context where their mere presences signify and where their actions follow from choice and greatly count. And the objects in nature also, by their mere presence, signify, and can fulfill a purpose by their obstruction to human effort.[33]

This moves the allegory from the precise into the ambivalent realm familiar to modern readers. Some find that the poem draws its life from its mythic roots and its meaning from subconscious response to primordial symbols. It represents a fertility or vegetation rite, involving the yearly slaying of a king.[34] Or the Green Knight is the master of a *rite de passage*, an initiation into mysteries by which Gawain is enabled to return in a cycle of rebirth.[35] The Green of primitive nature and the Gold of civilization [36] struggle throughout and end in a draw:

> The whole poem is, in its very texture—its imagery and rhythm—an assertion of belief in life as contrasted with winter deprivation and death; and it seems finally to discover within the antagonism between man and nature, between human and other-than-human, an internal harmony, even a kind of humorous understanding.[37]

Or again:

> The poem is not an allegory, and we cannot advise substitution of a concept such as "the Life-force" whenever the Green Knight appears. . . . [But] he testifies to an assumption that moral behavior, though of vast importance, is subservient to and dependent on something even more primary—creative energy. In the poem, Gawain and his "society" humbly come to terms with the Green Knight.[38]

The poem has even been pushed back into the collective memory of man through the Vedic myths of India, where:

> Disenchantment is more than magic; it is a liberation of the sun from the darkness by which he had been obscured and eclipsed. But the sacrificial death of Indra is also a making of many from one . . . and the release of the imprisoned principles. . . . The restoration of a lost head builds up again the divided deity, whole and complete, and therewith the sacrificer himself.[39]

This study of Indra as a remote picture of Gawain ends with the words of Jessie Weston:

> The Grail and related romances repose eventually not upon a poetic imagination, but upon the ruins of august and ancient ritual, a ritual which once claimed to be the accredited guardian of the deepest secrets of life.[40]

The right use of such criticism assumes that a myth is meaningful, presenting a universal and ever-emerging pattern. It is used consciously by modern writers, subconsciously by medieval writers, for a purpose. In the Middle Ages "the prevailing use of the allegorical method brings nearer to the surface of the literary work the unconscious mythic quality that underlies all literature." Here the journey–initiation–quest pattern brings out a specific theme: "A semi-allegorical presentation of the whole history and meaning of the Round Table." [41] Critics are reminded that the author of *Sir Gawain* "is a Christian and not a Druid in disguise." "For all their Catholic civilization and chivalry, Arthur and his court are alike vessels of the life instinct which, with the assistance of grace, they can make beautiful in the working. The poem then speaks that Catholic sacramental view of life which Puritanism was to vitiate." [42]

The fourteenth century had a whole set of artistic and ritualistic symbols which could be counted on to evoke the right psychological response. The "things that signify" carried their meanings boldly. Liturgy, heraldry, astrology, alchemy, each had its language spelled out in stained glass, carvings, and illuminations. Birds, animals, jewels, garments, designs could talk to each other in a counterpoint story. Interpretation can be pushed too far, but suggestive power is always at work. Colors, for instance, speak in *Sir Gawain:* green and gold for the Challenger, red and gold for the Hero. Morgan, with her yellow skin, is properly clothed in black. Is it significant that when Gawain appears before Bercilak after passing (with reservations) his tests, he wears a mantle of blue, sign of loyalty, lined with white, sign of purity? [43]

Symbolic objects in balance resolve the tensions of the poem: the shield and the green girdle, for instance. The pentangle on Gawain's shield can be traced back through Jewish legends from Spain to Byzantium, and from there to the East where it is found on Babylonian pottery. The Pythagoreans saw in 3 + 2 the number of perfection, the blend of odd and even, and "the endless knot" became associated with the wisdom of Solomon. The Poet elaborates on the five pentads in terms of the familiar codes of penance and of courtly virtue (640–51). The girdle of fairy color with its magical powers is an ambiguous symbol. Through it Gawain fails; he then uses it as a sign of his victory, and ends by wearing it as he wears his shield: as a symbol of his ideals.

The animals of the hunt can also be seen as "extended metaphors." *Bestiaries* and handicraft arts had traced character sketches of deer, boar, and fox, drawn from natural history, scripture, and legend. The hunt and castle scenes are so interwoven as to bring out their correspondences. On the first day the lady "finds herself, like her husband, hunting noble game," the antlered deer, while Gawain displays the adroitness of the same. On the second day he is more aggressive, like the boar. On the third he sinks to the craftiness of "the foul fox." [44]

Juxtaposed symbols may clarify but not compose a consistent allegory; only a basic theme like that of the quest can control the whole poem. Such a theme may produce allegory as ambiguous as *Moby Dick* or as precise as *Pilgrim's Progress*. One interpretation, after "a thorough examination of the image-creating ideas of the times," [45] attempts to give the story a definite congruence: Gawain seeks salvation, his own and that of the court. The Challenger, in the green of Christian hope (he is also Bercilak, radiant with the fiery glow of grace) is the Word of God (Christ) under two aspects: he strikes to save and renews by refreshment. Gawain overcomes foes who have all the vicious connotations given them by sermons. He is welcomed by Fortune (Providence in league with the Word) under her adverse and favorable aspects in the persons of the two ladies. He is scathed by his temptations and descends into the valley of despair (Virgil's Inferno) only to be saved by his encounter with the Word.

It is baffling to find the Green Knight, lately a fiend, as a Christ-figure, but medieval symbols could carry more than one meaning, and these could be antithetical. So much the more exciting to recognize the right one in context! It may be questioned whether a particular interpretation was the one meant by the author, but medieval writing did not require a specific intention. In the *Ovid Moralisé* and the *Expositio Virgilianae Continentiae* Christian critics uncovered values that might have astonished Ovid and Virgil. Vincent of Beauvais said that it was the business of a poet to re-express things that really happened, to change them into new shapes—with a certain beauty. The principle could work in reverse:

In this respect, too, the writer of *Gawain and the Green Knight* shows the mark of the great poet: he infuses conventional allegorical connections with real life, he achieves the highest type of allegory—a type that even in the Middle Ages was the exception rather than the norm—where the artistic appreciation of material things combines harmoniously with their allegorical meaning.[46]

This is what gives to *Sir Gawain*—in its lighter way—the power of the *Divine Comedy* to carry a man through a great adventure which, at each step, "speaks otherwise." It speaks through things that are themselves allegorical precisely because, as realities, they are integrated with other realities that make up the universe. The poem keeps its artistic integrity; it tells its secret to no one but lets everyone understand.

Pearl

If Sir Gawain is a fellow-pilgrim of Dante, he journeys only through an exciting Purgatory and comes to rest in a sociable earthly paradise. He does not visit hell and is not aiming at heaven—just yet! The seeker in *Pearl* has known a deeper suffering and reaches the verge of the Beatific Vision. If the dream vision is less read than the romance, it may be because of Dante's warning at the beginning of the *Paradiso*:

> Tempt not the deep, lest, losing unawares
> Me and yourselves, you come to port no more.[1]
>
> (II, 5-7)

The poet-narrator calls himself a jeweler; he must "cleanly enclose" his thoughts in clear gold. The *littera* of this poem calls for the most elaborate and demanding craftsmanship. The vocabulary is still vigorous, still courtly, but no longer heroic; it is more brilliant, subtle, and delicate in texture, a "polychromatic vocabulary." The wording of a spiritual experience must be both theologically exact and existentially personal. The speaker not only narrates; he thinks aloud, cries aloud, and speaks to another mysterious but well-known person in the groping language of conversation. Sudden shifts in the use of "you" and "thou" show a poignant tension between awe and familiarity. This paradoxical "fugue-like poem" plays on the varied meanings of the same word (usually a key word): *spot* as "stain" and "place," *deme* as "judgment" and "thought," *paye* as "payment" and "pleasure." Yet there is an astonishing bareness of expression in this intricate speech.

The prosody is the French four-beat line assimilated into the Anglo-Saxon alliterative line, or the alliterative cadence modified by the French syllabic beat. The balance eludes definition. Four "lifts" are set between "dips" of a varying number of syllables, and cause the line to hover between a classical iambic–anapestic movement and the freer rise and fall of the Teutonic hemistich with its frequent "clashing stress." A light caesura breaks most of the lines. Alliteration is found two, three, or four times in single lines, but about one quarter of the lines have none. Many lines read ambiguously because the final *e*, which was no longer pronounced in conversation, remained in poetry as an archaism. This strictly controlled metric pattern approaches what Eliot describes as free verse at its best: a constant evasion of and return to a basic pattern.

The rhyme scheme cuts the flow of sound into brilliant facets: *ababababbcbc*. In about seventy of these twelve-line stanzas there is a division by sense-pauses into quatrains; in some the final quatrain balances the octave as does the sestet in a sonnet. The stanzas are linked by concatenation; the last word of one is picked up in the first line of the next in a near-refrain. The linking fails only at line 721. The last line of the whole poem picks up the key word of the first, clasping the twenty-cluster necklace. This elaborate stanza form, showing concatenation and refrain, is used in some twenty other lyrics, mostly from the West Midlands. *Pety Job*, a poem "full profitable to sinners in compunction," with a Latin refrain, is the closest to *Pearl:* "Thy visitation, Lord, has kept/My spirit that is within me." Stanza-linking by echoed words, phrases, or thoughts is also found in some northern romances like *Sir Percival*. The practice, frequent in this area, may be due to Celtic verse heard in the songs of Welsh bards as late as the fourteenth century. Nowhere does it link sound with sense more artfully than in *Pearl*.[2]

The *sensus* is disarmingly simple. A man (the poet or a fiction?) has lost a pearl (it or her?). Rebelling, he falls asleep on the site of his loss. In a dream he meets his pearl in a maiden (his daughter or a symbol?) who rebukes, comforts, and enlightens him, then leads him to within sight of heaven. He tries to reach her by crossing, unbidden, the separating stream, and wakes a wiser man. He tells his "very avisioun" without once addressing the reader. So basic an experience would be banal if it were not unique each time: loss, recovery-with-a-difference, acceptance. But in making it into a lyric drama, the narrator (the "central intelligence," as Henry James would say) has changed this simple pattern into something extraordinarily rich by his use of contemporary "objective-correlatives."

Other-worldly as the poem is, the Poet (as always) uses real life as his prime matter. The time is August, the place is a garden, a park-like "pleasaunce" or "erber" rich in spices, with flowery turf. Gilly-flowers, gromwell (sometimes called "pearl-plant"), ginger, and peonies all had medicinal value, but:

> They are brought together in a way that is independent of time and space. . . . intended as symbols, as is made clear by their being made to bloom together in a manner quite removed from their known natural habits.[3]

The dream garden is exotic, metallic, done in mystic blues and silvers, yet it is real: there are pear trees here, and the pearly gravel crunches underfoot. The "maiden of dignity" wears a dress that would have honored the court of Edward III. The Dreamer speaks to her in a natural tone, calling on specific memories. Metaphors of experience are used for the ineffable, as when he stands before a mystery like "a hawk in a hall." When he wakes into earthly life again, peace comes with the thought of daily mass. There is a convincing sense of actuality throughout this journey into the mystical.

"Holy Writ" (as the Poet always calls it) is the basic source, as in the Homilies, but the vision is a parable rather than an *exemplum*. It draws on the Bible some 130 times, by quotation, citation, allusion, or echo, balancing texts or interweaving them. The fragrant garden of the Song of Songs is the setting for the Bride of the Lamb: "You are all fair my love, and there is no spot in you" (IV:7). The Old Testament (in passages from Genesis, Exodus, Wisdom, Ezechiel, and Daniel) throws light on New Testament themes, in the manner of medieval exegesis. The words of Isaiah are even blended with those of John the Baptist (822–28). The Gospel of St. John (XII:24) gives doctrinal depth to the metaphor of the seed in the ground (31), and all four evangelists are drawn upon for the gospel scenes. Central to the whole argument is the parable of the workers in the vineyard (Matt:XX:1–16). The deepest theological issues in the poem (the operations of grace, the salvation of the innocent, the unity of the Mystical Body of Christ, redemption through His death) are drawn from the First Epistle to the Corinthians (echoed six times) and the Epistle to the Hebrews: "And by that will we have been sanctified through the offering of the Body of Jesus Christ once for all" (X:10). The last sections expand the description of the New Jerusalem in the Apocalypse.

The Poet takes his Scripture straight, without apocryphal flavor, but he probably knew manuals of exegesis, such as those by Bede, Hamo, and Rupert, in which the significance of the twelve jewels was traced back through Ezechiel to the description of the High Priest's ephod in Exodus XXVIII. These commentaries help to elucidate difficult passages such as lines 689–92, in which 690 is defective in the manuscript. The underlying scriptural text makes it plain that Solomon is speaking of Wisdom who "rescued from troubles those that served her. When a righteous man fled from his brother's wrath, she guided him on straight paths; she showed him the kingdom of God and gave him knowledge of angels" (Wis. X:9–10).

The Church Fathers had given symbolic meanings to Scripture which became traditional. Pearl's white crown "with figured flowers wrought perfectly" (208), like the "two crowns" in Chaucer's *Tale of St. Cecilia*, bears an interpretation going back through St. Boniface and Aldhelm to St. Jerome who declared that "a crown of red flowers signified martyrdom and one of white flowers virginity."[4] The date of the "high season" on which the vision occurred can be variously given, as patristic teaching clarifies the poem's own imagery. Lammas, August 1, is the feast of harvesting and first fruits; August 15, Feast of the Assumption, fits in with the marian images; August 6, the Transfiguration, stands for the glory of the resurrection of the just. Peter the Venerable connected this last idea with that of harvesting:

Rightly, therefore, the disciples were called by Christ, in spirit, onto a hill, since after the resurrection of their immortal bodies the saints will be lifted by Him from the depths to the heights, from humble things to exalted, from earthly to heavenly. They shall truly be led on high, since the cockle will not be left with the true wheat but will be bound into bundles for burning by angelic harvesters. The wheat, at the Lord's command, will be gathered into His barn.[5]

The dreamer and the maiden both quote Scripture in the syllogistic way of university schoolmen debating doctrine. While technically accurate, their discussions are charged with emotion. These were no mere contributions to the theological arguments then current; the salvation of the innocent and the equality of merit are of personal concern. St. Augustine, the doctor of grace, is at their core. He had written against Pelagius who denied man's need of grace. Semi-pelagians were active in the fourteenth century, especially at Oxford where Bishop Bradwardine countered them in his *De Causa Dei contra Pelagium*. The maiden exalts the grace of God as the ground of all salvation, including that of the baptized infant. She is thoroughly Augustinian, and the dreamer, with some reluctance, allows her argument. But he reacts violently, declaring, "Then Holy Writ is but a fable" (592), when she further claims that in heaven the innocent will receive equal reward with the just, according to the parable of the vineyard. She reiterates: "Each man alike He there pays,/whether little or great his reward may be" (603-4).

Debate on this point had begun long ago, when St. Jerome attacked the heretic Jovinian for asserting equality of reward among the saved. Here it is the dreamer who sides with Bishop Bradwardine in denying such equality. Since Pearl is made to win the debate over his objections, a claim has been made for semi-heretical, or at least "evangelical," leanings on the part of the Poet: "The theological argument in *Pearl* is seen to be, at least in one respect, a most interesting and remarkable anticipation of sixteenth-century Protestantism." [6] Many critics have controverted this claim of Carlton Brown.[7] They recall the distinction between the essential "light of glory" which attends the Beatific Vision, and the accidental glory which varies with the merits of each soul. In a sermon on the parable of the vineyard St. Augustine had said:

> We shall all be equal in receiving our earning, both the first and the last to come; for that penny is eternal life, and in eternal life all have equal share. However, they will shine by diversity of merits, some more and some less, but what pertains to eternal life

is the same for all. There, in one mode will be found chastity in marriage, in another the crown of suffering.[8]

Moreover, patristic exegesis also said that the "the eleventh hour" applies to persons of any age who go into the vineyard only at the hour of death. The arguments of the dreamer and the maiden can thus be harmonized, and patristic thought is the pattern of the Poet's thought. The fact that the dreamer accepts this harmony without carrying the argument to a conclusion shows that his problem was no mere intellectual dilemma. To a soul in agony, crying "I want to know why," progressive enlightenment comes with humble acceptance of the mystery of pain. Like Dante, who questioned Picarda in the First Heaven, he is satisfied with the answer: "In His will is our peace."

The word "courtesy" carries the tale from the biblical plane to that of romance. To illustrate the exquisite manners of the court of heaven, the Poet boldly makes the maiden say: "By courtesy, as says Saint Paul,/members of Jesus Christ are we" (476). They are united in love as the Church is united to form the Mystical Body:

> For just as the body is one and has many members, and all the members of the body, though many, are one body, so it is with Christ. . . . The eye cannot say to the hand "I have no need of you," nor again the head to the feet, "I have no need of you.". . . But God has so adjusted the body, giving the greater honor to the inferior part, that there may be no discord in the body, but that the members may have the same care for one another. If one member suffers, all suffer together; if one member is honored, all rejoice together. (I Cor. XII:12, 21, 25–26)

Knights and ladies will feel at home before so "gentle" a King, with the Queen at His right hand: they will be kings and queens themselves. Small wonder that the Poet feels like a churl, a *blose*, when he blunders so rudely in speaking to his exquisite Lady.

Spiritual romances began and ended, like the tales of the Arthuriad, at a king's court. It is often a matter of lover and beloved seeking each other. Christ, seen at the end of *Pearl* as "the Lamb my Lord with a wide wound" (1135), will take the hazard upon Himself, as in the *Ancren Riwle:*

> A lady there was who was beset all about with foes and her land destroyed, and she all poor within her earthen castle. Yet a

mighty King's love was set upon her. . . . Like a noble wooer, He came to prove His love and to show her by knighthood that He was love-worthy, as knights used sometimes to do, and for His sweetheart's sake raised His shield in fight, like a keen knight pierced on every side.

Or again, as in the Welsh allegory *The Christian Way*, it is the soul who, like a crusader, must find the way to the King whose home is as jewel-like as the dreamland of *Pearl:*

In a fair castle crowning a lofty mountain dwelt my love Christ. Fairer than all other castles in the world was this one, and beautiful the gardens and pleasances within its walls. Weary of war, weary of the din of strife . . . I lay down one day to rest from the heat of the sun, and straightway came to my mind the vision of the castle of my First Love. Many days I journeyed, impatient to draw near to the castle. . . . Presently I saw that the path no longer led upward in the direction of the castle, but down towards a gloomy chasm. Then would my heart freeze, but my soul fiercely cried: "My Love is waiting, still waiting." Then I saw a brief glimpse of my Love's banner waving in the bright sunshine beyond the valley. By so much the nearer I drew to the castle, so grew it fairer to my eyes, and at length I beheld my Love standing in the gateway, radiant in the sunshine that shone on His face and glittered on the rubies that adorned Him.[9]

To fall asleep in a garden of delights was a fashion set by "Clopinel's Clean Rose," and followed by most dream allegories. In the *Romance of the Rose:*

> I went alone in my playing,
> To the small birds listening,
> As they did their best, many a pair,
> To sing on boughs blossoming fair.
> Jaunty, gay, full of gladness,
> Towards a river I would press,
> That I heard running fast nearby.
> Fairer playing never saw I
> Than what I found by that river fair.
> From a hill there standing near
> The stream came down strong and bold.
> Clear was its water, and as cold
> As any well. . . . .

> The bottom was paved everywhere
> With gravel full of bright stones.
>
> (99–121)

The Poet evokes the personifications of the *Romance* only indirectly. He shrinks from *luf-Daungere* (11) who, to him, is love's fear of losing his pearl forever. In the *Romance* the original Daunger:

> Jumps from the place where he was hid.
> Right great he was, and black of hue,
> Sturdy, hideous, as all knew.
> Like sharp quills did his hair grow,
> His eyes were red as the fire's glow,
> His ugly nose turned up. (1331–37)

Perhaps Reason (52), who could have brought calm to the Poet, is a similar evocation; Mirth may be personified in the passage where the dreamer sees a watered garden (139–40), as in the *Romance:*

> In places I saw wells there,
> In which never frogs were,
> And in fair shadow was every well;
> But their number I can't tell.
> Of small streams that by some device
> Mirth, through conduits caused to rise.
> Through which the water running by
> Made pleasant sounds. (1383–90)

One passage is taken directly from the *Romance*. When the Poet wonders at Pearl's endowments (745–54) he echoes the lines in which the Lover complains that he cannot describe Nature, since even Aristotle's ingenuity would fail, and even Pygmalion could not "carve Nature's mould" since "her face is fresher than the fleur-de-lys" (16013, ff.).

In many allegories, womanly guides of great wisdom and beauty instruct the bewildered protagonist, as Pearl instructs the dreamer. In the *Romance*, the Rose as a person plays no active part; she whom the flower represents is simply a woman "so worthy to be loved" that she must accept the book written for her. She is finally plucked, but she has taught her lover no lesson. Other personifications, among whom is Reason, see to his education. After Daunger's threats:

> A long while stood I in that state,
> Until she saw my madness great,
> She, lady always upon guard,
> Who from her tower looked outward.
> Reason men call that fair lady
> Who from her tower right quickly
> Came down to me without delay.
> She was neither young nor gray,
> Nor tall, nor short, nor fat, nor lean,
> But best, as in the right mean.
> Her two eyes were clear and light
> As any candle that burns bright,
> And on her head she had a crown.
> She seemed indeed a great person,
> For round her head her bright circlet
> Was full of gems richly fret.
>
> . . . .
>
> God gave her might and sovereignty
> To save men from their own folly,
> And whoever will trust her lore
> Will offend Him nevermore.
>
> (3195–3216)

Reason failed to convince the Lover to give up his folly, but another queen-like figure found a more docile pupil. In *Piers Plowman* Long Will saw:

> A Lady lovely of face, clothed in linen,
> came down from a castle, and called me graciously,
> and said, "Son, sleepest thou? Seest thou these people,
> how busy they be, and all in a maze?"
>
> . . . .
>
> I was afraid of her face, though she was fair,
> and said, "Mercy, Madame, what does this mean?"
>
> (B. I, 4)

When she has explained the gospel concerning the reasonable use of things:

> Then I had wonder in my wits what this woman was
> who showed such wise words from Holy Writ,
> and asked in the high name, as she went away,
> what she truly was who taught me so well.
> "Holy Church am I," said she. "Thou shouldst have known me."
>
> (B. I, 78)

So also Grace-Dieu, in *The Pilgrimage of Man*, appears in beauty and in regal garments beyond a stream, to help an obtuse pupil.

Another figure, both real and allegorical, plays a part closer to Pearl's than any other lady of high romance. In the *Divine Comedy* Dante sees Beatrice (an actual woman who for him is grace) in a garden, the earthly paradise on the top of Mount Purgatory. She is standing in the chariot of the Church, beyond a stream. Song arises from her retinue, and :

> So, even so, through cloud on cloud of flowers
> Flung from angelic hands and falling down
> Over the car and all around in showers,
>
> In a white veil, beneath an olive-crown
> Appeared to me a lady cloaked in green
> And living flame the color of her gown.
>
> And instantly, for all the years between
> Since her mere presence, with a kind of fright
> Could awe me and make my spirit faint within,
>
> There came on me, needing no further sight,
> Just by that strange, outflowing power of hers,
> The old, old love, in all its mastering might.
>
> (*Purgatory*, XXX, 28–34)

Like the Pearl-Poet, Dante is rebuked, then comforted. Beatrice reveals his foolishness:

> Stop sowing tears and listen; thou must know
> By another way, and quite reversed
> My buried flesh ought to have made thee go.
>
> Nothing in art and nature, last and first,
> Gave thee such joy as those fair members, wrought
> To clothe me once, now in the earth dispersed.
>
> And when my death brought that best joy to nought,
> What mortal thing should there have been whose clutch
> Could draw thee to it in thy hankering thought?
>
> Rather shouldst thou, at the first tingling touch
> Of these delusions, have made haste to spring
> Up after me, who was no longer such.
>
> (*Purgatory*, XXXI, 46–57)

Unlike the Pearl-Poet, Dante is drawn through the separating stream. But he too must come back to tell about it.

Basic to the allegorical thought of the whole of the Middle Ages is Boethius' *Consolations of Philosophy*, a sixth-century work in which the earliest of these womanly guides of unhappy men appears. She is Lady Philosophy,

> a woman of majestic face with burning eyes that pierced deeper than the ordinary vision of men, and with bright color suggesting endless vigor, although she seemed so old as not to belong to our age, and her stature varied. Sometimes she was of the common height of men, sometimes her head reached to the highest heavens, and when she rose to her full height she penetrated heaven itself and the gaze of men could not follow her. (I, Prosa 1)

Boethius had lost all that earth can offer. Philosophy is both severe and comforting, and leads to goodness:

> Therefore be firm against vice and practice virtue; lift your soul to worthy hopes and offer humble prayers on high. For, if you do not shrink from the truth, a great obligation of virtuous action is laid upon you, since all you do is open to the sight of the Judge who sees all things. (V, Prosa 6)

She discusses the nature of happiness, true and false, and the crucial problem of God's seeming injustice, and concludes that earthly love must be renounced for spiritual. Parallels with *Pearl* in theme and treatment are close, but where Boethius was helped by philosophy alone, the later dreamer finds in his Lady the spokesman of grace, "and this is the ground of all my bliss."

Boethius' book was a *consolatio*. Poems of consolation form a long elegiac tradition, coming from the same source as the pastoral tradition: the laments of Sicilian poet-shepherds such as Theocritus for an untimely death. The mourning of Thyrsis for Daphnis began the pastoral writing that remained linked to the form of the elegy through the Middle Ages and the Renaissance, and then from Milton to Matthew Arnold. There are two fourteenth-century elegies which may have influenced *Pearl*.

Boccaccio wrote *Olympia* in 1361, after the death of his five-year-old daughter Violante. The imagery is classical; the figure of the pastor and his flock had long been blended with that of the Good Shepherd. Here the grieving father, a shepherd named

Silvius, wakes from sleep in the middle of the night. A maiden appears to him, radiant and full grown, in a shining light; her name is now Olympia. The father questions her:

> I wailed thee, daughter mine, on mountain heights,
> in woods and far-off glades, and called thee oft.
> But me, if I be worthy, tell what haunts
> have held thee this long day. Who gave to thee
> thy robe so white, entwined with yellow gold?
> What light shines in thine eyes ne'er seen before?

To comfort him she sings a hymn in honor of Codrus—Christ—who has brought her to the top of Mount Olympus. As she departs the father accepts God's will; the last lines are a fore-echo of the "pastures new" of *Lycidas:*

> Whither, my daughter, whither fleest thou,
> leaving thy father tearful? Ah, she passed
> to upper air, and drew the scents she brought.
> With tears my life I'll dree, and fare to death.
> Boys, drive the calves afield! Lo, Phosphor gleams
> and Sol emerges now from misty shade.[10]

The second elegy is no eclogue, but a youthful dream-allegory of Chaucer. *The Book of the Duchess* is full of high spirits despite its mournful subject: the death of Blanche, Duchess of John of Gaunt. Chaucer tells his readers that he must fall asleep in order to dream, for which he must rehearse a story involving Morpheus. In his dream he finds the May morning so spritely that he takes to the woods, where he finds the black-clad John sitting under a tree. John lovingly describes his lost "White," who is no heavenly vision but a refreshing lady a little on the plump side. The picture is far removed from that of the Pearl-Poet's "Special Spice," but idealistic:

> And which a goodly softe speche
> Had that swete, my lyves leche!
> So friendly, and so wel ygrounded,
> Up al resoun so wel yfounded,
> And so tretable to alle goode
> That I dar swere wel by the roode
> Of eloquence was never founde
> So swete a sownynge facounde,

. . . .
> Trouthe himselfe, over al and al
> Had chose hys maner principal
> In hir, that was his restyng place.
>   (919–26, 1003–5)

Another of Chaucer's fair ladies resembles Pearl more closely: Alceste, Cupid's queen. She appears in the Prologue to *The Legend of Good Women* where Chaucer is playing with another literary fashion, "the cult of the marguerite," or daisy, celebrated by the French poets who influenced him: Deschamps, Froissart, Machault, Chaucer loved the English "day's eye" so much that he would rise before dawn to watch it open at the sun's touch. Thinking of his flower he falls asleep "in the jolly month of May," and:

> Me mette how I lay in the medewe thoo,
> To seen this flour that I so love and drede;
> And from afer com walkyng in the mede
> The god of Love, and in his hand a quene,
> And she was clad in real habit grene.
> A fret of gold she hadde next her heer,
> And upon that a whit corowne she ber
> With flourons smale, and I shal nat lye;
> For al the world, ryght as a dayesye
> Ycorounded ys with white leves lyte,
> So were the flowrouns of hire coroune white.
> For of o perl fyn, oriental,
> Hire white coroune was ymaked al.
>   (F. 210–22)

So the Poet first sees Pearl:

> A well-set crown she wore, that girl,
> of no other stones than marjory,
> high-pinnacled, of clear white pearl
> in figured flowers formed perfectly.
>   (205–8)

In the Vulgate the word for a pearl is *margarita*. The play on its triple meaning—a jewel, a flower, and girl's name—is a link between the *sensus* of the poem and its *sententia*. The pearl, its dominant symbol, must hold its meaning. In Scripture, the pearl has a tiny parable all its own: "The Kingdom of heaven is like a merchant in search of fine pearls who, on finding one pearl of great value, went and sold all that he had and bought it" (Matt. XIII: 45–46). In *Pearl* it is stated unambiguously that the peerless gem that the maiden wears is this same pearl beyond price: "Upon my breast it now lies, see!" (740). But this simple scriptural significance could unfold bewilderingly. In the fourth century Ephrem the Syrian wrote in *The Pearl of the Seven Rhythms on the Faith:*

> On a certain day a pearl I did take up, my brethren. I saw in it mysteries pertaining to the Kingdom, semblances and types of the Majesty; it became a fountain and I drank out of it the mysteries of the Sun. I put it, my brethren, upon the palm of my hand that I might examine it. I went to look at it on one side and it proved faces on all sides.[11]

In this manner the complex literary tradition of the pearl grew throughout medieval literature.

Margarita was the proper name of a girl whose life and death first translated the natural qualities of a pearl into a symbol that took its luster from the gospel parable. Saint Margaret of Antioch (Marina in the Greek Church) suffered martyrdom for her virginity in the persecution of Diocletian; her feast day is still kept on June 20. No records of her are found outside legend; the earliest Greek version is already spectacular. Her cult spread in Latin versions after its appearance in the *Martyrology* of Rabanus Maurus; the maiden of quick tongue and strong heart became one of Europe's favorite saints, especially in England where virgin-martyrs appealed to the heroic-minded Anglo-Saxons. The sensational episode of the dragon who swallowed the maiden after losing an argument with her, and then split open and released her, was declared "frivolous and apocryphal" by Jacobus de Voragine when he wrote the tale into the *Legenda Aurea*. There he connected the mystic significance of her name with the qualities of the pearl as given in manuals of natural history:

> "Margaret" is used for a certain precious gem which is called *margarita:* this gem is white and small and powerful. The blessed Margaret was white by virginity, small by humility, and powerful through the working of miracles. For this stone is said to be powerful against effusions of blood and against the passions of the heart, and for the strengthening of the spirit.

Virginity had already been connected with precious stones in the Liturgy. In the Divine Office for the feast of St. Agnes, January 21, the martyr sings:

> Depart from me, for I am already claimed by another Lover. He has clasped my right hand and my neck with precious stones, and He has hung priceless pearls in my ears. He has placed His seal upon my face that I may admit no other lover. He has bound me with a ring of faith and adorned me with immense jewels. Christ has set me about with ornaments and with shimmering precious stones.

The gospel and the communion antiphon of the mass for virgins told of the priceless pearl, and formed the basis for homilies. Manuals for preachers compared virginity to "that precious stone, the pearl for which the merchant seeking heaven gave all that he had to buy," and a special homiletic tradition grew up after 1250.[12] Vincent of Beauvais, referring to current scientific notions, wrote in the *Speculum Morale:*

> The dew of heaven, received into the ocean-shell, and kept there, is changed into a precious white stone; so the grace of God, descending from heaven, kept in the shell of a humble heart, there generates the determination to keep virginity, and in this perseverance, like to the hardening of the precious stone, is worthy to be compared to the kingdom of heaven. Also, the pearl has the power against the falling sickness, and virginity against a fall into sensuality. (I, 3)

The pearl became the symbol of many other things. In patristic exposition it was compared to: the contemplative life, the sweetness of heaven, the preaching of the gospel, Mary, Christ, the Trinity, and the souls of the just. In Rabanus Maurus' *Allegoriae in Sacram Scripturam:*

> Margarita means heavenly desire, as in the gospel, "Having found a precious pearl," that is, having conceived a desire of heaven in the mind. Margarita means spiritual sign, as in the gospel, "cast not your pearls before swine," that is, do not hand over interior mysteries to the unclean. Margaritas means righteous men, as in the Apocalypse; twelve gates are twelve pearls, through which holy men, by their faith in the apostles, have entry to the kingdom of heaven. Margaritas means earthly delights, as in the

> Apocalypse: The woman (the harlot of Babylon) was adorned with pearls, because the falseness of this glitters with earthly pleasure. (*P.L.* XII, 996)

The abrupt shift from good to bad significance in the last symbol is a reminder that any created thing can be abused. In the fourteenth century pearls were lavishly used on clothing and for decoration, and were often signs of luxurious ostentation. Royal inventories list enormous collections, with Edward III as a leading fancier. Popular ideas concerning pearls were drawn from lapidaries, or manuals of precious stones combining science, symbolism, and mysticism with downright superstition. *The Peterborough Lapidary* says:

> Margarita is the chief of all stones that are white and precious, as Isidore says. And it has the name margarita because it is found in cockle and mussel shells, and in shellfish of the sea. The breeding is done in a shellfish and it is engendered by the dew of heaven, the which dew the shellfish receiveth at certain times of the year, from which dew the pearls come. Some are called "unions," and they have a good name, for one only is ever found, and never two together. And the white margaritas are better than the yellow, and those that are conceived of the morning dew grow dim in the air of eveningtide. . . . And they are best when white, clear and round. And they have the power to strengthen in all cases, and some say that they strengthen limbs and members. . . . And the best and noblest margaritas come from India, and from Old Britain. . . . And it is thought that none grow larger than half a foot.

It is not surprising that literary references to the popular jewel, heavy with symbolism, appear in the writings of the Pearl-Poet's contemporaries. Gower, in his *Mirroir de l'Ame*, compares a virgin to a "très-fine marguerite" (16837 ff.), small and white and honored by God Himself, and in *Vox Clamantis* he parallels "Pearl pleasant to a Prince":

> As the white margarita pleases above precious things,
> So the dedicated virgin pleases God in her cloister.
> (IV, 65960)

And more than one of the key words in *Pearl* are found in a passage from *The Book of the Knight of the Tour Landry:*

(77)

This is found in the gospel of the virgins which our gentle Lord
Jesus preached and taught to the people. He was speaking of good
and pure women, and He said: "A precious marguerite is like to
them." And this was marvelously said, for the marguerite is the
precious pearl, round, clear, white and clean. And when it is clear
and clean, with no spot to be seen, this precious pearl is called a
marguerite. And so God showed us the value and worth of a
good and pure woman. For she is clean and spotless, that is, she
who is not married and remains a virgin, or chaste, and also she
who is married and remains pure within the sacrament of
marriage, without allowing herself to be touched by any other
man than the husband whom God destined for her and gave her,
and also she who lives pure in widowhood. (Chap. XIX)

The most elaborate development of the pearl theme is Sir Thomas
Usk's *Testament of Love*, c. 1386, a long prose allegory in which
the courtly love convention is treated with the earnestness of
Boethius' *Consolations of Philosophy*, its model. The narrator
grieves for the loss of "Lady Precious Margaret" whom he had first
found when "a mussel in a blue shell had enclosed her." Another
Lady comforts him, Love herself. In their long dialogue full of
allegorical episodes they return constantly to: "This jewel, as
precious a pearl as womanly woman is by nature, in whom goodness, virtue and the fair shaping of limbs and features all accord.
And it pleases me to liken this Pearl to Philosophy" (III,l). The
symbols are drawn together at the end:

Also I pray that every man may perfectly know what was the
intention of my heart in writing this treatise. How is it that
visible manna in the desert was spiritual food for the Children of
Israel? Bodily also it was, for it nourished men's bodies, and yet,
nonetheless, it signified Christ. Even so a jewel betokens a gem, a
power-bearing stone or else a pearl. Margarita, a woman, betokens grace, learning, or the wisdom of God, or else Holy Church.
If bread, through power, is made holy flesh, what is it that our
God says: "It is the spirit that giveth life; the flesh profiteth
nothing." Flesh is fleshly understanding; flesh without grace and
love is worth nothing. "The letter slayeth, the spirit giveth living
understanding." "Charity is love, and love is charity." (III, 9)

Usk explained his meaning; the Pearl-Poet did not. "Great poetry
can communicate before it is understood," said Eliot of Dante.

Pearl communicates. But readers, like the dreamer, want to understand, and for over eighty years critics have argued with all the heat of a medieval debate over the poem's *sententia*.

The tropological level is not hard to find; anyone can step onto it from his own experience when he reads line 9: "But O! I lost it!" Loss, desire, struggle, questioning; the astonished refinding; the need to press on through a second loss; the hard-earned willingness to wait for final possession—at peace with Another's will. The analogical level is made visible in the New Jerusalem, over the narrow but as yet unpassable stream. But what is the allegorical significance of the whole?

This begs the question. Is the poem an allegory at all, or is it autobiography? The first editor wrote: "The author evidently gives expression to his sorrow for the loss of his infant child, a girl two years old. . . . He represents himself as visiting the child's grave." [13] Subsequent editors enlarged:

> The poet had married. . . . A child, a sweet girl radiant in innocence, had blessed this union. The father concentrated all his affection upon the child, and so exclusively that we are led to believe that the mother had not long survived her birth. The dearest ideals of the thoughtful poet were embodied in his daughter. But the pitiless hand of fate tore her away at the tenderest age. The poem describes the father's feelings at her death, and tells how he was comforted. [14]

And again:

> The poet had married; his wedded life had been unhappy; the object of his love had disappointed him and had perhaps proved unfaithful. . . . But his wedded life had brought him happiness—an only child, his "little queen." He perhaps named the child Marjory or Marguerite; she was his "pearl"—emblem of holiness and innocence. But his happiness was short-lived; before two years had passed the poet's home was desolate. His grief found expression in verse. A heavenly vision of his lost jewel brought him comfort and taught him resignation. On the child's grave he placed a garland of song. [15]

And again: "The poem is undoubtedly an elegy." [16]

None of these critics denied that an elegy could also be symbolic. As one wrote: "Here, as in the *Divine Comedy*, the allegory is lifted almost to symbolism by its earnestness and intensity and by its evident mysticism, which is connected with a well-known passage in the Apocalypse." [17] Yet when criticism in the scholarly journals began, a dichotomy was created between the literal and the symbolic interpretations. The first articles drew attention to the wealth of meaning that the poem took from its cultural milieu, and claimed that it was in no sense autobiographical but purely allegorical.[18]

This invited a search for a key to the allegory, one dominant significance that would unlock the rest. One such key symbol was found in the Holy Eucharist. There are numerous references in patristic writing to Christ as a pearl, and some to the Host as a pearl, with the Mystical Body as "the Great Pearl." The structure of the poem could parallel that of the mass. Perhaps the Poet's vision took place in church before some altarpiece such as "The Adoration of the Lamb" by the brothers Van Eyck. "Within the frame of the Great Pearl the poet sees his lost Pearl in the presence of the Lamb of God. She teaches him that through the Eucharist he can be united to his Pearl as part of 'the Great Pearl'." [19] Another possible key was "innocence," presented in terms of marian imagery. The Blessed Virgin is the archetype of innocence; in medieval commentaries she is "adorned with the pearls of all virtues." The imagery in *Pearl* is drawn from such works as Albertus Magnus' *De Laudibus Beatae Mariae*, in which "Mary is figured in nearly every person and thing mentioned in Scripture." The maiden will not allow herself to be mistaken for "the Queen of heaven's blue," but she shares the prerogatives of this "Phoenix of Araby." [20]

Pearl, a Study in Spiritual Dryness vehemently denied the elegiac nature of the poem. It has nothing to do with a lost child:

> Boldly, I call *Pearl* a spiritual autobiography, a study of dryness and interior desolation. The author was a monk who had enjoyed a beginner's fervor for the two years of his noviceship. . . . He is speaking indeed to a dream-child, but this child is not the ghost of a dead infant. It is the personification of his own soul in the state of such potential perfection and happiness as is congruous with it at this time of his life. The Pearl is symbolic of this same state, and is used interchangeably with Maiden or Child to indicate it.[21]

The Pearl is, further, "a symbol of peace. . . . It is found in the religious life, upon the word of the poet's own vision. . . . It is his hope of heaven, of the Beatific Vision." This interpretation is supported by references to spiritual biographies such as those of Ramon Lull and Henry Suso. Another critic followed the same lines, but less specifically:

> The poem, though cast in elegiac form, is not autobiographical but parabolical; it was designed to illustrate the doctrine of divine grace. . . . The figure of a child lost in infancy is used as a literary device. [The author] writes with all the fervor of the mystic and contemplative soul, not that of the bereaved father.[22]

But the elegiac and allegorical interpretations are not mutually exclusive; they must be harmonized. It was shown that there is no single "key" to the allegory which, in its shifting nature, can throw various lights on the content of the poem.[23] The next interpretations followed these lines. One made the poem the story of a real jeweler who has lost a pearl and is inordinately distressed. He identifies the maiden of the vision with his lost treasure. Their dialogue reveals that she is the symbol of his own soul who shows him his potential glory and leads him to the renunciation that will insure it.[24] Another and more comprehensive view sees the poem as "a Catholic Paradise Lost and Regained." The settings of garden and hill are Eden and Calvary, the fall and the redemption, and the maiden is the human soul. The whole poem "in its studied ambiguity and contrapuntal technique [is] a biblical epic of the soul, in delicate miniature, seen in the epitome of one man's passionate experience." [25]

Interpretation then swung in the direction of the New Criticism; the poem is "not so much a secret allegory as a work of art in which art and meaning are one." Analysis must "take into account the complete scope of the imagery of earth and water, images which make the *Pearl* a picture of two worlds and the means of transition between them, a vision embracing heaven and earth." [26] Newman once said that images used together correct each other. And so the poem is "an elegy along the lines of spiritual adventure. The central adventure is resurrection, and here images are boldly mixed: a jewel in the ground is a germinating seed." [27] Or again, the structure of the poem is pictured as concentric circles around the parable of the vineyard. The theme—a realization of God's free giving that leads to resignation—is seen in images of lavishness:

overflowing water, overspreading spices, overwhelming light and color.[28]

One study claims that the poem was created for a practical purpose, that it is a homily in which a pastor addresses his audience with "a message of salvation and of its attainment through God's gracious *cortayse* and men's childlike acceptance of His bounty." [29] But most recent studies see the poem as essentially dramatic. It is "a non-allegorical unfolding of the pearl symbolism along dramatic lines." [30] In a drama the protagonist is central. The dreamer's grief and struggle for understanding give the poem its appeal. He reaches a mid-point between heaven and earth, between problem and solution, and his acceptance of the fact of death from a heavenly point of view is the central theme. "By a *rite de passage* he has journeyed to a strange land and returned initiated into a more meaningful life." [31] Or again, the art of the poem can explain its total meaning through the progression of its dramatic plot, "the pattern of ideas and emotions arranged as thesis–antithesis–synthesis." This dialectical order controls the substance of the poem and "leads to a high vision of salvation which enables the protagonist to go on living. . . . The whole poem is devised to present a vision of salvation so compelling that we wish to attain it." This vision of paradise is the high point. The poem ends with "Amen. So be it." The mystery remains.[32]

In summarizing these varied interpretations, one may conclude that none is wrong or would have been disowned by the Poet, but none is the only correct view. The Poet has used symbolism in the parable of the vineyard and the pearl of great price, but:

> Symbolism succeeds only in as far as it approaches true allegory, which is the expression of conscious experience of a thing or concept by means of words which do not literally represent it. . . . Like all great poems of any age, *Pearl* is fundamentally allegorical; its meaning is the experience of learning what heavenly justice and courtesy are, of learning that man can use his free will properly only by freely consenting to the greater will of God. . . .
>
> The girl who appears in *Pearl* is herself an allegorical figure, for she expresses to the poet and to us, through her words and actions, the most important experiences the poet wishes to convey. The question of her actual existence is as irrelevant to the meaning of the poem as is the question of the name of the poet;

but we must not therefore fall into the error of assuming that she is an abstract symbol. Within the poem her existence as the poet's lost daughter is absolute and complete—as real as the existence of the dreaming poet himself, who is also an allegorical figure and not a symbol. If critics of *Pearl* have in general tended to regard the girl as symbolic and the poet-narrator as real, the reason is partly that our modern habits of symbolic thought lead us into a false separation of experience and expression, of fact and imagination. . . . There are signs that the twentieth century is on the road to recovery of an understanding of the allegorical habits of thought which lent such richness to the medieval view of the world.[33]

So the small dazzling figure of Pearl is left standing at the close of the Middle Ages, looking toward the twentieth century. Behind her is the *Divine Comedy*, of which her story is a radiant miniature. Before her are the Renaissance, the Reformation, the Enlightenment, the Industrial Revolution, and the atomic-cosmic age. No wonder that her language has become archaic! But if we are indeed recovering the allegorical habit of thought, she will be more easily understood now than in any age between ours and her own.

As the variety of interpretation shows, she has the elusive ambivalence of modern imagery. Yet when she "speaks otherwise" it is in positive terms. Her tone is the tone of Beatrice, full of authority; she expects assent to truth, and she purifies love till it burns with joy. She could not be negative, neutral, or nihilistic; she is not the symbol in Steinbeck's *Pearl*, a gem beyond price which is good yet brings misery, which is beautiful yet wrecks reality. Rather, she blesses with her presence, like the Lady in White met in the garden-in-the-desert of Eliot's *Ash-Wednesday*, and:

> Because of the goodness of this Lady
> And because of her loveliness, and because
> She honors the Virgin in meditation
> We shine with brightness.

Like the Lady, she is at home, sure of herself, among paradoxes. Is she prayer? Is she purity? She wears:

> White light folded, sheathed about her, folded.
> The new year's walk, restoring
> Through a bright cloud of tears, the years, restoring
> With a new verse the ancient rhyme.

Saint Erkenwald

This poem is found in MS Harleian 1150, described in the British Museum catalogue as "a paper book in folio, consisting of diverse tracts." The script is that of the late fifteenth century, and one entry (an abridgement of the *Speculum Christiani*) is dated 1477. It contains religious and didactic pieces such as sermons, stanzaic "Instructions for Parish Priests," expositions of feasts from *Legenda Aurea*, "Five Church Tales," and metrical lives of the saints, some from the *South English Legendary*. One legend, found nowhere else, bears the title *De Erkenwaldo*.

The whole manuscript is in the West Midlands dialect, with a mixture of eastern and northern forms; it shows peculiarities not shown in the Cotton manuscript, as it was written seventy-five years later. The names of Booth and Massey in the margins connect the book with the Northwest. One distinguished member of the Booth family, Lawrence Booth from Barton, Lancashire, became Dean of St. Paul's in London in 1456. The manuscript might well have been in his library, since *Saint Erkenwald* tells of a miracle worked in that very cathedral.

The hero-saint of the poem had a splendid tomb in St. Paul's, but his cult had fallen into neglect. So, in 1386, Bishop Robert de Braybrooke wrote a pastoral *Monitio* to his diocese:

> By the advice and with the consent of the deacons and chapter of our cathedral church, we decree that the feasts of the Conversion and Commemoration of this apostle [St. Paul], and also the days of the Deposition [April 30] and Translation [November 14] of Saint Erkenwald shall be celebrated with veneration and with the solemnity due to the sacred day of Sunday, by all the followers of Christ in our city and diocese.[1]

Perhaps the Bishop thought that a poem in honor of Saint Erkenwald would help in this revival of the honor due to him, and if the Pearl-Poet were in London that year he may have been asked to write it.

The *littera* of the poem gives internal evidence of his authorship.

The meter and quatrain structure are like those used in *Patience* and *Cleanness*. The homiletic tradition was closely linked with hagiography; sermons used saints' lives as *exempla*, and sometimes a complete biography would be given from the pulpit on the appropriate feast day. The *Acta Martyrum*, dating from the times of the catacombs, became patterns for the longer *Acta Sanctorum*, and gradually great cycles of saints' lives evolved, the *Legendaries*. These highly uncritical biographies were ardent with hero-worship; they tingled with the excitement of the miraculous. They were an enthusiastic blend of a little history and much legend, and could bring home their moral lessons entertainingly. In *Saint Erkenwald* the same craftsmanship and insight shown in the poems of the Cotton MS have made a work of art out of such a story.

The *sensus*, the tale itself, is unknown elsewhere. Its hero belongs to history; he was named Bishop of London in 674. Four Latin *Vitae* exist in manuscript, one of which was printed by the Bollandists in the *Acta Sanctorum* for April 30. Erkenwald was the son of King Anna of East Anglia who died in 654. Some versions say that his father was a less-authentic King Offa. He and his sister Ethelburga were won to Christianity by the Roman missionaries. Both entered monasteries; then, as Bede says in the *Ecclesiastical History*:

> At the time when Sebbit and Sighere, of whom we spoke before, were ruling over the East Saxons, Theodore appointed Erkenwald to be their bishop in the city of London. Both before and after he was made a bishop his life and conversation were most holy, as signs of his heavenly power even now bear witness. . . .
>
> Before he was made bishop this man had built two illustrious monasteries, one for himself and one for his sister, Ethelburga, and established excellent regular discipline in both. His own monastery was near the river Thames at Chertsey, that is Ceorot's Island in Surrey. The convent where his sister ruled as mother and teacher of women was at Barking in the province of the East Saxons. While ruling over this convent she always acted as the worthy sister of a bishop, leading an upright life, and constantly and devotedly caring for the needs of her subjects, as heavenly signs attest. (IV, 6)

Later chronicles wove in many stories. William of Malmesbury wrote in the *Gesta Pontificum Anglorum*:

Both recent report and former memory clearly affirm that he was a worker of miracles. One of the most notable occurred while he was being carried on a litter because of illness. When he came to the shore of a raging torrent, he and his companions hesitated, as he was so infirm that he could not cross it either on foot or on horse-back, and it was feared that even a boat could not withstand the violence of the waters. Suddenly the waves grew calm and the river quietly subsided along its banks. As soon as the Bishop and his company had crossed over, the stream, which had gathered behind him in a crest of tossing waves, returned to its course. (II)

The Bishop died while visiting his sister at Barking where, according to the *Acta Sanctorum:*

Till the last moment of his life he vigorously comforted those standing around him with words of eternal life. As soon as his holy soul had left his body and had been carried by angels to heaven, such a sweet fragrance remained that it filled the whole house in which his body lay with marvelous sweetness. (April 30)

Accounts of the Bishop's miracles fill ten folio columns of the *Acta,* but not one of them resembles the story told by the Pearl-Poet.

All this happened in the "Golden Age" nostalgically described by Bede: "Never were there happier times since the English came to Britain . . . for the people eagerly sought the new-found joys of the kingdom of heaven, and all who wished to learn to read the Scriptures had teachers ready" (IV, 2). The events given in the first lines of the poem are found scattered through such records as the *Chronica Majora* of Matthew Paris: the driving of Christian Britons into Wales "with swords and flames" (I, 251); the arrival of St. Augustine to convert "the barbarous Saxons," who, "driven by their pagan superstitions had destroyed Christianity in that part of the island where they lived" (I, 255); and the changing of the pagan temples into churches.

Medieval poets rarely made a distinction between history and legend. Bishop Erkenwald is authentic, but the long-buried British judge whom he restored to life belongs to the dubious days when "what is now London was called New Troy," so named by the Trojan Brutus with whom early histories of Britain all began. Geoffrey of Monmouth's *History of the Kings of Britain* goes on to tell of the troubled reign of King Belin and of his conflict with his brother Brennius (called Beryng in the poem) in 354 B.C. This king, when peace was made, "renewed his father's laws everywhere throughout the kingdom, rejoicing always in doing steady and even-handed justice" (III, 10), through such honest judges as the one restored by St. Erkenwald.

The Pearl-Poet may have found this episode in the form of an oral tradition clinging to the shrine of St. Paul's cathedral. It is, perhaps, significant that its famous analogue, the recalling to life of the Emperor Trajan by the prayers of Pope Gregory the Great, is told in the *Chronica Majora* just before the account of St. Augustine upon which the Poet probably drew. He may simply have adapted the event to his own purposes. This widespread tale was first told in 713 by a monk of Whitby; Bede does not mention it. Paulus Diaconus in the ninth century told how Trajan had once put off an important battle in order to do justice to a poor widow, and:

> When Gregory was walking through the forum of Trajan he remembered and marvelled at the story of the widow. Recalling the mercy of this judge, he came to the basilica of St. Peter's, and there for a long time he wept over the mistaken beliefs of so kind a prince. And the following night he received an answer that he had been heard in his plea for Trajan. (*P.L.*, LXXV, 104)

The Emperor was thus delivered by prayer and tears. The scene in which Erkenwald wins the same grace for the British judge is more vividly told. The Poet may have been helped in his description by another legend:

> About the year of the Lord 1200 it was reported that in Vienna the head of a certain dead man, whose lips and tongue were intact, spoke intelligibly. When the Bishop asked him what he had been while living he answered: "I was a pagan and a judge in this place; my tongue never pronounced a false sentence, and thus it could not die until, regenerated by baptism, I might go to heaven, since I had merited this grace from God." And when the head was baptized, at once the tongue fell into dust and the soul flew off to God.[2]

The story of Trajan also had been extended to include an excavation and a speaking head. A tale by John de Bromyard concerning the finding of a head in St. Paul's had become attached to memories of the excavations of Roman dead. It is possible that another famous story current in Belgium concerning a judge named Erkenbald, whose integrity was rewarded by a miracle of the sacred Host, had been blended with that of St. Erkenwald because of the similar names. It was left for the Pearl-Poet to raise the legend, wherever he found it, to artistic excellence.

If legend and history are confused in medieval narrative, legend and Christian teaching are apt to be confused in modern commentaries on the legends. The theological import of *Saint Erkenwald* can only be clarified by making a much-needed distinction between the three meanings of the Latin term *inferus*, and of the English term "hell," which translated it in Old and Middle English writings. These "lower regions" included the hell of the damned, the limbo of the Patriarchs, and the limbo of the unbaptized. The first is an irrevocable state; legend does not condone the final release of a soul condemned through its own fault. The second ended when the act of redemption was accomplished; Christ's visit to the limbo of the Patriarchs (the saved who lived under the Old Testament) is based on Scripture and expressed in the Nicene Creed: "descendit ad inferos." The widespread story of Christ's "Harrowing of Hell" amplified this fact of doctrine with legendary material drawn from the apocryphal *Descensus ad Inferos;*[3] its most powerful literary expression is found in *Piers Plowman* where Christ comes to lead out from the dominion of Satan "those that be worthy" (Passus XVIII). The third "hell" is the abode of the virtuous pagan souls unsanctified by baptism. The *Divine Comedy* places this third hell within the confines of the first, but the souls there are not damned: "They sinned not, yet their merit lacked its chiefest/Fulfilment, lacking baptism" (*Inferno*, IV, 34), and they live in "a noble seat" set "in a fresh meadow." The geographic lines, so to speak, between the three "hells" were not clearly drawn; neither, at times, were the thought-lines. Moreover, the word "damned" was used for any kind of condemnation, not only for final perdition.

The British judge tells St. Erkenwald that he was left behind at the harrowing of hell. He was not damned for sin; he belonged in the limbo of the unbaptized. The miracle worked for him was the Pearl-Poet's answer to the question that exercised many medieval thinkers: the salvation of the good heathen. Langland had answered it in his downright way:

> "Yea, baw for books!" said one who broke out of hell
> named Trajan, a true knight, as the Pope witnessed;
> for he was dead, and damned to dwell in pain
> as an unchristian creature. . . . .
> Thus loyal love and truthful living
> pulled out of pain a pagan of Rome.
>
> (B, XI, 136–228)

Dante found Trajan shining star-like above the eye of the eagle of justice in the sixth heaven, and was told:

> One from hell (where spirits never grope
>   Back to right will), into his flesh and bone
>   Returned; this was the guerdon of living hope,
>
> The living hope that nerved the orison
>   Made unto God to raise him up, and dower
>   His will once more with motions of its own;
>
> Which glorious soul, when for a little hour
>   It thus resumed the body whence it came,
>   Believed in Him that hath the saving power,
>
> And, so believing, loved, with ardent flame
>   So bright that at the second death 'twas found
>   Worthy to join our high celestial game.
>
> (*Paradise*, XX, 106–17)

The case of the British judge also bears a haunting resemblance to the second soul that Dante saw in the eagle's brow: Ripheus, described in the *Aeneid* as "the one man among the Trojans most just and observant of the right" (II, 426–27). The amazed Dante heard the eagle say:

> The other, by a grace from such deep ground
>   Gushing that no created eye can plumb
>   Its hidden well-springs where they run profound,
>
> On righteousness spent all his earthly sum
>   Of love; when God from grace to grace unsealed
>   His eyes to the redemption yet to come.

> Then he, believing in the truth revealed,
> The stench of pagan filth could no more bear,
> And scourged the vice with which the land was filled.
>
> Ere ever baptism was, a thousand years,
> He was baptized. (*Paradise*, XX, 121–28)

Saint Thomas would have approved of the answer of all three poets. He had written in the *Summa Theologica*:

> In answer to the incident of Trajan it may be supposed with probability that he was recalled to life at the prayers of Blessed Gregory, and thus obtained the grace whereby he received the pardon of his sins and in consequence was freed from punishment. The same applies to all those who were miraculously raised from the dead. . . . According to higher causes, in view of which it was foreseen that they would be raised to life, they were disposed of otherwise. (III, Supp. Q.71, Art. 4, Obj. 4)

The *sententia* of a saint's life lies open in the telling; *Saint Erkenwald* is a straightforward story. It is as edifying as the homilies, without oratorical framework or *moralitas* or *exemplum*. It is as vivid as *Sir Gawain* in its specificness, its swiftness, its narrative integrity, its ethical earnestness. But in thought it links most closely with *Pearl*; it completes one of the central themes of the dream vision: "The mercy of God is great enough." To convince the dreamer that she has been fitly rewarded in heaven, the maiden quotes Psalm XXIV; two sorts of men are saved:

> The one whose hands have done no ill,
> the one whose heart is clean and light.
> (680–1)

These are the righteous and the innocent; she herself fulfills the first case: "The innocent is saved by right." When St. Erkenwald asks the judge to tell of his reward in heaven he quotes the same Psalm:

> For as He says in His truthful Psalmbook:
> "The righteous and the innocent ascend ever to me."
> (277–78)

Surely he fulfills the second case, for he had led a supremely righteous life! But the judge explains that God's mercy could not come to a "dull pagan," a "faithless fellow who fell short of the law which Thou, Lord, art praised by" (285–86). The Bishop's compassionate tears become the means by which the sacrament of regeneration is effected. Heaven opens. In *Pearl* the dreamer had leaped too soon toward the possession of his joy. He was checked, left on earth to wait in yearning peace. But the soul of the British judge had waited long enough in the shadows of desire. It "leaped swiftly with joy unleashed" (335) to God's supper-table, while in London "all the bells in town boomed out together" (352).

Saint Erkenwald, in its simplicity and mature artistry, may well be the Pearl-Poet's last work, closing a life in which joy had won out over pain through the power of faith.

SYNTHESIS

"What any great writer has to say can be written in the palm of his hand." If this adage be true of the Pearl-Poet, some image basic to his art may be found to express some truth basic to his thought. One dominant image is that of the rarest of earth's products: jewels. His poetry has the quality of living light reflected from the facets of gems, well-set. Ephrem the Syrian easily held in his palm the pearl in which he saw "faces on all sides." Just as easily a poet could write in his palm the Augustinian saying: "Beauty is the splendor of order."

Jewels were familiar things in the Pearl-Poet's world. In folklore they were thought to shine by their own light; Lambkin in the ballad called out to the lady:

> You have two bright diamonds,
>   As bright as the stars;
> Put one on each finger,
>   And they'll show you downstairs.

In fairy tales they gave invisibility; in real life they were worn for protection against accident, disease, and temptation. In the lapidaries their magic "virtues" were given as natural qualities: a diamond "defends a witless man against foes," a sapphire "does away sorrow." In social life jewels stood for luxury and nobility. Brought from the Orient, they honored crowns, swords, and church vessels. They were symbols of the lofty, the precious, the mysterious.

The Pearl-Poet uses jewels as sheer adornment and lets them speak as symbols. None are mentioned in *Patience*, though the leaves of Jonah's bower glint like the jeweled leaves in *Pearl*'s dreamland. But the Orient opens in *Cleanness*. Jewels sparkle, reverently or profanely, at Belshazzar's feast, and a pearl is the core symbol of the theme: the clean soul approaches Christ, the cleanest of pearls. In *Sir Gawain* jewels flash from the garments and trappings of court life, from the diamond circlet on the knight's head, and from the gems "in clusters of twenty" in the lady's hairnet. The total goodness of the hero is put into the same core symbol: "As a pearl by a white pea so is Gawain among knights" (2364). In *Saint Erkenwald* pearls are the only jewels on the robe of the just judge, but more precious are the tears that "poured in a bright stream" (330) from the bishop's eyes as "a gleam flashed lightly through the low abyss" (334). As for *Pearl*, it is by common consent the "jewel" of Middle English poetry, jewel-like in language, structure, and theme. The herb garden where flower colors "shine now brilliant against the sun" (28) is like a manuscript miniature done in gold-leaf and lapis-lazuli. The stream and the garden of vision have undergone the alchemy of the philosopher's stone. The jewels in the New Jerusalem are more than magical, more than visionary; they are Revelation. In the closing prayer "we all" shine as pearls for a Prince's pleasure.

The Poet gives his work a jewel-like quality, even when no gems are mentioned, by the alchemy of style. It is found in the fine-edged phrasing, as when the moon rises "before the day-gleam dies away" (1094); in the cloisonné grouping of pictures, as when animals, birds, and fishes leave the ark, each darting off to its own home; in the little insets that stud the larger scenes, as when Bercilak rides off to hunt while "ruddy-red through the cloud-banks the sun was rising" (1095). It is found in unexpected flashes of light, in the "stone-sparks" that fly from the hooves of Gryngolet; in the sparkle of humor in unlikely places, as when the dreamer stands "like a dazed quail" (1085) before the towers of heaven. It is found in a certain tactile hardness which is at the same time delicate, a diamond-surfaced emotion: "I would have pierced His mystery!" (1194). Everywhere is the mysterious suggestion of something hidden yet self-revealing, as in the depths of a precious stone; as in the face of Pearl herself, white and lustrous and "grave as a duke or earl" (211). And everywhere is the sense of the gem-high value of each of earth's joys; the ark opens "merrily on a fair morning" (493), and "many a merry mason" sings as he works. This poet is like Marco of the Millions who, returning from a far land, casually spilled his gems onto the supper-table.

Jewels are small *exempla* of "the splendor of order": symmetrical, juxtaposed in patterns, luminous. Order and splendor were basic notions in the medieval theory of beauty, derived from classic philosophy and sublimated into a Christian theophany by St. Augustine. Order was fundamental. "Measure and proportion are the elements of beauty," [1] said Plato who, as the poet-philosopher, could see through order "beauty shining in brightness." [2] "Beauty consists in order united to magnitude," [3] said Aristotle. These ideas led to a theory of art that used "intermediary links," seeing the sensible world as a poem or myth symbolizing spiritual essences. Plotinus then laid the basis of the Neo-Platonic view of beauty as primal unity and the splendor of the good. It does not rest only in symmetry, for the simple thing without parts can radiate beauty with the energy of light. Beauty has the power to attract, to awaken love. Beauty and being are identical, but the One is beyond being, and "material things become beautiful by communication in the thought that flows from the Divine." [4] As the Pseudo-Dionysius said: "God is the cause of the harmony and the clarity of the universe." [5]

St. Augustine, building on Plotinus, sought God as "Beauty ever ancient, ever new." [6] He wove his aesthetic theories through his whole philosophy. His views on the fusion of the transcendentals in beauty have been well summarized:

> Beauty is had when both the unity and the order of a thing, that is to say, its ontological truth and goodness, are manifested. . . . The luster of truth may illuminate the intellect without bringing delight, but beauty which implies truth is a delightful illumination. The good may bring delectation to the will, but unless this good has splendor—as when the splendor of order is spoken of—and brings delight through the illumination of the intellect, beauty is not had. Beauty is the delightful illumination of goodness and truth, simultaneously enlightening and gladdening. The delightful splendor of being which is beauty is the shining out of truth and goodness in which goodness is made visible and truth brings joy. [7]

St. Augustine himself turned all this into a prayer:

> I call upon Thee, God the Truth, in whom and from whom and through whom all things which are true have truth; . . . God the Good and the Beautiful, in whom and from whom and through

whom all things good and beautiful have goodness and beauty; God, intelligible light, in whom and from whom and through whom all things that shine with intelligibility have their intelligible light.[8]

St. Thomas drew the Augustinian aesthetic into Scholasticism: "For beauty includes three conditions: integrity or perfection, since those things that are impaired are by that very fact ugly; due proportion or harmony; and lastly brightness or clarity." [9] And again: "Those things are beautiful which please when seen." And since the intellect delights in light, "splendor is the root of beauty."[10] These quiet statements are the culmination of the almost ecstatic medieval view of nature; irradiated by the sun, the cosmos became a theophany irradiated by Christ, and all symbols, whether drawn from nature or from the Bible, became the links by which God draws all into the concord of a single harmony. The vision of God became the condition of all universality.[11] It was *splendor*, *claritas*, the joy-bringing dynamism of beauty, that stirred the artists: manuscript illuminators, craftsmen of stained-glass windows, singers who saw Our Lady as "Lantern of Light," and the Pearl-Poet. T. S. Eliot has pinpointed the intellectual basis of this artistic theory:

> It is ultimately the function of art, by imposing a credible order upon ordinary reality, and thereby eliciting some perception of order in reality, to bring us to a condition of serenity, stillness and reconciliation, and then to leave us, as Virgil left Dante, to go on to regions where that guide can avail us no further.[12]

A perception of order was the Pearl-Poet's inheritance. He found order on the plane of faith, in the Bible as unfolded through Christian doctrine. He found it on the plane of philosophy, in the hierarchy of being that moved up from stones through plants, animals, men, angels, to God. The cosmos revolved around its own "still point," the unturning world. The love of the First Mover, communicated from the Empyrean downward from sphere to sphere, drew each object to its right end—for man, the direct perception of Himself. The Poet found this hierarchic order reflected in civil society. Feudalism was a system of reciprocal loyalty and protection, conditioned by a chivalric obedience. Obedience, rooted in respect, flowered into courtesy. That this idealistic system could be mocked by human malice and folly was only too evident in the fourteenth century, and the Pearl-Poet was no escapist. He neither condoned nor satirized; he neither raged nor turned heretic. He recalled his age to "the splendor of order" in his own artistic way. Like Ephrem the Syrian he looked at the jewel in the palm of his hand: "Thou dost not hide thyself in thy bareness, O Pearl . . . Thy clothing is thy light, thy garment is thy brightness." [13]

He saw observance of right order as a free act, to be performed graciously and enthusiastically. Jonah in *Patience* foolishly tried to escape the order of individual vocation planned by his "gentle Lord"; only when brought back by force into the pattern could he be a "gentle Prophet." The sinners in *Cleanness* maliciously broke the very structure of the natural law, or failed to revere the divine law; disaster had to follow. Only those who, like Nebuchadnezzar, saw their own place in this order, were saved. In *Sir Gawain* the whole action turns on the hero's loyalty to his king, to his promise, to his host, to his own honor; it permeates his manners, his speech, his heart, and his mind, "Sir courteous Knight." In *Saint Erkenwald* the judge who had never swerved from justice was brought miraculously to his reward.

Pearl projects the pattern of right order into a fourth dimension of spiritual experience. Pearl herself is a human soul in possession of all that human longing can reach out for; she is in God, she sees the world through the heavenly eyes of wisdom. The dreamer is a human soul groping and blundering and rebelling in the face of a call to higher understanding. By "grucchyng" he balks at the conditions for being God's creature. His obedience turns not upon the breaking or keeping of a commandment, but upon the willingness to say "yes" to God's love—the highest name for His will. "And in His will is our peace." [14]

Order, when reflected in art, reveals its inherent splendor. The Pearl-Poet saw this as purity, as cleanness. Why is the pearl, worth less in pennies than other stones, valued above them? "What cause could there be but its clean color?" (119) "Clean" is a key word in every poem. Even in *Patience* where there are no pearls, Jonah "may well need to wash his mantle" (342), and the beatitude of the clean of heart promises God to pure eyes. *Cleanness*, a long excoriation of filth, glories in clean raiment, clean vessels, clean married love, and the virginal cleanness of Mary and her Son. In *Sir Gawain*, romance moves on the plane of exquisite courtliness that deals in clean words and clean thoughts, the perfect behavior that safeguards a clean life. In *Pearl*, the soul who seeks God like a bride seeking her lover wears the pearl of great price. She is "crowned in clean virginity" (767). Like Chaucer's *Tale of Saint Cecilia, Pearl* is a poem of consecrated chastity, the "splendor" of an order wholly supernatural, endowed with the elation and the vigor of fire. The poet who wrote it could have said the words of a twelfth-century mystic (like himself, nameless) who saw the center of such love as a pearl:

> Let us draw near to Thee, and let us exult and be glad in Thee, remembering Thy Heart that we have found in the dug field of Thy body. Who could throw away this pearl? Rather I will give all things. I will sell the thoughts and desires of my mind and buy it, casting all my care in the Heart of the Lord Jesus, and without fail it will care for me.[15]

If the splendor of order gives beauty, beauty gives the Pearl-Poet his dimension in fourteenth-century literature. Chaucer shows the breadth of his times, humanity with its lovable foibles through the whole range of society on a spring pilgrimage. He is preoccupied with the goodness of people—or with their badness, lovable or otherwise. Langland shows the depth of his times, the rightness and wrongness under the surface; he is preoccupied with leading his worker-pilgrims to seek Saint Truth. The Pearl-Poet shows the heights to which those times could rise; beauty is his answer to the challenge of reality. His ordered world is beautiful, from the little fern under Jonah's feet to the turrets of the New Jerusalem. The cities that went up in smoke once stood "among the loveliest places on earth"; they need not have burned, leaving a Dead Sea for remembrance.

"That is called beautiful the very sight of which gives joy," [16] wrote the serious St. Thomas. The Pearl-Poet's joy is felt in the bounding movement of his lines, or in their bare tranquility. His joy is unafraid. He has faced Poverty with Patience; he has turned from the handwriting on the wall to the Gracious Lord on His throne; he has waited through a long Limbo. He has given up his pearl in exchange for its eternal possession. His are the whimsy, the sanity, the certainty, the courage, and the serenity of Christian joy:

> In the throng that praised the Lamb so well
> I too was caught with great delight.
>
> > *(Pearl,* 1125–26)

THE POEMS

PATIENCE

I

Patience has its good points, though not often pleasant.
When heavy hearts are hurt by something hateful
long-suffering may cure them and cool them off,
for she quells every evil and quenches malice.

If a man can bear sorrow, bliss will overtake him,   5
but if too angry to wait his suffering gets worse.
Then it's better to bear the blow sometimes
than throw my rage around, though I think I'm ill-used.

Once, on a holy-day, I heard at high mass
Matthew telling what the Master taught His followers: 10
eight blessings He promised them, each one a boon;
each merits in its own way, in a different manner.

Happy are they who have poverty in their hearts,
for theirs is heaven's kingdom to keep forever.
Happy they also who hold to meekness;   15
they shall rule this world, and have all they will.

Happy too are they who weep when they are harmed,
for they shall find comfort in many countries.
Happy also they who hunger for righteousness;
they shall be amply fed, and filled with good things.   20

Happy also those who are pitiful in heart,
for all manner of mercy shall be meted to them.
Happy also are the clean of heart;
they shall see with their own eyes their Savior enthroned.

Happy too are they who hold their peace;   25
it is good to call them the gracious God's sons.
And happy are they who can steer their own hearts,
for theirs is heaven's kingdom, as I claimed before.

All eight of these blessings have been promised us
if we honor these ladies, being like them in virtue: 30
Dame Poverty, Dame Pity, Dame Penance the third,
Dame Meekness, Dame Mercy, and merry Cleanness,

then Dames Peace and Patience, put in afterwards.
Happy he who has one—better to have all!
Since I'm brought to that pinch that is called Poverty,   35
I shall provide Patience too, and play with both of them!

In the text these two are yoked in a team.
They fill the same formula, from first to last;
because of their wisdom they win the same reward
and, in my opinion, they are of one kind.   40

For where Poverty appears she will not be put out,
but lingers where she pleases, likable or hateful;
where Poverty pinches, though a man think it painful,
no matter how he mumbles he must suffer much.

So Poverty and Patience must needs be playfellows.   *45*
Since I've settled for both, I had just better suffer!
It's easier to put up with them and praise their ways
than to kick and be wrathful, and come out the worse.

If a destiny befits me and I'm due to have it,
what good will it do to disdain or despise it?   *50*
Or if my Liege Lord pleases to bid me so live—
to ride or to run or to roam on His errands,

what good is grumbling but to make me grouchier?
Better had He not made me—in spite of myself—
if I then must bear trouble and a bitter reward   *55*
after doing His bidding, as bound by my hire!

Did not Jonah in Judah once play such a joke?
Being sure of himself he got into a scrape.
If you will wait a little, and listen for a while,
I shall put you wise about it, as Holy Writ tells us.   *60*

I I

Once upon a time, in the territory of Judah,
Jonah was enjoined to be prophet to the Gentiles.
God's call came to him; he was far from glad!
It came with stern words whispered in his ear.

"Rise rapidly," He says, "and go straight off;   *65*
take the way to Nineveh, with no more talk,
and in that city sow my sentence all around.
At the right time and place I will put it in thy heart.

"Indeed, they are wicked, those who dwell in that land;
they show such malice that I can stand it no more,   *70*

but must at once take vengeance on their villainy and venom.
Now go for me, swiftly, and speak out my message."

When the voice that had stunned his mind was stilled,
his wits grew wrathful; wildly he thought:
"If I do His bidding and bring them this tale,   75
then be taken in Nineveh, my troubles begin!

"He tells me those traitors are towering rogues.
If I come with these tidings they'll take me straight,
pin me in a prison, put me in stocks,
torture me in tight chains, twist out my eyes!   80

"What a marvelous message for a man to preach
among so many foes, such cursed fiends!
But if my gracious God wills me such grief,
for the sake of some sin wants me slain,

"at any peril," said the Prophet, "I'll approach no nearer! 85
I'll go by some way He's not watching over;
I'll take off for Tarshish and tarry there awhile
and surely, when I'm lost, He'll leave me alone."

Then Jonah rises swiftly and sets out at once
for the port at Joppa, in a jittery tantrum;   90
for nothing would he put up with any such pains,
though the Father who made him were unmindful of his
        safety.

"Our Sovereign sits," he said, "on so high a seat
in His glowing glory, that He gives little heed
if I be taken in Nineveh and stripped naked,   95
ripped apart on a cross by a crowd of ruffians."

So he goes to the port, seeking passage;
he finds a fair ship ready for sea-faring,
haggles with the mariners, and hands them pay
to carry him to Tarshish as quick as they can.   *100*

Then he hurries on board while they handle their gear;
they catch up the cross-sail, fasten the cables,
weigh their anchors nimbly at the windlass,
and readily fix the spare line to the bow-sprit.

They tug at the guide ropes; the great cloth falls   *105*
while they swing to larboard and luff to the wind;
at their back a cheerful breeze fills the broad sail
and swings the sweet ship swiftly from harbor.

Never a Jew so joyful as Jonah was then,
when he had daringly escaped the Lord's dominion!   *110*
He fancied that the One who formed the whole world
had no power to molest any man at sea!

Oh, the silly wretch! Since he would not suffer
he has put himself in the grip of a far worse peril.
What a foolish fancy he felt in his mind: *115*
if he slipped from Samaria God could see no further!

Yes, he looked far abroad; he had better be sure!
A word of the King was well known to him;
noble David on his throne had put it thus
in a psalm he had written in his Psalter: *120*

"O fools among the people, ponder this sometimes;
understand in time, though steeped in folly:
do you think that He hears not, He who made ears for all?
Surely He is not blind who shaped every eye!"

But Jonah dreads no blow—like a man in his dotage, 125
for he was far out at sea, faring on to Tarshish.
But, believe me! in time he was overtaken,
for he shot far short of his aim, shamefully.

The Wielder of knowledge, wise in all things,
always awake and watching, has tricks at His will! 130
He called on the same powers He created with His hands;
they wakened more wrathfully since with wrath He called:

"Eurus and Aquilo who live in the east,
blow, both of you, at my will, on the blue-black waters."
No time passed before they did what He told them, 135
so willing were they both to work at His bidding.

At once from the north-east the noise begins,
with both winds blowing on the blue-black waters.
Rough cloud-rack rose, casting a red light;
the sea sighed dismally, a strange sound to hear. 140

Winds wrestled together on the sombre water;
the waves, driven wild, weltered so high
before crashing to the abyss, that clustering fishes
dared rest nowhere on the rough sea-bottom.

When the wind's breath, the waves, and the boat all met, 145
there was no joy on the ship that Jonah was in!
It reeled all around on the rough waves;
the gale bore down behind till it burst its gear.

The helm and the stern were hurled in a heap;
first many ropes broke, then the mast as well. 150
The sail swayed to the sea; their craft must sup
on the cold water. Then a cry arose!

Yet they cut the cords and cast out everything;
many boys leaped about, baling and heaving,
scooping out the sea water that couldn't escape.   155
Though a man's lot be loathsome, life is still sweet!

They were busy casting their bales overboard,
their bags, their feather-beds, their bright clothes,
their chests, their coffers and all their casks—
trying to lighten their craft in hope of a calm.   160

But as loud as ever was the wind's uproar,
angrier the waters and wilder the streams.
Then, weary and worn out, aware of no help,
each called on the god that could get the best for him.

Some offered to Vernagu their solemn vows,   165
some to chaste Diana, some to stern Neptune,
some to Mahomet or Mergot, to the moon and the sun,
each man where he liked and where his heart lay.

Then the most alert spoke out, well near despairing:
"I think there's a liar here, some lawless wretch   170
who has grieved his God and goes round among us!
See! We're sinking for his guilt, lost for his sin!

"I move that we lay lots, every man of us,
and the one who loses—let him be thrown out!
When the guilty one is gone, can we not guess   175
that He who rules the storm will pity the rest of us?"

They assented to this, and all assembled;
each was dragged from his hole to take what might happen.
Lightly, a steersman leaped under the hatches
to look for more men and bring them to the lots.   180

No man failed to come that he could find
save the Jew, Jonah, dozing in a dark corner.
He had fled, in fear of the roaring flood,
to the bottom of the boat where he lay on a board.

Huddled on a wooden drain, away from heaven's wrath,   *185*
he had slipped into heavy sleep and snored, slobbering.
A man poked with his foot, bade him perk up:
he's enchained—may Raguel raise him from his dreams!

Taking hold of his clothes they hauled him out,
pulled him up by the breast, set him on the board   *190*
and questioned him roughly: What reason had he,
while trouble was striking, to sleep so soundly?

They drew up their lots and soon dealt them out;
sure enough—the lot fell at last to Jonah.
At once they yelled at him, asking loudly: *195*
"What the devil hast thou done, doting wretch?

"What seekest thou at sea, sinful rascal,
destroying all of us with thy wicked doings?
Hast thou, fellow, none to govern thee, no god to call on,
that thou canst fall asleep when nearly slain?   *200*

"What land art thou from? What art thou looking for,
let loose in the world? What is thine errand?
See the doom dealt to thee for thy bad deeds!
Give glory to thy God before going overboard!"

"I am Hebrew," said he, "of Israel born.   *205*
I worship the One, I trust, who made all things,
the whole world, with the sky, the wind and the stars,
and all who dwell in it, with one word only.

"For my sake trouble has come at this time;
I have grieved my God and am found guilty.   *210*
So, carry me to the edge and pitch me over,
or you'll have no good luck, I guess truly."

He showed them by signs that they understood
that he had fled from the face of the fair Lord.
Such tormenting fear fell on them then   *215*
that they took to their oars and let the fellow alone.

The men hurried to row with those long oars,
since their sail had slipped over onto one side.
They hauled and they heaved to help themselves,
but all was needless labor, for nothing worked.   *220*

In the bubbling black water their oars broke;
they had nothing in their hands that could bring help.
No comfort could they find, no counsel either,
but to pass a just sentence on Jonah right there.

First they prayed to the Prince whom prophets serve   *225*
to give them grace never to grieve Him,
lest with sinless blood they stain their hands.
The man whom they killed might be His own!

Quick, by top and by toe they took hold of him;
they lurched him straight into that loathsome sea.   *230*
Hardly was he tossed out when the tempest ceased,
and the ocean settled down as soon as it could.

Then, with torn tackle, tottering on the waves,
for a while the stiff currents still battered them,
steadily driving them on through the deep   *235*
till a gentler wave quickly washed them ashore.

When they reached the land their praise arose
to our merciful God, in Moses' way,
with sacrifice sent up, and solemn vows;
they granted that truly He alone was God.   240

While they went wild with joy, Jonah still dreaded;
he who would not bear pain finds his well-being in peril!
The fate of that man, after falling in the water,
would be hard to believe but for Holy Writ!

III

Now Jonah the Jew is judged fit to be drowned;   245
they had shoved him out of that shattered ship.
As Wyrd would have it, a wild, wallowing whale
was beaten up from the bottom. It floated by the boat,

aware of the man then tumbling overboard;
quick, it swung to sweep him in, mouth open to swallow! 250
While his feet were still held, the fish promptly seized him;
untouched by a tooth, he tumbled down its throat.

Then it swings and sways to the sea-bottom,
among many rough rocks and rolling sands,
with the man in its maw, maddened with dread.   255
Little wonder then that he suffered woe!

Had not heaven's high King, through the power of His
          hands,
watched over the wretched man in demon Warlow's guts,
who could have lived there, by any law of nature,
or what life go on for so long inside it?   260

But he was helped by the Sovereign who is seated on high,
though hopeless of well-being in the fish's belly
and driven through the deep, in the dark wallowing.
Lord, cold was his comfort, and his care huge!

He knew every bit of bad luck come to him: 265
tossed from boat to beast in the foaming waves,
thrown into its throat, with no more threats,
like a mote through a church door, so mighty were those
      jaws.

He glides in by the gills through the gluey filth,
reeling along the guts—they seemed like a road—   270
head over heels, still hurtling about,
then blunders into a space as broad as a hall.

There he makes his feet fast and fumbles about,
then stands up in the stomach that stank like the devil;
there, in fat and in slime as savory as hell,   275
a bower was built for one who could bear no trouble!

There he lurks, looking round for some leeway
in each nook of the navel, but finds no place
to rest or recover in, only reeking mire
in the guts he goes through. But always, God is sweet!   280

There he lingered at last, and called to His Lord:
"Prince, now show some pity to Thy prophet!
Though I am foolish and fickle and false at heart,
put aside Thy vengeance, by the power of mercy.

"Though I have played false, the very scum of prophets,   285
Thou art God; all good things are of Thy giving.
Now have mercy on Thy man and on his misdeeds,
and prove easily Thou art Lord on land and on water."

Then he hid in a nook and held on tight
where no filthy defilement was felt about him.   290
There he sat down as sound, save for the darkness,
as in the boat's bulk-head where he had slept before.

So in that beast's bowels he abides alive
three days and three nights, thinking ever of the Lord,
of His might and His mercy and His moderation.   *295*
Now, in care, he knows Him whom he knew not in
        pleasure!

The whale wallows on through the deep wild places
of many rough regions, in a rancorous mood;
for that mote in his maw made him, I guess,
—though such a little thing—feel sick around the heart.   *300*

And the man, as he sailed on, heard ever more surely
the heavy sea on the whale's back, beating on its sides.
There and then, promptly, the prophet took to prayer
in this wise, as I gather; his words came with a rush:

I V

"Lord, I have called to Thee in my crushing woe;   *305*
Thou hearest me in this hole. From the belly of hell
I called; Thou hast heeded my hoarse voice.
Thou hast dropped me in the deep sea, in its dim heart.

"The flow of Thy great floods has folded me round;
all Thy water-gulfs, Thy groundless pools,   *310*
the struggling currents of Thy endless streams
like a dashing dam are driving over me.

"Yet I say while I sit on the sea-bottom:
full of care, I am cast away from Thy clear eyes
and shut from Thy sight; yet surely I hope   *315*
to walk again in Thy temple and keep tryst with Thee.

"I am wrapped in water, to my woeful pain;
the abyss holds the body that I abide in.
Ever-heaving waves play over my head;
I, a man, have fallen down to the foot of the mountains. 320

"Sea-banks, like bars, hold—so strong
that I cannot reach land; yet Thou rulest my life.
Thou shalt save me, a man, while Thy justice sleeps,
through Thy strong mercy, much to be trusted.

"When the onrush of anguish overwhelmed my soul, 325
well I remembered my royal Lord,
praying Him for pity's sake to hear His prophet,
till my cry for help enters His holy house.

"I have mulled over Thy mighty works many a long day,
but now I know well that those unwise men 330
who trust in vanity and in vain things
will forego mercy for what amounts to nothing.

"But devoutly I vow, on my very honor,
to offer solemn sacrifice when I am safe,
and give Thee, for my welfare, a perfect gift, 335
holding good Thy bidding; here is my pledge!"

Then our Father severely bids the fish
spit him out promptly on some dry space;
at His will the whale turns and finds a beach
where he brings up the man, as our Lord bade him. 340

He was swept up on the sand in his soiled clothing;
it may well be he needed to wash his mantle!
The shores that he saw as he sat down there
were of the very regions he had renounced!

Then a wind of God's word stirred the man again: 345
"Wilt thou never go to Nineveh, by no way at all?"
"Yes, Lord," said he, "only let me have grace
    to go at Thy pleasure; nothing else does me good."

"Rise! Approach and preach. See, here is the place!
    My wisdom is locked in thee; let it loose here!"   350
At that the man rose as rapidly as he could,
    and that very same night he drew near to Nineveh.

It was a wide city, wondrous in breadth,
    and to walk through it was a three days' deed.
For one day's journey Jonah went straight on,   355
    speaking no word to men met on the way.

Then he cried out so clearly that all could know
    the true trend of his message; he told it this way:
"Yet forty days shall come to their full end,
    then Nineveh shall be taken and brought to nothing.   360

"Truly, this same town shall be tilted to the ground.
    You shall plunge up-side-down in the deep abyss
    and swiftly be swallowed by the swart earth;
    all those who live here shall lose their sweet lives."

His speech sprang through the place and spread all around
    to the citizens and young men who lived in that city.
Such terror caught hold of them, such cruel dread,   365
    that all changed color and were chilled to the heart.

And the man would not cease, but kept on saying:
"The very vengeance of God shall make this place
        void!"   370
Then the people piteously murmured their plaint
    and were dismal at heart, dreading the Lord.

They put on harsh hair-shirts that bit in hard,
bound to their backs and to their bare sides;
they dropped dust on their heads, and with dim hope
    besought   375
that penance might please Him who complained of wrong-
    doing.

Still he cries through the country, till heard by the king
who straightway arose and ran from his throne;
he tore his noble robes from his naked back
and huddled in the midst of a heap of ashes.   380

He sharply asked for haircloth and clasped it about him,
sowed sacking on top of it and sighed coldly.
There, dazed in the dust, with tears dropping down,
he wept wondrously for his wicked deeds.

Then he said to his officers: "Assemble in a hurry;   385
send out a decree, drawn up as by myself,
that all living beings in the bounds of this city,
both men and beasts, women and their babes,

"each prince, each priest, and each prelate
shall all freely fast for their false works.   390
Stop infants from sucking, even if they howl,
let no beast graze on heather, nor even on grass,

"let them not go to pasture, nor pick at the weeds,
put no ox to hay nor horse to water.
All shall cry out, hunger-pinched, clearly, strongly,   395
till the uproar reaches Him who will feel rueful pity.

"Who knows, who can tell if He will be pleased,
He who acts handsomely in his nobility?
His power, I know, is great; though He be displeased,
He will show mercy in His mild moderation.   *400*

"If we leave off playing with our loathsome sins,
and quietly take the path He plans out Himself,
He will turn from His anger, abandon His wrath
and forgive our guilt, if we believe He is God."

Then all believed in His law and left their sins,   *405*
performing the penance that the Prince bade;
and God, as He had said, forgave through His goodness
(though He had pledged otherwise) and put vengeance
        aside.

V

Then a heavy sorrow settled down on Jonah.
He grew wild with Our Lord, like a wrathful wind,   *410*
and hard anger lashed at his heart; he calls
in prayer to the High Prince, speaking out his pain:

"I beseech Thee, Sire, judge this Thyself!
Have not my own words now come to pass,   *414*
what I said in my country when Thou gavest command
to come to this town and preach Thy tidings?

"I knew well Thy courtesy, Thy wise long-suffering,
Thy bountiful goodness, Thy benign grace,   *418*
Thy long patience with failure, Thy delayed vengeance.
Thy mercy is meeted out, though we miss the mark widely.

"I knew well, when I had mustered what words I could
to menace all the proud men who dwell in this place,
with prayer and penance they might make their peace,
and therefore I tried to flee far into Tarshish.

"Now take away my life, Lord; it lasts too long!   425
Bid my death-blow come quickly, bring on my end.
Sweeter to perish at once, it seems,
that longer spread Thy message that makes me a liar!"

Then the voice of our Sovereign sounds in his ear,
upbraiding this fellow in a stern fashion: 430
"Hark, man! Is this right, to rage so wrathfully
for anything I have done or ordained for thee yet?"

Jonah, thoroughly glum, gets up grumbling
and sets out for the east part of those high places,
and in a field comfortably crouches down to wait,   435
watching in that place what should come to pass.

There he built himself a bower, the best he could make,
of hay and of ferns and a few wild plants,
for the place was a plain, with no pliant groves
to shield him from the sunshine or cast any shade.   440

He huddled in his little booth, his back to the sun,
and there fell asleep, slumbering soundly all night,
while God, of His grace, bade grow from that soil
the fairest woodbine a man could ever find.

And when at dawn the Lord sent a new day,   445
the man awakened under the woodbine
and glanced up at the leaves that glimmered green;
a more praise-worthy leaf-hall no-one ever possessed!

It was broad at the bottom and curved above,
walled on either side, a house, as it were,   *450*
with a round hole on the north-side but nowhere else,
and all shut in greenery that cast cool shadows.

The man glances up at the green, graceful leaves
waving so softly in a cool wind;
bright sunlight shone round, although no shaft,   *455*
not even a few flecks, could fall on him.

Then the fellow was glad of his gay lodging;
he lies lolling in it, looking towards town,
so pleased with his woodbine that he wallows under it—
the devil he cares about food that day!   *460*

And he kept laughing as he looked round his lodging,
wishing it were in the land where he must live,
high upon Ephraim or the hills of Hermon.
"Sure, a nicer dwelling was never mine to own!"

And when night drew near he needed a nap.   *465*
He slid into dull sleep, sluggish under the leaves,
while God raised up a worm that grubbed at the root;
withered was the woodbine by the time the man waked!

Then God warned the west to waken softly,
and told the wind, Zephyrus, to blow up warm,   *470*
to let no cloud come before the clear sun;
it must rise up right broad and burn like a candle.

The man awoke from his wandering dreams
and blinked at his woodbine that was rudely blighted;
all faded and wasted were the fine leaves.   *475*
The bright sun shrivelled them before the fellow saw it.

Then the heat welled up and burned horribly;
the warm wind from the west scorched the weeds.
The man was perishing on the ground, unprotected;
his woodbine was gone. He wept for sorrow.   *480*

With burning hot anger he cried out bitterly:
"Ah! Thou Maker of men, what mighty scheme is this,
to destroy Thine own man more than all others,
with trouble of every sort, and never spare me?

"I got myself some comfort and now it is gone,   *485*
my woodbine so proud that protected my head.
Now, I see, Thou art set on taking away my solace.
Why not bid me die? I have endured too long!"

Then our Lord spoke out to him in straight words:
"Is this right, Sir, all thy proud rancor,   *490*
so much wrath over a woodbine that grew up at once?
Why art thou peevish, man, over so little?"

"It's not little," said he, "but more like my right.
I wish I were wrapped in the earth's rubble!"
"Then think over this, Sir: if thou art so sore,   *495*
do not wonder if I help my own handiwork.

"Thou hast worked up such anger over thy woodbine,
yet never toiled to tend it for an hour's time.
At one stroke it flourished, at the next it faded—
so little to thy liking that thou wouldst lose thy life!   *500*

"Then blame me not for wanting to help my own work,
showing mercy to heedless ones who moan for sin.
First, I made them myself, from matter of my own,
then long I guarded and led them on their way.

"And if I lose my travail after so long a time,   505
  overthrowing yonder town when it had turned to me,
  the sorrow of that sweet place would sink into my heart,
  so many malicious men now mourn in it!

"And some in that crowd are innocent because crazy,
  and little babes at the breast who are not blameworthy,
  and women without wits who could not tell   511
  one hand from the other, for the whole of this world,

"or know a ladder's rung from the upright bar,
  or what rumor is talked about on their right hand
  or on their left, though they lose their lives for it.   515

"And there are dumb beasts in the bounds of that city
  that never can sin and so come to grief.
  Why should I show wrath to them, since men will repent,
  come to know me for king and acknowledge my words?

"Were I as hasty as thou, great harm would be done here;
  did I bear things as thou dost, very few would thrive!
  I cannot be malicious who am known to be mild,   522
  for malice should never go unmixed with mercy.

"Be not so gruff, good man, but go forth on thy way!
  Be steadfast, be patient in pain and in joy.   525
  For he who is too ready to rend his clothes
  must sit down in worse ones and sew them together."

So when poverty pinches me, and pains enough,
softly, with long-suffering, I must settle down.
For penance and pain prove this plainly: 530
patience has its noble points—not often pleasant!

CLEANNESS

I

Cleanness! Should one praise it in keeping with its nature,
reckoning up the reasons for doing so rightly,
he must find fair forms in fashioning his speech,
or, doing the contrary, be caught in great trouble.

For mighty angry is the One who made all things   *5*
with a fellow who is filthy in following Him,
such as men of religion, who read and sing
and approach His presence, and are called priests.

They go into His temple and turn toward Him;
with reverent piety they reach His altar.   *10*
They handle His own body and use it, both;
if cleanness enclose them, they carry off merit.

But if they counterfeit service and lack courtesy,
outwardly honest and all filthy within,
they are sinful themselves, altogether stained;   *15*
they loathe God and holy things, and goad Him to anger.

He is so clean in His court, that King who rules all,
so honored by his household, so handsomely served
by angels adorned in all that is clean,
both within and without, in their bright robes!   *20*

Were He not careful and exact, with no loathing for evil,
it would be too marvelous; such a thing might not be!
Christ said so Himself when He spoke once
in praise of eight blessed things, and promised reward for
      them.

I remember, among others, one place in Matthew   *25*
where cleanness is disclosed in very clear words:
the man clean of heart shall come to a fair end;
he shall gaze on our Lord with great delight.

This means: that sight shall be seen by no-one
who has any uncleanness about him anywhere,   *30*
for the One who drives filthiness far from His heart
cannot abide a man whose body it touches.

So, go not to heaven in torn garments,
in a beggarly hood, with hands unwashed.
For what earthly lord who holds to his honor   *35*
would be pleased if a boy came in poorly attired,

when he was solemnly placed on a rich seat,
above dukes on the dais where dainties are served?
Should a tramp hurry in, right up to the table,
in stockings rent at the knees and patched rags,   *40*

his overcoat torn and shoe-toes out,
for even one such thing he should be hauled off,
well-blamed, perhaps with a big buffet;
hustled to the hall-door and shoved out—hard,

forbidden forever to enter that city   45
on pain of imprisonment, being put in the stocks;
he should be sent flying for his unseemly clothes,
though he never does wrong again, in word or in deed.

If he would be unwelcome to a worldly prince,
the High-King in heaven would be harder on him,   50
as Matthew, in the mass, says of that rich man
who made a great banquet at his dear heir's marriage,

and sent messengers to say that all should gather
and come to his feast in becoming outfits.
"For my bulls and my boars are baited and slain,   55
my well-fed fowls are fattened for slaughter,

my well-fed poultry and partridges too,
while flanks of wild swine, with swans and cranes,
are all crisped and roasted to the right point.
Come quick to my court before it gets cold."   60

When they knew of his call, all those who should come
made excuse by a dodge that let them escape.
One had bought an estate, he said on his honor:
"I must turn out at once, take a look at that homestead."

Another also refused, and offered this reason: 65
"I have got what I yearned for, some yokes of oxen,
and since hirelings bought them, I must hurry off
and be on the spot to see them plowing."

"And I've wedded a wife," the third said warily.
"Excuse me to the court, for I cannot come."   70
Thus they all drew back, each one with denial,
till none entered the palace, though each was pressed.

The lord of that land had no liking for this
and disdained such doings; angrily he declares:
"To their own sorrow they have forsaken me;   75
    their wrong-doing is more blameworthy than a heathen's
        rage.

"Then go forth, my men, through the great streets,
    and beset this city on every side.
Wayfaring fellows, on foot and on horse,
    men and maids both, the best and the worst,   80

"urge them all, lovingly, to linger at my feast;
    bring them cheerfully to my mansion, as though they were
        barons,
till this palace, brim-full, is properly filled.
    Those other wretches, I warrant, were not worthy."

They came and went, the guards of that country;   85
    they brought the young knights they met by the banks,
the squires who followed them swiftly on horseback,
    also many on foot, the free and the bond.

When they came to court they were cared for politely,
    placed by the steward, settled in the hall   90
where the well-mannered marshal made them sit down;
    seats were arranged for them according to rank.

After that the servants said to the sovereign:
"See, Lord, with your leave, as you told your liegemen,
    at your word and bidding we have brought in   95
many strange fellows, and there's still more room."

The lord said to his men: "Go out still further,
far out in the fields, and fetch more guests;
look in glades and groves where men may be lurking,
folk of whatever kind, and call them in here.   *100*

"Be they noble, be they humble, neglect none of them,
be they agile or lame, be they one-eyed,
be they both blind and blundering cripples,
my house must be cram-full in every corner.

"Certainly those men who said no to me   *105*
and set me at nought at the same time,
shall never sit in my hall nor taste my supper—
not one sop of my pottage, though they are perishing!"

The sergeants, when he said this, swaggered out
and did the deed called for, as he had decreed;   *110*
the palace was filled with people of all sorts,
not all sons of one wife, with a single father!

Whether worthy or worse off, they were well-placed,
the best always first, and the brightest attired,
the noblest and best-dressed on the high dais,   *115*
then, lined up below them, lots of people,

and according at each man ranked, by his clothing,
so, at meat, his needs were met by marshals.
The clean-clad in the crowd were by no means neglected,
yet the simplest in that hall was well-served to the full,   *120*

with fine manners, good food and elegant music,
all the courtesies a lord should show in his land.
They began to feel glad, after a good drink,
and each man made himself at ease with his comrades.

II

In the midst of the meal the master thought   *125*
of going to see the crowd that was gathered there,
to give proper cheer to the poor and the rich,
rejoice them with his smile and warm up their spirits!

So he bustles from his own room into the broad hall
to the best men on the benches, bade them be merry   *130*
and cheered them by his manner, then moved further on
from table to table, talking mirthfully.

But, crossing the floor, he found with his eye
one not very handsomely arrayed for a holiday,
a thrall poorly clothed, thrust into the throng   *135*
in no festive garb, but all fouled with work.

The fellow was not dressed to deal with good men;
the great lord, displeased, was bent on punishing him.
"Tell me, friend," said he, with a fierce look,
"how didst thou get here in such foul garments?   *140*

"The clothes thou hast on are not fit for a holiday;
fellow—that's no dress for a bridal feast!
How canst thou draw near this house—for thine undoing—
in so ragged a robe, all rent at the sides?

"What an ungodly man in that miserable gown,   *145*
to honor me and my palace in a poor stingy way,
and yet so prompt to push into my presence!
Dost thou think me so low-down as to like thy coat?"

The other was abashed at these angry words;
he lowered his head, looking at the floor.   *150*
Discomforted in mind, lest he draw down more wrath,
he found no words ready to fling back.

Then the lord spoke out, crying wondrously loud,
and called to his torturers. "Take him," he bids.
"Bind both of his hands behind his back   155
and fasten harsh fetters to his feet, quickly.

"Stick him tight in the stocks, and then stake him
deep in my dungeon where woe dwells forever,
with grieving and weeping and the hard grinding
of angry teeth, to teach him to be decent."   160

Thus Christ compared the Kingdom of Heaven
to this sumptuous feast to which many are summoned.
All are lovingly bidden, the bad and the better sort,
all those hallowed at the font, to enjoy that festival.

Be careful, in coming, that thy robes be clean   165
and decent for the holy-day, lest thou meet with harm;
if thou approach that Prince of noble peerage,
he hates hell no more than men who are soiled.

What, then, are these robes in which thou art wrapped,
which should show up brightly, as do one's best clothes? 170
They are thy deeds, truly, the things thou hast done
in living by the wish that lies in thy heart:

that these deeds be found noble and fair in thy life,
well-shaped, well-formed for foot or for hand,
and all thy other limbs clad in like cleanness.   175
Thou canst then see thy Savior on His royal seat.

For many faults a fellow may forfeit bliss
so as not to see his Sovereign—not only for sloth;
for pompousness and boasting and swelling pride
a man is thrust roughly into the devil's throat.   180

For covetousness, treachery and crooked deeds;
for perjury, man-slaughter and too much drink,
for theft and quarreling, a man may come to grief;
for robbery and ribaldry and false reasoning,

for disinheriting, depriving widows of their dowry, *185*
for breaking up marriages and buying wenches,
for treason and treachery and tyranny as well,
for false defamations and for feigned laws,

a man may miss that joy so justly praised;
for such wrongs as these he may suffer much pain, *190*
and never more come to the Creator's court,
never catch sight of Him, for unsavory deeds.

III

I have listened, and heard from learned clerics
(and also, as is right, I have read myself)
that the well-mannered Prince who rules paradise *195*
is displeased with anything that points towards evil.

But never, in any book, have I found noted
that He more wrathfully dealt with the works He made,
or more revenged the vileness of vice and sin,
or willed to grow hot with anger more hastily, *200*

or more suddenly inflicted fatal vengeance,
than for filth of the flesh that fools get into.
For then, I find, He leaves his liberal ways,
fiercely ready to punish with wrath in His heart.

The false fiend was guilty of the first felony   205
while still in heaven, and lifted on high.
Endowed with more beauty than all bright angels,
he, rude as a churl, chose his own reward.

He saw only himself, how handsome he was,
and so forsook his Sovereign, and said these words: 210
"I shall place my throne near the pole-star,
and be like the Lord, maker of heaven aloft."

When he let fly these words, wrath lighted on him;
the Lord, by a hard doom, drove him to the abyss.
Yet, His anger was measured, His mercy no less,   215
though He then lost the tenth part of His princely retinue.

Though the felon was so proud of his fair robes,
of his glorious glamor that gleamed brightly,
as soon as the Lord's doom drove down on himself,
more, in dense thousands, were thrown out violently.   220

Fiends, all pitch-black, fell from the firmament;
whirling down in the first swoop, as thick as snow,
hurled into hell's hole like a hive swarming,
the fiends fell in tangles, forty days on end,

before the stinging storm could become stilled;   225
as meal strained in a small sieve thickly smokes,
so from heaven to hell that horrid shower went on
all over the world, everywhere the same.

Yes, it was a fierce outburst, a big vengeance,
yet the High Being was not angry—nor the wretch
        reconciled;   230
wilfully, he would never acknowledge God's worth,
nor pray for pity, so proud was his will.

Thus, though the blow was strong, he sorrowed little;
cast down into woe, he became no better.
But again vengeance woke and overtook men   235
through the fault of one man who failed in loyalty,

Adam, disobedient, ordained for bliss
where, hidden in paradise, his place was prepared,
living there in pleasure for a length of time,
then inherit the home that the angels forfeited.   240

But, when Eve egged him on, he ate an apple
that poisoned all the people who came after them,
by a law that was given by the Lord Himself,
and a penalty put on it and held to plainly.

Forbidden was the fruit that he fell to taking;   245
the doom is that death that destroys us all.
The vengeance was measured throughout by mercy,
then amended by a maiden who never had a mate.

I V

But the third time all thriving things were spoiled;
merciless anger and much wrath were shown   250
because of the earthly filth that folk got into,
those living in the world with no leaders.

They were the fairest in form and in face also,
the mightiest and merriest that were ever made,
strongest, most stalwart to go on their feet,   255
and they all lived longer than other people.

They were the first off-spring that the earth bred,
sons of the noble ancestor who was called Adam,
to whom God had given everything good,
all the blameless bliss anybody could have,   *260*

and those who lived next were most like that man,
so that none since then were so fair to see.
No law was laid down but to look to nature,
keep to it and follow its whole course in cleanness.

Then they turned filthy by fleshly deeds,   *265*
contriving practices contrary to nature,
using them basely, each on the other,
harming one another by their bad habits.

They fouled their flesh strangely, till the fiends saw
that the daughters of noblemen were delightfully fair,   *270*
and formed fellowships with them in human fashion,
thus engendering giants by their evil jesting.

These were immoderate men, mighty on earth,
who were all famous for loathsome feats;
he who most loved a fight was famed as noblest,   *275*
the biggest trouble-maker was held to be best.

Then evils on earth grew up in earnest
and multiplied many-fold among mankind.
For strong men in the world so warred on each other
that the One who made all began to be angry.   *280*

When He knew that each country was inwardly corrupt,
each man roaming off from the right way,
a strong indignation then stirred His heart.
As one turns things over, He thought to Himself:

"It grieves me much that I ever made man;   285
  I must down and do away with those dotards on earth,
  and drive from the world's face all those clothed in flesh,
  from men to beasts, from birds to fishes.

"All shall be struck dead and driven from the earth,
  those to whom I gave souls; sorely I repent   290
  that I myself made them. If I may, hereafter,
  I shall be more wary to watch for their tricks."

There was one man then living in the world
  always ready and righteous; he ruled himself well.
  In the dread of the Lord he spent his days;   295
  walking ever with God, his grace grew greater.

His name was Noah, as is well enough known;
  he had three strong sons, and they had three wives.
  Sem, indeed, was one, the second was Cham,
  and the handsome Japhet was the third engendered.   300

Now God in His anger spoke out to Noah
  in wild wrathful words; His will was roused:
"The end of all flesh that moves on earth
  has come before my face; I must carry it out.

"Their unseemly doings sicken me within,   305
  their filth vexes me, their vileness grieves me.
  I shall strike, in my grief, and destroy all together,
  both men and their lands, and all things living.

"But make a home for thyself—that is my will,
  a closed coffer of trees cleanly planed;   310
  work out dwellings in it for wild things and tame,
  then plaster it with clay till it's comely inside,

"and daub, on the outside, the nail-driven joinings.
  Thou shalt make that boat thus, in length and breadth:
  three hundred cubits keep it in length,   *315*
  of fifty more, neatly cross-wise, form the breadth,

"and see that thy ark is thirty in height,
  with a wide window in it, well-made, high up,
  a cubit each way, exactly square,
  and a safe-shutting door set in one side.   *320*

"Have halls inside it, and many hide-outs,
  stalls and cow-bins and well-bound pens;
  for I shall waken water to wash the whole world
  and kill all quick things with a quaking flood.

"All that moves and stirs with the spirit of life   *325*
  I shall lay waste in my wrath, all that dwells in the world.
  But thus shall I keep firm my covenant with thee
  who hast ruled thyself reasonably, being always righteous:

"Thou shalt enter this ark with thy noble off-spring
  and thy wedded wife. With thee take also   *330*
  the mates of thy happy sons; this household of eight
  I shall save, of all living men, and slay those others.

"Lay hold of a couple of each living beast,
  enclose seven pairs of each clean, comely kind,
  but keep only one pair of unclean in the ark,   *335*
  saving for me the seed of every species.

"And mix with the males the meet she-beasts,
  each pair by pair to please one another;
  fill thy coffers with all the food to be found,
  sustenance for yourselves and those same creatures."   *340*

Eagerly the good man goes about God's bidding
in heavy dread of danger; he dared not to do otherwise.
When all was fitted and forged, fully ready,
the Lord spoke to him in these words, seriously:

V

"Now, Noah," said our Lord, "art thou all ready?   345
Hast thou closed thy chest with clay all about?"
"Yes, Lord," said the man, "by Thy leave now
all is done at Thy word, with Thee guiding my wits!"

"Enter in, then," He warned. "Take thy wife with thee,
thy three sons, without doubt, and their three wives;   350
as I have bidden, bring the beasts in too,
and when you are stowed in, fasten yourselves safely.

"When seven days have passed I shall swiftly send
such a rushing torrent, a rain so heavy
as to wash the world of its filthy works.   355
No flesh in the land shall be found alive

except the eight of you shut in this ark,
and the seed of the various beasts I shall save."
Now Noah never stops—he begins that night
till all are stowed away as the voice ordered.   360

The seventh day came soon, when all were gathered
to dwell in the boat, the wild beasts and tame.
Then the abyss boiled over and the banks broke,
each well-spring brimmed up into wild streams;

no sea but what burst its bounds all at once,   365
each great, streaming lake swept up towards the sky;
many clustering clouds were cut into shreds
rent into rain-rifts rushing down on the earth,

unceasing for forty days. And then the flood rises,
overwhelms the woods and the wide fields;   370
for when water from the sky and from the earth met,
all who must suffer death were drowned in it.

Then moaning arose when the horror was seen—
nothing for it but death in the deep stream!
The water grew wilder; it washed over homes,   375
crashed into houses and caught those who dwelt there.

First they took flight—all those who could flee;
women with their babes left the buildings,
stepped up the bank where it was steepest
and hurriedly rushed to the high hills—fast!   380

But it was all needless; nothing could stop
the torrents of rough rain and rolling waves
till each hollow was brimfull to the bank's edge,
and every deep dale dammed up to the brink.

The highest moor-mountains were dry no more,   385
and the folk flocked there in fear of vengeance.
Then wild things from the wood floated on the water;
some swam through it and thought themselves safe,

some climbed to a high spot and stared up to heaven;
ruefully, loudly, they roared for dread.   390
Hares, harts also, ran to the high places,
bucks, badgers and bulls hurried to the banks,

all crying in their need to the King of heaven,
calling for rescue to their Creator.
The confusion was proof that His mercy had passed,   *395*
His pity withdrawn from the people He hated.

By the time the flood rose and flowed over their feet
each man saw well that he had to sink;
friends, in their fear, fell clasped together,
to endure their destiny and die in company.   *400*

Lover looks to his loved one and takes his leave,
to end all at once and to part forever.
When forty days had passed no flesh stirred on earth
ungnawed by the flood with its fierce waves,

for it climbed up each cliff, fifteen cubits   *405*
over the highest hill that huddled on earth.
All must rot in the mud, every being
in whom a spirit once stirred—no struggling availed—

save the man below deck with his strange household,
Noah, who called often on the name of our Lord,   *410*
one of eight in the ark—as the good God allowed;
all those in the ship were sure to stay dry.

The ark was heaved high by hurtling currents,
cast up in strange places right near the clouds.
It weltered on the wild flood and went as it liked,   *415*
driving over the deep sea; it seemed in danger

without mast or tie-rope or trusty bow-line,
cable or capstan to clasp hold of the anchors,
oars, or hand-helms hasped to the rudder,
or a swaying sail that could seek out a haven.   *420*

It floats on through the strife of the fierce winds.
Wherever the water rushed, it re-bounds,
often rolling around and rearing on end;
without our Lord as leadsman, bad luck to them!

In Noah's life-span (to lay down a sure date),   425
the six hundredth of his age, with no odd years,
in the second month, the tenth day exactly,
all the springs welled up and the waters flowed.

The flood lasted thrice fifty of the days following;
each hill was hidden under gray waves.   430
All beings that lived in the world were laid waste,
all that floated or flew or went on foot.

It was lucky for the remnant, driven by the rack,
that all species lodged there had been led within.
When the Lord of the heavens Himself was pleased   435
to remember the man awaiting his mercy,

He wakened a wind to blow on the waters.
The seas that had been so large then lessened
as He sealed up the ponds and stopped the wells
and bade the rain cease; right away it abated.   440

Then all the lakes shrank, locking together,
when one hundred and fifty hard days had passed,
while the lifting vessel lunged all about
wherever the wind and the weather threw it.

It settled down, one soft day, sinking to ground;   445
it rested at last on a rising rock,
the mount of Ararat in the Armenian hills,
which in the Hebrew tongue is called Thanes.

Though the ark was caught in the crags to stay,
the flood did not cease nor fall to the valley;   450
but the highest crests were a little uncovered,
till the man on board could see the bare earth.

He threw up the window and thence sent out
a messenger from his household to hunt out land,
the rank raven who was always a rebel;   455
he was coal-colored, that untrusty crow!

He takes to flight and fans the wind,
flies to a great height to harken for tidings.
He croaks comfortably when he finds carrion
cast up on a cliff where the crests lie dry.   460

He smacks the smell of it and hurries straight there,
falls on the foul flesh, fills his belly
and at once forgets yesterday's orders,
what the chieftain who ruled the ark had charged him.

The raven reels on, recking little   465
how the people fare if he can find meat;
but the man on shipboard, who was sure of his coming,
cursed him bitterly, with all such beasts!

He seeks another herald, settles on the dove,
brings out that bright one and blesses her, saying: 470
"Go, worthy creature, to win us a dwelling;
drive over this dim water to find dry land.

"Bring tidings to announce bliss to us all!
Though the first bird is treacherous, be trustworthy always!"
She whirled through the winds on her swift wings,   475
straight on all day long, for she dared not alight.

When she finds no land to put her foot on
she circles the coasts and comes back to the boat,
alights at evening-tide and sits on the ark;
at once Noah takes her and brings her in neatly.   *480*

On another day Noah takes the dove again,
bids her cross the water to seek banks once more;
she skims through the skies and scouts about
till night draws near, and then she seeks Noah.

V I

At evening-tide the dove hovered down on the ark;   *485*
she stood on the threshold and waited, quite still.
See! She brought in her beak a branch of olive,
all gracefully overgrown with green leaves.

So our Lord sent them this sign of safety,
of His peace-making with the placid beasts.   *490*
There was joy then in that well-jointed vessel,
and great comfort in that clay-daubed ark.

Merrily on a fair morning in the first month
that falls earliest in the year, on the first day,
the men in that boat laughed and looked outside   *495*
where the waters had waned and the world had dried.

Each one praised our Lord, yet they lingered on
till tidings came from Him who enclosed them there.
Then God's word came to gladden them all,
bidding draw near the door; He would deliver them.   *500*

They went to the wicket; it soon swung wide.
Both the man and his sons went straight out;
their wives walked with them and the wild beasts behind,
fiercely pressing and thronging, thrown thickly together.

Of each good species Noah picked a special one;   *505*
he raised up an altar, reverently hallowed it,
and set on it a sacrifice of each species
that was comely and clean; God cares for no other.

When the beasts were burned wholly and the vapor borne up,
the savor of his sacrifice sought out even Him   *510*
who speeds or spoils all; He speaks to the man
with kind comfort, secretly, in courteous words:

"Now, Noah, no more; I will never curse
the whole mainland, for no man's sins.
For I see this truth well: that all men's wits   *515*
are thrown into folly by the thoughts of their hearts.

"It has been and will yet be, that from babyhood
the whole mind of man is inclined to malice.
I shall never again strike all at once, suddenly,
to destroy all for man's sin, in the days of this earth.   *520*

"But increase now; go forth and grow into many;
multiply on the earth, and may honor come to you!
Seasons shall cease not for you, nor seed nor harvest,
nor heat nor hard frost, nor rain nor drought,

nor the sweetness of summer, nor the sober winter,   *525*
nor night nor day, nor the new years,
but all run on, restless; you shall reign over them!"
So He blesses each beast and bestows the earth on them.

His plan was made clear when the wild things escaped:
each bird in the flight that its feathers served for,   530
each fish to the flood where it uses its fins,
each beast to a field—those that bite on grass.

Wild snakes then writhe to their holes in the soil;
the fox and the pole-cat make off to the forest,
harts to the high heath, hares to the gorse-lands,   535
lions and leopards to the lake-valleys,

eagles and hawks to the high rocks,
while the web-footed fowl hurry to water,
and each beast at a bound goes where it best likes.
The four men seize empire over the earth.   540

See! What avenging woe for wicked deeds
the high Father brought on the folk that He made!
Those He well cherished He chastised severely,
undoing the villainy that vanquished His graciousness.

So be wary now, man, who would be honored
in the beauteous court of the King of bliss,   545
that thou never be found with filthy flesh,
lest the waters of this world fail to wash thee.

No man under the sun is truly well-mannered
if cluttered with sins that make him unclean;   550
one speck or spot may speed his dismissal
from the sight of that Sovereign who sits on high.

Since such is shunned in those shining houses,
a man must be bright as a burnished beryl
that is round on all sides, with no blemish seen,   555
unmarred, unstained, like a marjorie-pearl.

VII

When the Sovereign on His throne so sorely repented
that ever He had made man to live on earth,
since men fell into filth, He took fierce vengeance
by slaying all the flesh that He had formed.   *560*

He grieved that He had reared men, had given them
      sustenance,
and then undone them. This was hard, He thought;
for when this grievous sorrow sank into His heart
He courteously made a covenant with mankind,

measured by His pity and His merciful will,   *565*
that never, for any sin, would He smite all at once,
and kill all things living for some crime done,
for as long a time as the earth should last.

For no wrong was that ordinance ever undone,
yet He took wondrous vengeance on wicked men
      afterwards,   *570*
when fiercely, for the same fault, he ruined a fair land
in His angry ire that alarmed many.

All was for the same evil, that miserable slime,
the venom and villainy and vicious filth
that bespot man's soul when his heart is unsound,   *575*
till he cannot set his eyes on his Savior.

He hates all evil like stinking hell,
but none troubles Him more, by night or day,
than indecent harlotry, self-degradation.
One unashamed of such baseness should be disgraced!   *580*

Savor this in thyself, man; though thou live sottishly
and rave like a fool, reflect sometimes:
if the One who gave sight to each bright eye
had Himself been born blind, that would be a wonder!

And if He who aptly fitted ears to each face   585
had lost His own hearing, that would leave you marveling!
Never trust such a tale, find it untrue;
there is no deed so hidden that it darkens His eyes.

No man is so wary and so still in his work
but what it flies straight to Him before it is thought of.   590
He is a searching God, the ground of all deeds,
piercing the reins and the heart of each person.

And if He finds a man all fair within,
his heart honest and whole, that man He honors,
and sends clear sight to see His own face;   595
others He puts down harshly, driving them from His home.

This the doom of fine men for deeds of shame:
He so abhors their sin that He swiftly scatters them;
He cannot bear to wait, so He kills speedily.
That was shown—and promptly—by a punishment   600
    once.

VIII

Old Abraham sits in his land, all alone
at his own house-door, under a green oak.
Bright glittered the beams from the broad heavens;
in the height of the heat wave Abraham waits.

He had shrunk into shadow under shimmering leaves,   605
then beheld on the road three handsome young men.
They were gracious and fair, good to look at;
that is easy to believe by what happened afterwards.

When the man lounging there under the leaves
had caught sight of them, he hastened straightway.   610
As if before God the good man went towards them,
greeted them as one Being, and said: "Gracious Lord,

"if ever Thy man has earned merit on earth,
linger, I humbly beg, for a little while.
Do not pass by Thy poor one, if I dare so pray,   615
but abide with him, resting under these boughs.

"I shall willingly bring you a little water,
and see to it—fast—that your feet are washed.
Rest here by this root; I shall search around
for a morsel of bread to bring strength to your heart."

"Go forth," said the men, "and fetch what Thou wilt;
we shall wait by the trunk of this wide-spreading tree."
Hurrying indoors, he hastened to Sarah,
commanding her to be clever and quick, for once.

"Mingle three measure of meal to make cakes,   625
under the hot ashes hide them straightway.
While I fetch something fat, stir up the fire
promptly, at this point, to make some pottage."

He went to the cow house and brought a calf
that was tender, not tough, bade the hide be torn off,   630
and told his servant to boil it swiftly;
so he, at this command, quickly dressed it.

The man then makes haste to bare his head,
takes a clean cloth, casting it on the grass,
puts carefully on it three unleavened cakes,   635
then brings some butter and sets it by the bread.

Proper portions of milk he puts down beside it,
and then the pottage in a decent platter.
Like a steward at a good feast he served in fine fashion,
with serious and sweet manners, such as he had.   640

And God, like a glad guest, made good cheer,
as one pleased with his friend, and praised the feast.
Abraham, hood thrown back, arms folded,
placed food for the Ones who wield almighty power.

They said, as the three of them sat together,   645
when the food was taken off and they talked graciously:
"I shall come here again, Abram," they said,
"before thy life's light fails on the earth.

"Then shall Sarah conceive and bear a son
who shall be Abraham's heir, and after him obtain,   650
with wealth and with honor, the worthy people
who shall hold in heritage what I have in store for them."

The woman behind the door laughed in derision,
and said just to herself—that foolish Sarah:
"Trust that to be nonsense, that thou shouldst teem!   655
I so far on in age, and my lord also!"

Truly, as the Writ says, they were of ripe age,
both the man and his wife; such a work had failed them;
for many long days before this they were barren,
and Sarah without seed in that same time.   660

Then our Sire on His throne said: "See! Sarah laughs,
not trusting the tale that I told to thee!
Does she think anything hard for my hands to work?
Yet verily I am pledged to the promise I made.

"I shall appear again soon and give what I promised,   665
and indeed send to Sarah a son and an heir."
Then Sarah stepped out and answered; certainly
she had never laughed—at nothing they had said!

"Enough now; that's not so," the Lord said then,
"for thou didst laugh low. But let's leave it alone."   670
With that they got up quickly as if they must go,
turning their eyes towards Sodom, all together.

For the city nearby was set in a vale
no more than two miles away from Mambre
where that same man lived to whom our Lord came   675
with warning words to show him the way.

Then God moves on, the good man follows Him.
Thus Abraham came along to convey them
towards the city of Sodom that had then sinned
with the fault of filthiness; the Father threatened   680

and said to the man who was following Him:
"How turn my heart away from trusty Abraham,
and not make clear to him my dire counsel?
Since he is chosen to be the forefather of children

"from whom folk shall come to flood all the world,   685
and each child of that man's blood shall be held blessed,
I must inform him of my angry will,
and now disclose to Abraham my whole design.

I X

"The great sound of Sodom sinks into my ears,
  and the guilt of Gomorrah goads me to wrath;   690
  I shall go to that land and look around for myself
  to see what they are doing—the din rises so high.

"They have learned a lust that I like ill,
  they have shown in their flesh the worst of faults:
  each man takes for mate a man like himself   695
  and they join filthily, in female way.

"I granted them a great power, privately taught them,
  and devised it, in my plan, singularly dear;
  I set love in it, the sweetest of gifts,
  and I myself planned the play of lovers.   700

"I made it an action more joyous than others;
  when two true ones had so joined together,
  such mirth should arise between a man and his mate
  that pure paradise, nearly, should prove no better,

"as long as each virtuously deals with the other;   705
  at a still, secret word, unguided by sight,
  a love-flame joining them lashes so hot
  that no evil in the world can ever slake it.

"Now they have spurned my plan and scorned nature,
  taking up in contempt an unclean custom;   710
  I think to smite sharply for such a stain,
  that men be warned by them world without end."

Then Abraham was awe-struck; all his mood changed,
facing the hard hate that our Lord foretold.
Deeply sighing, he said: "Sire, by your leave,   715
shall sinful and innocent all suffer the same pain?

"Could my Lord be pleased to lay down such a doom,
wreaking one vengeance on the wicked and the worthy,
throwing on the wrong side those who caused Thee no
      wrath?
That was never Thy fashion, Thou who formed us all!   720

"Now, if fifty fine friends were found in yonder town,
in the city of Sodom and also Gomorrah,
who never failed in Thy law but always loved truth,
righteous and reasonable and ready to serve Thee,

"shall they fall for the fault of those other fellows,   725
joined in one judgment and in one justice?
That was never Thy way; it would be unnamable,
Thou art a God so courteous, so kind in spirit!"

"No, for fifty," said the Father, "and for thy fair speech,
if found among that folk clean from their filth,   730
I shall forgive the guilt, through my grace alone,
and let them pass unsmitten, in peace, for this once."

"Ah, blessed be Thou!" he said, "so bounteous and good,
holding all in Thy hand, heaven and earth!
But I've gone far in talking, so take it not ill   735
if I ask a little more, I—dust and ashes.

"What if five fall short from the number of fifty
and the remnant be righteous, how rests Thy will?"
"For five short of fifty," said God, "I'll forget all,
and withhold my hand from hurting those people."   740

"What if forty be good and the others at fault?
 Wilt Thou shortly harm all, and shape it no other-
      wise?"
"No, if forty are sin-free, I shall forego a while,
 and make void my vengeance, though I find things vile."

Then Abraham honored Him and thanked Him humbly: 745
"Blessed be Thou, Savior, so simple in Thy wrath!
 I am but vile earth and black ashes,
 to speak thus with a Master who is almighty!

"But I have begun with my God, and He thinks it good
 if I, like a straying fool, serve Thy liberality.   750
 What if thirty pure men be punished in yonder towns,
 how could I think that my Lord would not love them?"

Then God in His goodness gave this answer:
"For thirty in that rabble I shall hold back my wrath,
 surely sparing my anger in accord with my attributes,   755
 and restrain my rancor for thy righteous words."

"What, for twenty," the man said, "wouldst Thou make
      trouble?"
"No, if thou yearn for it I shall yield them grace;
 if only twenty be true I shall trouble them no more,
 but deliver all that region from their rank deeds."   760

"Now noble Lord," said Abraham, "only one more word,
 and I shall try no further to help those fellows;
 if ten trust men in that town do Thy tasks,
 wilt Thou temper Thy mood till they mend their ways?"

"I grant it," said the great God. "I give thanks," said
    the other.   765
Then the man ceased and said nothing further,
and God passed along through those green ways
while the man led Him on with a look from his eyes.

As he looked around while our Lord went by,
he still cried out in a voice full of care: 770
"Meek Master, be pleased to remember Thy man;
Lot, my dear brother, lives with those people.

"He sits there in Sodom, Thy poor servant,
among the evil men who have grieved Thee much.
In destroying that town, temper Thine anger,   775
as Thy mercy moves Thee to spare Thy meek one."

Then he goes on his way, weeping for care,
towards the sea of Mambre, mourning sorrowfully;
there he lingers all night in a house, in his longing,
while the Sovereign sent some into Sodom, to spy.   780

X

His message was sent into Sodom, right then,
that very evening, by two angels
moving modestly together like pleasant young men,
while Lot, at his lodge-door, lounged all alone

in a porch set near the gates of that place   785
that was royally built—he was rich himself.
Staring into the street where strong men were playing,
he saw those two fair men walking together.

They were both bold youths with beardless chins,
hair waving royally, like raw silk,   790
in color like the briar-flower where the bare skin
    showed;
and clean was the look of their clear eyes.

Clear white were their robes, and well became them;
fine were their features. Both were faultless,
with nothing amiss, for they were angels,   795
as he sitting near the gate soon understood.

Rapidly Lot rose and ran to meet them;
he bent to the ground, bowing very low,
and said earnestly: "Sirs, I beseech you,
alight at my lodge and linger within.   800

"Come to your servant's cottage, I crave it this once;
I shall fetch a vessel to wash your feet.
I urge you for one night to stay near me;
in the merry morning you shall make your way on."

They answered no; they would enter no house,   805
but quietly in the street where they were standing
they would spend the long night, lodging outside.
House enough for them the heaven's above!

Lot urged them so long with loving words
that they agreed to go in, and grudged it no more.   810
He brought them straightway into a building
royally arrayed; he had always been rich.

The men were welcomed—his wife knew how—
and his two dear daughters devotedly greeted them;
they were modest maidens, not yet married,   815
attractive and sweet, and suitably arrayed.

Then Lot, all alert, looks about him
and orders his men to prepare a meal.
"Be careful that it's unleavened, whatever you cook,
and don't serve anything with salt or sharp flavor."　　*820*

By this, I think, the woman was worked up to spite,
saying softly to herself: "These rude striplings
like no salt in their sauce; that's no sane reason
why other folk do without, because they are fussy."

Then she flavors with salt each of her services,　　*825*
against the bidding of the man who forbade it;
she reviled them scornfully, though she knew their reasons.
Why was she—wretch—so mad? She made our Lord wrath-
　　ful!

They sat down to supper and were soon served,
the guests glad, light-hearted, gracious in speech,　　*830*
winningly handsome when they had washed;
by the wall were the trestles, and the table also.

When the men had supped and were sitting awhile
before going to bed, the city was agog;
all who could wield weapons, the weak and the strong,　　*835*
surrounded Lot's house to seize the young men.

In a great rabble those folk fell on his gates;
like a scared scout-watch they raised a cry.
With heavy clubs they clattered on the enclosing walls,
and in sharp shrill voices shouted out these words:　　*840*

"If thou lovest thy life, Lot, in these dwellings,
let us have those young men that came here lately,
we must teach them love, as our lust craves,
in the fashion of Sodom with fellows passing through."

Ho! They spouted and spoke such despicable filth,   *845*
Ho! they yelped and bragged of such yeasty dirt
that the wind and the weather and the world yet stink
from the vomit cast up by those vile words.

The good man stared at the talk, stunned by the noise;
sharp shame shot through him and his heart shrank,   *850*
for he knew the custom those wretches carried on.
No grief had ever dazed his mind so deeply.

"Alas!" said Lot then; he leaped up nimbly
and sprang from his bench to the broad gates.
Ho! He wavered not at harm from those wicked knaves   *855*
but passed through the door to meet the peril.

He went through the wicket and wafted it after him
till the latch clicked and it closed behind.
Then he spoke to those men in measured words,
for he hoped to chasten those harlots with civility.   *860*

"Oh, my noble friends, your notions are so strange!
Be off with your dire din; don't damage my guests.
Away! This is villainy; you make yourselves vile.
If you are fine gentlemen, your jokes are bad ones.

"I'll show you a better way, befitting nature: *865*
I've a treasure in my house, my two fair daughters
who are maidens untouched by any man yet;
in Sodom, though I say so, are no sightlier girls.

They are full-grown and ripe, ready for marriage;
it will give more pleasure to possess those fair ones.   *870*
I bestow on you these two, so lively and beautiful;
play with them as you like and leave my guests alone."

Then those rank rebels raised such a noise
that their horrible harlot speech was hurled in his ears.
"Hast thou forgotten that thou art a foreigner,   *875*
a stranger, a churl? We'll chop off thy head!

"Who made thee a justice to blame our jesting,
who came as a boy to town, though a rich man?"
Thus they thrust and thronged, throwing words in his ears,
and put him in sore straits with their strong pushing.   *880*

But the young men, all ready, ran out just then,
knocked open the wicket and made their way to him;
they took him by the hand, hurried within,
and stopped the gates stone-hard with stalwart bars.

Those cursed people blew a loud blast together,   *885*
they blustered as blindly as ever Bayard did.
At Lot's house they failed to find an entrance,
milling around all night, for nothing at last.

Then they made off, those fellows who had failed in
      their sport,
each rambled away to what rest he could get.   *890*
But those who stayed indoors were suddenly wakened
by as ugly an ill-hap as earth ever suffered.

XI

The red daylight arose in the dawn
when the mirk of midnight could last no more.
Right early those angels roused the man;   *895*
alarmed, they got him to rise, for God's sake!

He rose up fast, his heart full of fear.
They commanded him quickly to catch up all he had:
"With thy wife and thy men and thy winsome daughters,
   we urge thee, Sir Lot, to save thy life.   *900*

"Go fast from this country, before thou art crushed,
with thy company, in haste, till thou findest a hill.
Go swiftly, on foot; look before your face,
   but be never so bold as to glance behind.

"Never halt your steps but go straight on, fast,   *905*
till you reach a refuge; take no rest.
We shall ruin this town and wholly wreck it,
   with all those wicked people promptly cast down.

"We shall punish at once the whole land and its people.
Sodom shall suddenly sink into the ground,   *910*
the land of Gomorrah shall go down into hell,
   and each region of this country clatter into heaps."

Then Lot spoke out: "Lord, what is best?
If I take to my feet—since I must flee—
how hide from them that have kindled His hate,   *915*
   from the violence of His breath that burns everything,

"or creep from my Creator, not knowing where I'll come,
or if, foe-like, He follows me, before or behind?"
Said the Other: "No foe to thee is our Father
   who sees to thy safety among them that suffer.   *920*

"Now choose a dwelling-place that can protect thee,
and He who sent us shall save it for thy sake.
Thou alone art saved out of all this filth,
   with Abraham thy kinsman, who asked it from Him."

"The Lord! Be He praised through the whole earth,"
    said Lot.   *925*
"There is a city near by that is called Segor;
out on a round hill it stands, alone.
I would, if it please Him, escape to that place."

"Then go forth," said that noble One, "and never stop,
with those whom thou wilt; let them press on with thee, *930*
going straight along without looking back;
this whole land shall be lost long before sunrise."

The man wakened his wife and his winsome daughters,
and the two fine men the maidens were to wed,
but these thought it tittle-tattle and paid no attention;
though Lot spoke strongly, they lay quite still.

The angels urged the others with awesome warnings
and forced them through the gates, all four of them.
They were Lot and his wife and his lovely daughters,
who no longer sought safety in the five noble cities. *940*

Those angels then led them by the hand through the gates,
impressing them with the peril; they bade them be prompt:
"Lest you should be taken in the sins of these tyrants,
see that you obey; bustle out of here."

And they dared not swerve, but fled swiftly;   *945*
before heaven's first gleam they came to hill.
Up above, the great God grimly begins
to waken wild weathers; he calls up the winds,

and they wrathfully whirled and wrestled together
from earth's four corners, loudly quarrelling.   *950*
The clustering clouds were cast up in towers
where thick thunder blasts pierced them through.

The rains rolled down, riddled thickly
with fierce flashes of fire and flakes of sulphur;
all in smoldering smoke, smacking evilly,   955
it rushed over Sodom from every side,

striking into Gomorrah and loosening the ground;
Admah and Zeboim, all four of those cities,
were drenched in that rain, roasted and burned.
Fiercely it terrified the people of those towns.   960

For when hell heard those hounds of heaven,
it was wonderfully glad and opened wide.
At once it burst open the great bars of the abyss
and tore the whole region into huge rifts,

till all the cliffs split into little clouts   965
like loose leaves of a book that breaks in two.
When the breath of the brimstone stopped blowing,
the cities and suburbs had all sunk into hell.

Helpless were the great hosts of men within
when aware of the wrath that none could escape;   970
such an outcry, such wailing and yelling arose
that the very clouds clattered: "May Christ have pity!"

The man going to Segor heard that sound,
and the women who followed along the way;
their flesh shivered fearfully as they fled on,   975
going at a fast trot, not daring to turn.

Lot and his two dear lily-white daughters
followed with set faces, both eyes before them.
But the wretched woman who would not obey
glanced behind her back, to hear the burning.   980

So Lot's good-looking wife, over her left shoulder,
glanced once at the city. But no sooner done
that she stood stone-stiff, a stalwart image,
as salt as any sea, and so she yet stands.

They fled on without seeing, her fellow-travelers,   985
till they were brought to Segor, and blessed our Lord.
With glad hands lifted they praised Him heartily
for keeping His servants safe from such harm.

Then all were damned, drowned and done for.
The people of the little town leaped out for dread   990
into that accursed sea; all swiftly perished,
with nothing saved but Segor seated on a hill,

with the three left in it, Lot and his daughters.
For his wife was missing; she had stayed on the mount
as a stone statue that has a salt flavor,   995
for the two faults found in that untrusty fool:

first, at supper she served salt before the Lord,
and then she looked back, although forbidden.
For one, she stands in stone, for the other she is salt,
and all the beasts in that land like to lick her.   1000

Abraham was up in the morning, right early;
all night he had suffered much sorrow of heart,
and in longing for Lot had lain watching.
There he had left our Lord, who had gone aloft.

He turned his eyes, looking towards Sodom,   1005
among the loveliest places on earth,
like a part of Paradise that the Lord planted,
plunged now in a pit that seemed filled with pitch.

A rush of smoke-reek rose from the blackness,
ashes and cinders flew through the air,   *1010*
like a pot full of grease that boils on the fire
when bright burning brands are stirred beneath it.

Such violent vengeance made these places void
when fair people floundered and the fields sank.
Where four cities were settled is now called a sea,   *1015*
ever turbid and dull and dead by nature,

livid, black-bubbling, bitter to go near,
a stinking pool that destroyed sin;
for its smell and its smack and its smarting touch,
it is ever more doomed as the dark Dead Sea.   *1020*

For its deadly deeds endure there yet:
it is broad and bottomless, bitter as gall,
and nothing living can linger in that lake,
as it wars against each of the ways of nature.

Lay a lump of lead there and it floats aloft,   *1025*
set there a light feather and it sinks to the depths,
and where that water flows to wet the earth
no green shall ever grow, neither grass nor woods.

If a man is pushed in, by way of punishment,
though he dwell for a month in those horrible depths   *1030*
he must live on in that lake, lost evermore,
and never meet death, days without end.

It is cursed by nature, and its coasts also,
so the clay that clings to it brings a strong curse,
such as alum and alkatran that are both so acrid,   *1035*
sour sulphur, sandiver, and many such others.

There flows through that water in great wax-twists
the seething asphalt that spice-mongers sell.
Such is all the soil beside that sea
that it fiercely gnaws flesh and festering bones.   1040

There are also trees by that lake of traitors
that burgeon and bear very fair blossoms
and the loveliest fruit that grows in the fields,
oranges, pomegranates, and other fruits,

all as red and ripe and richly colored   1045
as anyone could want in such dainties—outwardly.
But when they are bruised or bitten in two,
no earthly good is there, only wind-blown ashes.

All these are still signs, tokens to trust in,
witnesses to foul deeds and the vengeance following   1050
when our Father destroyed the people's filthiness,
that all may know well that He loves the worthy.

If He loves clean behavior, He, our noble Lord,
and if thou dost covet to be known in His court,
to see that fair One enthroned, with His sweet face,   1055
clearer counsel I know not: thou must be clean.

Clopinel, in the course of his "Clean Rose"
gives advice to one who would have good-speed
with a lady he loves: "Look straight at her,
see how she bears herself, what she likes best,   1060

and be always like her, in body and in deeds,
follow the footsteps of that fair comrade;
if thou workest in this way, even though she were wicked
she would love the behavior that likens thee to her."

If thou wilt make love with thy Leader then,   *1065*
loving thy Lord loyally, and loved by Him,
conform thee to Christ and make thyself clean;
He is polished as smooth as the pearl itself.

Look: when He first came to the fair maiden,
by how comely a means He was enclosed there,   *1070*
when virginity was unvanquished, no violence used;
much cleaner was her body with God conceived in it!

Then, when He was born in noble Bethlehem,
in what purity was He brought forth! Though they were
          poor,
no bower is more blissful than a cow-bin was then   *1075*
no shelter more shining than that cattle-shed,

and none so glad in God as she who should groan;
for the sorest sickness was there made sound.
There was scent of roses where rot had once been,
there was comforting song where sorrow had wept.   *1080*

For angels with instruments, organs and pipes,
royal ringing viols and vibrant fiddles,
and all charming things that make hearts chastely glad,
were gathered round my Lady when she was delivered.

And her happy Babe was burnished so clean   *1085*
that the ox and the ass adored Him together.
They knew Him by His cleanness for the King of nature;
one so clean had never come from such an enclosure.

And if clean in His coming, He was courteous afterwards,
loathing and hating all that holds evil.   *1090*
Nurtured in nobility, He would never touch
anything ungodly, or that had ordure in it.

Yet the loathsome came to that man, such as lazars,
the leprous, the lame, and the lumbering blind,
the poisoned, the paralytic, those pained with fevers,   *1095*
dry folk and dropsical, and the dead last of all.

All called on that courteous One and claimed His grace.
He healed them with pleasant words, as they had prayed Him,
for whatever He touched turned healthy at once,
far cleaner than craftsmanship could ever make it.   *1100*

So clean was His handling that corruption shrank from it;
His touch was so good—He was both God and man—
and His fingers so skillful that He was not forced
to cut or carve with a keen-edged knife.

Thus He broke bread without any blade;   *1105*
it obeyed more freely in His fair hands,
fell apart more neatly when He portioned it,
than if all the tools of Toulouse were cutting it.

He whose court thou seekest is clean and careful.
Canst thou come to His country unless thou too art
     clean?   *1110*
We are sore and sinful and stained, each one of us.
"How see," we may say, "that Sovereign on His throne?"

Yes, that Master is merciful, and thou a vile man
all ugly with mire while living on earth.
Thou canst shine through confession, after serving
     shame   *1115*
and be pure through penance until made a pearl.

A pearl is held priceless among precious stones,
though it be not the dearest when bought with pennies!
What cause could there be but its clean color
for the honor bestowed on it above all white stones?   *1120*

For it shines so clear in its round shape,
without fault or stain, if it is a fine stone,
and though, in the world, it grows old from wearing,
yet the pearl is not impaired while still prized.

But if by some chance it is not cherished,   *1125*
And its brilliance dims as it lies in a bower,
just wash it reverently in wine, as is needful;
its own color will come back clearer than before.

So if a man be stained by something base
till polluted in soul, let him seek confession   *1130*
and be promptly polished, by doing penance,
brighter than beryls or embellished pearls.

But be wary, if washed in waters of confession
and polished as smooth as a shaven parchment,
soil thy soul no more in sin thereafter,   *1135*
or thou wilt sadden the Lord with thy sorry deeds

and entice Him to anger more surely than ever,
and to hate much hotter than before thy washing.
For a soul once reconciled and sacred to the Lord,
He holds as His own, and He will have it.   *1140*

If it then turns vicious, He takes its loss ill,
as though evil robbers had snatched it wrongfully.
Be careful of the vengeance; His wrath is kindled
when what was once His has become unclean.

Though it be but a basin, a bowl or drinking cup,   *1145*
a dish or large plate that once served the Lord,
He firmly forbids to defile it on earth,
so repugnant is wrong to the One ever righteous.

That was made plain in Babylon in Belshazzar's time,
when hard luck overtook him all in a hurry;   *1150*
for he treated vilely vessels used in the temple
in the service of the Sovereign some time before.

If you give me time I will tell about this:
the bad case of him who would not care for them
when his erring father had fetched them by force,   *1155*
robbing a religious shrine of all its relics.

XII

Daniel once described in a dialogue
(as proved expressly in his prophecies)
how the Jewish nobility and royal Jerusalem
were crushed by distress, drawn down to earth.   *1160*

For those people were found untrue to their faith
who had promised the high God to hold to Him ever;
He had hallowed them as His own, helping them at need
in many misfortunes—things marvelous to hear.

And they left their faith, following other gods;   *1165*
that awakened His wrath, and raised it so high
that He helped those faithful to the false law
to destroy those false to the true faith.

This was seen in the time when Zedechiah reigned
in Judah, he who judged the Jewish Kings.   1170
On Solomon's throne he sat with solemnity,
but he lacked loyalty to His gracious Lord.

He practiced abominations of idolatry,
and made light of the law of his own allegiance.
So our Father stirred up a foe on earth;
Nebuchadnezzar annoyed him mightily.

This one marched into Palestine with many proud men,
where he wasted the dwellings in those towns with war.
He harried all Israel, seized hold of the best,
and in Jerusalem besieged the noblest of Judah.   1180

He surrounded the walls with right strong warriors
—at each door a brave duke—and barred up those within;
for the town was big, with battlements aloft,
and packed full of stout men to stall those without.

The siege settled down around the city;   1185
skirmishing swiftly spread, scattering damage.
At each bridge was a moving tower, a bastion on wheels,
that seven times a day assailed the gates.

Trusty men in the towers made trouble within;
from a big broad parapet built on the walls   1190
they fought and fended off—all confused together—
while two years went by, without taking the town.

When a long time had passed, the people inside
found the food failing, and many were famished.
Hot hunger within hurt them more sorely   1195
than any blows from the strong men who stayed outside.

Then those routs were helpless in their rich houses;
since food was lacking they grew lean,
stuck there so strait they could not stray
a foot from the fortress to forage for goods.   *1200*

Then the king of that country takes counsel
with his best fighters how to form a trick;
they steal out on a still night without raising a sound
and fall heavily on the host, before their foes know it.

But before they can outwit the watch outside,   *1205*
the uproar spread wide under the skies.
Loud alarm was uplifted throughout the land;
nobles, roused from rest, ran for their outfits.

They snatched their hard hats and leaped on horseback;
clear clarion calls cried out aloft.   *1210*
Soon all were in a heap, hurtling mightily;
following the other army, they found them swiftly,

overtook them soon, tilted them from their saddles,
till each prince had put his peer on the ground.
Here the king was caught by Chaldean princes,   *1215*
outjousted with his nobles on Jericho's plains,

and given as prisoner to the richest prince,
Nebuchadnezzar, noble on his throne.
He was the happiest of men when he held his foes,
spoke spitefully to them, then spilled out their lives.   *1220*

He had each of the king's sons slain in his sight;
cruelly he gouged out the king's two eyes,
then bade him be brought to royal Babylon
and thrown into a dungeon to endure his fate.

Now see how the sovereign God settled His wrath!　　*1225*
It was not for Nabugo, nor for his nobles,
that Zedechiah was put down with strong pain,
but for bad behavior to his blessed Lord.

Had the Father who guarded him but been his friend,
and had he not failed by a want of faith,　　*1230*
all would have gone to Chaldea and the country of India
—and still have taken Turkey, with a little trouble.

Yet Nabugo would not stop this same undertaking
before stripping the town and tearing it to the ground.
He then placed over Jerusalem a gentile duke　　*1235*
called Nebuzaradan, to cause the Jews trouble.

He was master of his men, mighty in himself,
chief of his chivalry in leading a charge;
he at once broke the barriers and then all the city,
entering in earnest, with anger of heart.　　*1240*

Ho! The forces were meagre, the men were away,
the best surrendered to the city's master,
those who stayed were so bitten by baleful hunger
that one woman was worth the worthiest four.

Nebuzaradan, for that, would spare none of them,　　*1245*
but bade all be brought under the bare sword-edge;
they slew the fairest of the sweet maidens,
bathed babes in blood and spilled their brains.

Priests and prelates they pressed to death,
cut wide open the bellies of women and maidens　　*1250*
till their bowels burst out all over the ditches;
all whom they caught were killed woefully.

Those who slipped off unharmed by the keen sword
were bound and tied to horses, all bare,
fetters holding their feet under the foals' bellies,   1255
and cruelly brought to Babylon to bear their bad luck.

One-time noblemen sit in servitude and sorrow;
they are changed into churls and charged with work,
both pulling carts and milking cows—
they who sat in halls as sires and ladies.   1260

And yet Nebuzaradan would never stop
before marching on the temple with all his men,
beating down the barriers, bursting open the gates.
They slew at one stroke all who served therein,

pulled priests by the hair and struck off their heads,   1265
did deacons to death, knocked down clerics,
and killed, in their might, the maids in the temple
with a swing of the sword that slew them all.

Then they ran for the relics like wild robbers,
and pillaged the ornaments that pertained to the church, 1270
the pillars of pure brass with gold portraiture,
the main candlestick that carried the light.

and bore aloft the lamp that gave light always
in the Sancta Sanctorum where marvels were seen.
They carried off that candlestick, and also the crown   1275
of fine rich gold that was found on the altar,

the gridiron and the goblets garnished with silver,
the bases of the bright posts and shining basins,
precious dishes of gold and fair platters,
vials and vessels of virtue-bearing stones.   1280

Now has Nebuzaradan taken these noble things,
pillaged the precious place and packed off the goods;
the gold of the treasure-chest in great quantities,
with the house-ornaments, he put in hampers.

Spitefully and speedily he spoiled all the things   *1285*
that Solomon through many long years sought to make.
With all his wisdom and with clean workmanship
he had devised the vessels and the clean vestments;

with skill and with knowledge, in praise of his Sovereign,
he had adorned the house with its decorations.   *1290*
Now Nebuzaradan has brought all to nothing;
he has beaten down the city and burned it to ashes.

Then with legions of men he rides over the land;
he ravages in and out of the corners of Israel.
With loaded chariots he finds the chieftain,   *1295*
giving to the king the goods he had gathered,

presenting the prisoners taken as prey:
many a worthy man while the world lasts,
many a fine man's son, very noble maidens,
the proudest of the provinces, the children of prophets, *1300*

like Ananiah and Azariah, and also Michael,
and the great Daniel too, a noble diviner,
many proud mothers' children, more than enough.
And Nebuchadnezzar now rejoices

in conquering the king, winning the country,   *1305*
downing the bravest and direst in their armies,
with the leaders of their law laid on the ground,
and their choicest prophets now made prisoners.

What joy to behold such fine, rich jewelry!
When its glitter was shown him he wondered greatly;   *1310*
of vessels like these, so highly valued,
Nebuchadnezzar, till then, had never heard.

He received them solemnly, he praised the Sovereign
who was noblest of all, the Lord of Israel.
Such goods, such servants, such gorgeous vessels,   *1315*
had come from no country to Chaldean realms.

He tied them in his treasury in a trusty place,
fitly and reverently, as he thought right.
In this he did wisely, as you may here witness;
had he made light of them things might have gone worse. *1320*

That mighty one reigned through life, most royally;
as conqueror of each country he was called caesar,
emperor of all the earth, and also sultan,
then as god of that land his name was graven.

This all came through Daniel's power; he had declared   *1325*
that all good comes from God, and gave examples
till he clearly admitted this claim at last,
and God's masterful works often meekened his mind.

But all draws towards death, with dolor at the end;
a hero, however great, falls to the ground.   *1330*
And so Nebuchadnezzar, as he needs must,
for all his high empire, finds a grave in the earth.

Then the bold Belshazzar, who was his first-born,
was installed instead and established his reign.
He trusted that Babylon, the biggest of cities,   *1335*
could have no peer in heaven or on earth.

He began in the glory that the great man left him,
Nebuchadnezzar, his noble father;
till then no keener king had come to Chaldea,
yet he honored not Him who dwells in heaven.   1340

But false phantoms of fiends, formed by hands
with tools, from hard trees, to be heaved aloft,
and from stocks and stones, these he calls stout gods
when all gilded with gold and geared with silver.

There he kneels and calls, crying out for help;   1345
if they guide him rightly he promises reward,
but if they begrudge their grace, grieving his heart,
he picks up a great club and knocks them to pieces.

Thus in pride and arrogance he holds his empire,
in lust and in lechery and in loathly deeds.   1350
He had a wife to manage, a worthy queen,
and mistresses nonetheless, known as "ladies."

In his fair concubines, in curious robes,
in tasting new foods and in foolish fashions,
this man's mind was set on misshapen things,   1355
till the Lord of heaven willed to bring it low.

XIII

This bold Belshazzar once got an idea:
to vaunt a display of his own vainglory.
Not enough for the fool to do nasty things,
but the whole world must know of his wicked deeds!   1360

Belshazzar had his bidding cried aloud through Babylon
and the country of Chaldea; his call sprang wide:
all the great in the land must gather together,
and assemble on a set day at the Sultan's feast.

The man then planned to prepare a banquet   *1365*
for the kings of each country; they must come to it.
Each duke with his bodyguard and other brave lords
must appear in his court, admit their allegiance,

show him reverence, hearken to his revelry,
look at his mistresses and call them "my lady."   *1370*
These proud men were ready to praise his splendor,
the right bold barons of noble Babylon.

There moved toward Babylon so many men,
kings and strong rulers arriving at court,
so many landed lords bringing their ladies,   *1375*
that it would be troublesome to tell their numbers.

For the city was very broad, very big also,
set in the fairest site under the stars,
proud on a flat plain, the fairest of places,
encircled on every side by seven great rivers,   *1380*

and a wall wondrously made, arrayed on high
with well-cut battlements, cleanly carved,
tufted with towers every twenty spears' length,
thickly planted with palings placed crosswise.

The palace that covered the enclosure within   *1385*
was long and large, four-square likewise;
on each side the grounds stretched for seven miles,
and the Sultan's court was set in the middle.

It was a proud palace, surpassing all others
in workmanship and wonders, walled all about,   *1390*
with high dwellings inside, the hall in proportion,
broad-built, and so roomy that horses could run there.

When the fulness of time for the feast had come,
the nobility drew near and met on the dais,
and Belshazzar was brought in to sit on his bench;   *1395*
bright shone the stones in his stout throne.

The whole hall-floor was hidden by knights,
with barons sitting everywhere at the side tables;
none was placed on the dais but the proud man himself
and his fair concubines in their bright clothes.   *1400*

When all are seated the service begins.
Shrill trumpets strike up a loud sound in the hall
till the walls re-echo the ringing blast,
where big banners hang, bright-shining with gold.

There were men bearing roasts on broad platters   *1405*
that seemed to be silver and were used for serving;
they had arbors over them, cut at the edges,
pared out of paper and painted gold,

with fierce baboons above, beasts underneath;
between them birds fluttered through the foliage   *1410*
—all in azure and indigo richly enameled—
borne in the hands of men on horseback.

The noise of kettle-drums, the notes of pipes,
tambourines and tabors, twanged aloud;
cymbals and singing answered the sound   *1415*
while the beating of drum-sticks battered heavily.

Many times the servers circled the hall,
for the pleasure of the prince in the courses placed
where that lord and his mistresses lingered at table.
They pressed wine on him till it warmed his heart,   *1420*

rose into his brain, bemused his mind
and weakened his wits till he nearly went foolish;
he stares all around, then sees his wenches
and his bold baronage all about, near the walls.

So a wild madness welled up in his heart,   *1425*
and a craven idea then caught hold of him;
loudly the master calls for his marshal,
commands him to break open the coffers quickly

and fetch the vessels that his father had brought,
when Nebuchadnezzar, noble in his strength,   *1430*
had conquered with his chivalry and robbed the shrine
of Jerusalem in Judah—the deed of a Gentile!

"Bring them now to my board, fill them with beverage,
give a sip to these ladies whom I love from my heart!
If I show them this courtesy, they shall soon know   *1435*
there is no man more bountiful in his ways than Belshazzar."

This tale was told at once to the treasurer
and he, with his keys, unclosed many coffers;
many bright burdens were brought into the hall,
many side-boards covered with very white cloths.   *1440*

The jewels from Jerusalem, the gems so bright,
were handsomely arranged on one side of the hall;
the proud altar of brass was put into place,
and lifted above it the lovely gold crown

that had been blessed once by a bishop's hands,   1445
and bountifully anointed with the blood of beasts
in a solemn sacrifice whose sweet savor rose
to the Lord of heaven, in His praise alone;

it is set out now to serve Satan, the black one,
before the bold Belshazzar, with boasting and pride.   1450
Placed high on the altar were princely vessels
carved cunningly with curious craft.

Solomon took seven years, and several more,
with all the knowledge lent him by the sovereign Lord,
to design and carry through their clean workmanship;   1455
there were bright basins of clear burnished gold,

enamelled with azure, with ewers to match,
covered cups, very clean, arrayed like castles
fortified with battlements, with beautiful horn-corbels,
and filed-out figures of fantastic shape.   1460

The caps on the covers that rose over the cups
were carefully formed into long columns,
with pinnacles projecting plainly between them,
and all were embossed with branches and leaves,

with magpies and popinjoys portrayed in them   1465
as though proudly picking at the pomegranates;
all the blossoms on the boughs were pearls bright-shining,
all the fruits were formed of flaming gems,

sapphires and sardiners and sightly topazes,
almandines, emeralds, amethystine stones,   1470
chalcedonies, chrysolites and clear rubies,
peridots, pynkardines, and pearls everywhere,

in a pattern trailing cross-wise and set with trefoils
on each beaker and bowl, with birds all around,
graven on all sides of these goblets of gold   1475
and cups fretted with flowers and golden flies.

All these things were placed on the altar;
the candlestick, by some device, was soon carried in,
so that many praised it, adorned on its pillars
and bases of brass that bore up the structure,   1480

with bright boughs above, all embroidered with gold,
branches spreading over it, and birds there set
of many curious multi-colored kinds;
as though winging the wind they waved their feathers.

Among the leaves on those branches lamps were placed, 1485
and other lovely lights that gleamed lucently;
wide-brimmed candle-sticks clustered around it,
many a noble beast of burnished gold.

In that hall it was uncouth to waste wax candles
that should in truth stand in the real temple,   1490
before the Sancta Sanctorum where the true Sovereign
gave His spiritual message to special prophets.

Be certain that the Lord who rules the skies
was displeased at such playing in an evil place,
when rascals befouled His fair jewels   1495
once held so precious before His presence.

Some had been anointed in solemn sacrifice
at the summons of Him who sits on high.
Now a boaster on a bench imbibes from them
till he's drunk as the devil, bedazed where he sits.   1500

The Lord, the world's Maker, finds this so loathsome
that even as they play He plans His purpose;
but before harming them in His hasty ire
He gave them a warning that made them wonder.

Now all this ware serves to wait on gluttons,   *1505*
brought into that rich room and shined up brightly.
Belshazzar in a sudden fit bade it be used:
"Pour wine in this place! Waissal!" he cries.

Quick servants at once swept forward to do it,
seized cups in their hands to serve the kings,   *1510*
poured wine into bright bowls for the others, willingly,
each man attending to his own master.

Soon was heard ringing of rich metal
as men in that fine crowd ran to fill their cups,
and clattering of covers cast down by the ladies,   *1515*
like the sound of psaltery merrily singing.

The idiot on the dais drank with his whole might,
then drinks were poured for dukes and princes,
concubines and knights; because of their mirth
each drank from his cup the drink poured in.   *1520*

So these lords revelled long in their sweet liquors,
gloried in false gods, and called on the grace
of stocks and stones—still evermore;
no voice breaks from them, so bound are their tongues.

Those guilty ones named all the good golden gods,   *1525*
Beelphegor and Belial, Beelzebub also,
praising them highly, as though heaven were theirs;
Him who gives all good—that God—they forgot.

For this came a marvel that many men saw;
first the King knew it, then all the court: 1530
in that princely palace, on the plain wall,
facing the candlestick where it shone clearest,

there appeared a palm with a pen in its fingers,
huge and grisly, and grimly it writes;
nothing but a fist with no wrist to it   1535
is marking the wall-plaster and making letters.

When the bold Belshazzar beheld that fist
such a dazing dread dashed through his heart
that his face turned fallow, his color faded;
the sight struck a blow that stiffened his joints.   1540

His knees knock together, his thighs are numbed;
twisting his fingers, he lifts his face
and rages like a scared bull that roars with fear,
still gazing on the hand till it had engraved all
and scratched rune-like words on the rough wall.   1545

After scraping its script with a scratchy pen,
like a plough-share cutting furrows through clay,
it vanished wholly and they gazed on a void;
but letters were left there, large on the plaster.

As soon as the King, in his terror, could speak,   1550
he bade his men set to—the book-learned—
to find what the writing meant and unfold it clearly.
"For they frighten my flesh—those fingers so grim!"

Scholars set out to find the secret,
but not one was wise enough to read a word,   1555
or know what people's lore it was, or in what language,
or what tidings or tale the marks betokened.

Then the bold Belshazzar broke out into madness;
he bade them seek men through the whole city
who were wise in witchcraft, and other wizards   *1560*
who could deal with magic and divine letters.

"Call all to my court, these Chaldean clerics.
Unfold to them the marvel that has here befallen,
and call with a loud cry: 'He who makes the King wise
by expounding the speech spread out in these letters,   *1565*

" 'and makes this matter filter into my mind
till I truly know what the writing tells,
shall be fitted out gorgeously in purple gowns,
with a collar of clear gold clasped round his throat.

" 'As primate and prince of pure learning,   *1570*
he shall be third of those lords who thrive best,
the richest in my realm, riding with myself—
except for two only; he shall be the third.' "

This call was carried wide and many came.
Clerics from Chaldea known as the cleverest,   *1575*
like sage satraps who knew sorcery,
witches and valkyries went into that hall,

diviners of magic art who could read dreams,
sorcerers, exorcists and many such sages;
all looked at the letters, as little knowing   *1580*
as if looking at the leather of my left boot.

Then the King cries out and rends his clothing.
Ho! He cursed his clerics and called them churls;
he was in a hurry to hang those rascals;
the man was so brainless that he nearly went mad.   *1585*

She who was chief queen heard him chide that roomfull;
when she learned from servants where the cause lay
—such a reversal in the royal hall—
the lady, to enlighten the lord's doubt,
glides down the stairway and goes to the King.   *1590*

She kneels on the cold earth and addresses him
with words of worship, speaking wisely:

"Proud King," said the Queen, "prince of the earth,
may thy life last forever, for length of days!
Why rend thy robes without reflection,   *1595*
though these men know little about reading letters,

"when thou hast here a man, as I have heard often,
with the spirit of God who guides all truth?
His soul has the knowledge to make sayings clear,
to open each hidden thing in strange adventures.   *1600*

"He it is who so often uplifted thy father
in many hot fits of anger by holy speech.
When Nebuchadnezzar, at times, was annoyed,
he unfolded his dreams to the full truth,

"and by counsel saved him from a coward's fate.   *1605*
In time he answered clearly all he was asked
by the power of the Spirit present within him,
the best of the gods that bring good anywhere.

"For his divine learning and his deep sayings
thy bold father bade him be named Belteshazzar;   *1610*
he is now called Daniel, with knowledge of dark things,
who was caught as a captive in the Jew's country.

"Nebuzardan took him, and now he is here,
 a prophet of the province, prized through the world.
 Send into the city, seek him at once,   *1615*
 win him worshipfully to find ways to help.

"Although the matter spelled out there is mirky,
 he shall declare it as it stands on the clay."
 The Queen's good counsel was taken up quickly;
 the man was soon brought before Belshazzar.   *1620*

When he came to the King and hailed him courteously,
Belshazzar addressed him. "Dear Sir," he said,
"I am told by many that thou wert truly
 a prophet of that province that my father plundered,

"and thou hast in thy heart a holy cunning;   *1625*
 thy soul is full of wisdom to make sayings clear.
 Through the gift of God's Spirit who guides all things,
 thou revealest each hidden thought of heaven's King.

"Here a marvel has befallen; I will give much to know
 the sense of the writing that stays on that wall;   *1630*
 for the learned Chaldeans have all failed cravenly.
 If thy skill can reveal it, I shall reward thee.

"If thou canst read rightly, and unravel its sense,
 first telling the text of those intertwined letters,
 then giving the meaning of the inner matter,   *1635*
 I shall hold to the promise that I have pledged:

"to deck thee in purple cloth of the finest kind,
 with a necklace of bright gold about thy neck;
 then, third highest of those that throng after me,
 thou shalt sit here, a baron; I have bidden no less."   *1640*

Then Daniel boldly broke out in these words:
"Royal King of this realm, may our Lord counsel thee!
It is certainly true; the Sovereign of heaven
ever aided thy father and cherished him on earth,

"made him the greatest of all governors, 1645
wielding the whole world at his will and liking.
If any man did well, the King did well by him,
but the man he wished dead dropped down at once;

"the man he would lift was straightway aloft,
the man he would lay low was swiftly lowered. 1650
Such was the known way of Nebuchadnezzar,
his reign made stable by the strong Lord.

"In his heart he held on to hope in the Highest,
since all power passes down from that very Prince,
and while he kept all this close to his heart 1655
there was no man on earth of such might as he,

"till it happened in time that pride touched him
for his widespread lordship and royal life.
He had such deep insight into his own deeds
that he plain forgot the power of the High Prince. 1660

"Then he went on blaspheming and blaming the Lord;
with these words he made his own might like to God's:
'I am god of the earth, to govern as I like,
as the One high in heaven rules His angel hosts.

" 'If He made the fields and the folk in them, 1665
I have made Babylon, mightiest of cities,
laying each stone in it with my own strong arms;
no might but mine could make such another.'

"No sooner had these words slipped from his mouth
than an over-ruling voice rang in his ears: 1670
'Now Nebuchadnezzar has spoken enough;
now all thy principality has passed at once.

" 'Removed from the sons of men, thou must live on the moor,
walk in waste places and dwell with wild things,
like a beast nibble weeds and bracken on the heath,   1675
living with fierce wolves and with wild asses.'

"Then he departs, in his towering pride,
from his throne, his solemnity; he leaves all solace,
cast out, full of care, in unknown countries,
far in a distant forest where men never fare.   1680

"His heart roams insanely; he hopes for nothing
but to be a beast, a bull or an ox.
He forages on all fours, grass is his food;
he eats hay like a horse when the herbs wither.

"Thus he, once a rich king, is reckoned a cow   1685
while seven times summer went by, I trust.
By then many thick muscles muffled his body
that was covered and drenched with the dew of heaven.

"His hair got tangled, hung in shaggy mats
growing below his shoulders down to the groin,   1690
and, entwined twenty-fold, reached to his toes
where thick burs, like plaster, bound it together.

"His beard overspread his breast, down to the bare earth,
his brows bristled briar-like above his broad cheeks;
hollow were his eyes under shaggy hairs,   1695
all gray, like a falcon, with grim claws

"that were crooked and keen like the kite's nails.
 Eagle-hued he was, thus covered all over,
 till he knew right well who wields all power
 and can destroy kingdoms and restore them at will.   *1700*

"Then the wits came back to one who suffered woe;
 he had gained knowledge, he knew himself.
 Then he praised the Lord, and truly believed
 that none but He held all in His hands.

"Soon he was sent back, his seat restored;   *1705*
 barons gave him honor, glad of his coming.
 His head was covered in its proper color,
 and his state given back, fully granted to him.

"But thou, Belshazzar, his son and bold heir,
 hast seen signs with thine eyes and set them at nought,   *1710*
 ever lifting thy heart against the high Lord,
 with pride and blasphemy, with boasting cast at Him,

"with unclean vanities defiling the vessels
 first raised in His own house to His honor,
 hast brought them to thy barons, pouring beverages in
        them,   *1715*
 costly wines for thy wenches in a cursed hour.

"Thou hast brought to thy dinner drink in vessels
 first joyfully blessed by bishops' hands,
 praising those lying gods that never had life,
 made of stocks and stones that could never stir.   *1720*

"For such festering filth the Father of heaven
 sends into this hall these unknown sights,
 the fist with fingers that flayed thy heart,
 scratching the wall runishly with a rough pen.

"Without more ado, these are the written words   *1725*
   that I find in each figure, as our Father pleases:
   Mane, Techel, Phares, those three marks there
   threaten thee for thy vices in these three ways.

"I intend speedily to expound this speech;
   Mane means this: 'Almighty God   *1730*
   has counted out thy kingdom by a clear number,
   fulfilled faithfully to the farthest end.'

"To teach thee *Techel,* the term means this:
   'Thy proud reign is doomed to be placed on the scales,
   and too few faith-deeds are found in it.'   *1735*
   Phares, to test the truth, follows for those faults.

"In *Phares* I find, truly, this frightful saying:
   'Gone is thy principality, thou art deprived;
   thy reign is torn from thee, entrusted to the Persians,
   the Medes shall be masters, thou removed from honor.' " *1740*

The King commanded that the wise man be clothed
   in robes of fine cloth, as his promise claimed.
   Daniel was quickly decked in costly purple,
   with a collar of clear gold clasped round his neck.

A decree then went forth from the duke himself;   *1745*
   bold Belshazzar bade that all should bow to him,
   the commoners of Chaldea that belonged to the King,
   as to a prince close to him, in the third place,

higher than all others, save only two,
   to follow Belshazzar through towns and fields.   *1750*
   At once this was cried aloud, made known to the court,
   and all his followers were full of joy.

Daniel was decked out, but that day went by
and now night drew near full of disaster,
for no day ever dawned after that darkness   *1755*
before the doom fell that Daniel foresaw.

The hilarious festival goes on in the hall
with joyful feasting till the sunlight fades.
The color of the bright sky then turns somber,
the merry weather darkens; mists drive down   *1760*
from clouds aloft through the low meadows.

Each man hurries fast to his own home,
sits down to supper and sings after it;
each fellowship sets out on its far way that night.
Belshazzar is carried to his bed with bliss;   *1765*
let him rest as he likes! He arose never more.

For huge battalions of his battle-field foes
who had long sought that man to destroy his lands,
now suddenly assembled at the self-same time;
no-one dwelling there knew anything of them.   *1770*

It was noble Darius, the duke of the Medes,
the proud prince of Persia and Porus of India,
with many great legions and men at arms
who were spying for a chance to despoil Chaldea.

They thronged through the darkness in dense crowds, *1775*
slipped over the clear waters and scaled the walls,
lifted their long ladders and climbed aloft,
stealing stealthily into town before raising a sound.

Within one night-hour they had made an entry,
yet frightened no-one; further they passed on   *1780*
to the princely palace, approaching stilly;
then they ran in rush in a great rout.

Blasts from bright brass burst out on high,
cries rang from the sky, confusing many.
Sleeping men were slain before they could slip off;   *1785*
in a moment each house was harried throughout.

Belshazzar was beaten to death in his bed,
till his blood and his brains mingled on the bed-clothes.
The King, behind curtains, was caught by the heels,
pulled out by the feet and foully dishonored.   *1790*

He who that day daringly drank of the vessels,
is now cheaper than a dog lying in a ditch.

For the master of the Medes rose the next morning;
that day proud Darius was placed on the throne.
He seized the city unharmed, and settled peacefully   *1795*
with the barons thereabouts, who bowed before him.

Thus was that land lost for the lord's sin,
for the filthiness of the man who had befouled
the ornaments of God's house that had been made holy.
He was cursed for uncleanness, caught right in it,   *1800*

put down from his dignity for shameful deeds,
shut out evermore from honor on earth,
deprived too, I guess, of pleasures above;
too late now to look on our lovable Lord!

I have thus shown you, in three downright ways,   *1805*
that uncleanness cuts deep through the dear heart
of that joy-giving Lord who lives in heaven;
it stirs Him to anger and vengeance awakes.

He finds comfort in cleanness, He loves fit clothing;
they who are clean and fair shall see His face.   *1810*
May He send us this grace: to go gayly attired
for serving in His sight, where joy is unceasing.

Amen.

SIR GAWAIN AND THE GREEN KNIGHT

PART ONE

I

When the siege and the assault on Troy had ceased,
the city broken, burnt to brands and ashes,
the man who there twined the strands of treason
was tried for his treachery—it was such truly!
It was lordly Aeneas and his lofty kinsmen   5
who beat down the provinces and became possessors
of most of the wealth in the Western Isles.
At the time when great Romulus pressed on to Rome,
with boastful pride he builds up that city
and gives it his own name, as it is now called.   10
Ticius goes to Tuscany and takes on house-building,
Longobardus then founds new homes in Lombardy,
while far over the French sea Felix Brutus
settles Britain on its many broad banks
joyfully,   15
where war and woe and wonders
have reigned alternately,

and often bliss and blunders
in quick turns come to be.

2   When Britain had been built by this mighty baron,   20
bold men were bred there; they loved battling,
and as time moved on they stirred up trouble.
Marvels have happened in this place, more often
than in any other, since then, that I have known.
But of all Britain's kings who have carried on here,   25
Arthur, I have heard, was always the courtliest.
I intend to reveal a strange event in his land
such that some men hold it an utter marvel,
a baffling adventure among the wonders of Arthur.
If you will listen to this lay but a little while,   30
I will tell it straight off, as I heard it in town
by tongue,
as it is set, well-stocked,
in a story brave and strong,
with true letters interlocked,   35
told in this land for long.

3   This King was at Camelot at Christmas time
with many fair lords, the best of his followers,
all the gorgeous brotherhood of the gracious Round Table
in right costly revelry and reckless mirth.   40
Many a time these men tourneyed there,
jousting gayly; these gentle knights
then set out for the court to sing carols.
The feasting went on fifteen full days,
with all the meats and mirth that men could think of: 45
such noisy glee, glorious to hear,
such a fine din by day, such dancing by night!
All was high-hearted happiness in those halls and chambers
among lords and ladies, what each one liked best.
With the world's best delights they lived together,   50

the best-known knights, next to Christ Himself,
and the loveliest ladies that ever lived,
and he, comeliest of kings, who holds court there.
For all this fair company was in its fresh age
      in that hall,   55
   under heaven the luckiest men,
   with a king highest of all.
   How hard to find again
   so brave a troop at call!

4 While the new year was still fresh, a new-comer, 60
the nobility on the dais that day was served double.
As the King and his knights came into the hall,
the singing in the chapel softened to an end;
a loud cry then broke out from clerics and others,
Noel, celebrated new, its name called out often. 65
Then the gallant lords ran forth to give largesse,
cried New Year gifts aloud, gave them out by hand
and debated busily about these gifts;
the ladies laughed loudly, though they had lost,
and the winner was not sorry—you may well believe! 70
They kept up their mirth until meal-time;
after washing properly they went to their seats,
the better man placed first, as always seems best,
Queen Gwenevere, lovely, well-gowned, in the middle,
set out on the grand dais, adorned on all sides 75
with fine silks around her, a canopy over her,
treasured tapestries of Tharsia and of Toulouse
embroidered and set with the best gems
that would prove high-priced to buy with pennies
      any day.   80
   She, the loveliest there,
   glanced around with eyes of gray.
   That he saw one more fair
   no man could truly say.

5 But Arthur would not eat till all were served; 85
he was jolly in his youthfulness, and somewhat childish.
He took life lightly; little did he like
to lie down or sit still for very long,
so busy his young blood and his wild brain kept him.
Also, he was moved by another motive 90
that urged his noble spirit; he would never eat
on such a regal day till someone related
an unheard-of tale of some adventurous thing,
some great marvel that he might believe,
of princes, of arms, or of other adventures, 95
or till someone asked him for an able knight
to join with in jousting, to meet in jeopardy
and risk life for life, each leaving it to the other
to gain the advantage, as fortune might grant.
This was the King's custom when he held court 100
at each splendid feast with his courtly followers
in the hall.
And so, with his proud air
he stands up straight and tall
and fresh, that New Year there, 105
making mirth with all.

6 So there he stands, the strong King himself,
making graceful small-talk before the high table.
Good Gawain is placed there next to Gwenevere,
Agravain of the Hard Hand on the other side, 110
both sons of the King's sister, both trusty knights.
Bishop Baldwin presides at the table, above them,
and Ywain, Urien's son, eats beside him.
These were seated on the dais, honorably served,
while many true men sat at the side-tables. 115
Then the first course came in with a fine blare of trumpets
adorned with bright banners hanging down.
A new noise of drums and of noble pipes,

loud, wild warblings, awoke such a din
that many a heart leaped high at their strains.   *120*
Dainties were served up, delicate dishes,
plenty of fresh meat, and so many platters
that there was scarcely place in front of the people
to set down the silverware holding various stews
                              on the cloth.   *125*
      Each man served himself
      as he pleased, nothing loath;
      each two had dishes twelve,
      good beer and bright wine both.

7   Now I will say no more of their service,   *130*
for everyone knows well there was nothing wanting.
Another noise swiftly drew near, a new one,
that the Prince might have leave to take his life-food.
For scarce had the festal sounds ceased for a while
and the first course been fittingly served in court,   *135*
than there flings in at the door a gruesome fellow,
the mightiest on earth, measured by his height;
from the neck to the waist so square-built and weighty,
with loins and limbs so massive and long
that I judge he must have been half-giant on this earth.   *140*
A man still, I grant, one of the greatest
and handsomest—for his size—that goes on horseback;
for though in back and breast his body was forbidding
yet his belly and waist were worthily slim,
and his features fitted the form that he had,   *145*
                              cut clean!
      Men wondered at the hue
      that in his face was seen.
      He rode as a foe might do,
      and was, all over, bright green!   *150*

8   In green was this warrior decked—all his garments:
     a strait coat stretching down that stuck to his sides,
     a gay mantle over it, made fair within
     with close-cut fur showing, the lining clean
     and cheerful with bright ermine, his hood also,   155
     falling back from his locks and laid on his shoulders.
     Neat, well-gartered hose of that same green
     were fastened on his calf, with clean spurs beneath
     of bright gold upon silk strips richly barred,
     pointed shoes on his feet as he prances up.   160
     Indeed, all his vesture was like clean verdure,
     both the bars of his belt and other bright stones
     that were richly ranged in the clean array
     covering him and his saddle, upon worked silk.
     It would be too troublesome to name half the trifles   165
     embroidered on it, with birds and butterflies,
     gay, gawdily green, with gold everywhere.
     The pendants of his trappings, the proud cropper,
     his metal bit-studs, were brightly enamelled;
     and so were the stirrups that he stood in,   170
     like his saddle-bows and his fine tail-skirts
     that glimmered and gleamed all over with green stones.
     The horse that he rode was just as handsome,
                              surely.
                    A green horse great and thick,   175
                    steed hard to rein was he
                    with his fancy bridle; quick
                    like his rider he seemed to be.

9   This knight was a fine sight in his green outfit,
     the hair on his head matching that of his horse.   180
     Fair flowing locks enfolded his shoulders,
     a beard like a big bush hung over his breast;
     this, with the handsome hair hanging from his head
     was clipped off all around above the elbows,

hiding his upper arms, as though he had on   185
a king's hood-cape that enclosed his neck.
The mane of his horse was much like it,
well curled and combed, caught up in knots,
folded with gold thread about the fair green,
now a strand of hair, now one of gold.   190
The tail and the top-lock were twined in the same way,
both bound up with a bright green band,
set with rare stones to the end of the docked tail,
then tied with a thong in a thick knot above it
where many bright bells of burnished gold rang.   195
Such a mount on this earth, or such a man riding it,
had never been beheld by any eyes before
                              in that hall.
                    His look was lightning bright—
                    beholders all said so.   200
                    It seemed that no man might
                    stand up beneath his blow.

10   Yet he had no helmet, no hauberk either,
      no breast-shield, no plates of protecting armor,
      no shaft, no shield against shoving and smiting,   205
      but in one hand he carried a bob of holly
      that grows the greenest when groves are bare,
      an axe in the other, a huge one, monstrous,
      a cruel blade to talk of, if one could find words.
      Its head was as long as a whole ell-yard,   210
      the spike was fashioned from green steel and gold,
      the blade burnished bright with a broad edge
      as well-shaped for shearing as a sharp razor.
      The stiff staff-handle that the stern man gripped
      was wound with iron to the wand's end   215
      and engraved with green in graceful workmanship.
      A lace was twisted round it, tied at the top
      and along the handle in many loops

with lots of costly tassels attached to it
by buttons of bright green; it was richly braided.   220
This hero sweeps in and enters the hall,
driving towards the high dais, fearing no danger;
he hailed no-one, but from high up looked them over.
The first words that he spoke: "Where is," said he,
"the top-man of this get-together? Gladly I would   225
set my eyes on that man; to talk sense with him
                   I'm bound."
        On the knights his look he threw;
        he swaggered all around
        then stopped, and studied who   230
        was there the most renowned.

11   All turned with a long stare to look at the fellow,
for each man marvelled what it might mean
that a knight and a horse could have such a hue,
grown green as the grass—greener, it seemed,   235
glowing more bright than green enamel on gold.
The by-standers studied him, drawing stealthily nearer,
all wondering what in the world he was up to.
Many marvels they had seen, but such as this—never.
The folk there took it for a phantom or fairy spell.   240
So noble men were afraid to give any answer;
all were stunned at his voice, and sat stone-still
in a swoonlike silence through the sumptuous hall.
As if all had slipped asleep, their jesting sank down
                   suddenly—   245
        not, I think, due to fear,
        but rather to courtesy.
        Let him whom all revere
        ask who that man may be!

12   Arthur from the high dais watched this adventure;   250
he courteously showed reverence—he could not know fear—

and said "Welcome indeed, Sir, to this place.
I am called Arthur, master of this castle.
Alight graciously; linger, I pray thee,
and later we shall ask what thou art after."   255
Said the knight: "So help me, He who sits above;
it is not my purpose to stay long in this place.
But since thy renown, Sire, has risen so high,
and thy city, thy bold men, are held to be best,
most stalwart in their steel gear as they ride on steeds,   260
the strongest and worthiest that the world shows,
proved best to sport with in noble pastimes,
and since courtesy is here shown, as I have heard tell,
all this, truly, draws me here at this time.
Be sure by this branch that I am bearing,   265
that I travel in peace and seek no trouble.
For had I come fitted out in fighting wise,
I have a hauberk at home and a helmet too,
a shield and sharp spear shining bright,
and other weapons to wield, I know well, also;   270
but I want no war, so I wear softer raiment.
But if thou art as bold as all men say,
thou wilt graciously grant me the game that I ask,
                    by right."
                Arthur answered back   275
                and said: "Sir! Courteous knight!
                If thou cravest a battle-crack
                thou shalt not miss a fight!"

13 "No, I seek no fight, in faith I tell thee;
     there is no-one on the benches but beardless children.   280
     If I were wholly armed on my high steed,
     no man here could match me, their might is so weak!
     Thus I crave in this court a Christmas game,
     for it is Yule and New Year; here are many brisk knights.
     If any one in this house thinks himself so hardy,   285

had such bold blood and such a mad brain
as to stoutly dare strike one stroke for another,
I'll give him as a gift this rich gisarm,
this axe—it's plenty heavy—to handle at will,
and I'll take the first blow, bare as I now sit.   290
If any knight is so testy as to try out what I say,
let him run lightly to me and lay hold of this weapon.
I quit-claim it forever, let him keep it for his own,
and I shall take his stroke, standing stiff on this floor,
if thou grant me this doom: to deal him another.   295
                          So stay!
                 And let his respite be
                 a twelvemonth and a day.
                 Now hurry, and let's see
                 who has a word to say!"   300

14   If he had stunned them at first, stiller were they now—
     all the hall-retainers, the high and the low.
     The fellow on the steed turned about in his saddle;
     strangely he rolled his red eyes all around,
     bent his bristling brows, bright-gleaming, green,   305
     and waved his beard, watching who would rise.
     When no-one cared to speak he coughed loudly,
     cleared his throat pompously and called out:
     "What! Is this Arthur's house," said that hero,
     "of which much talk runs through so many realms?   310
     Where now your vain-glory, your power to vanquish,
     your fierceness, your grimness, your great words?
     Now the revelry and renown of the Round Table
     are overcome by the words of one man speaking;
     all are dazed with dread without one dint given!"   315
     Then he laughed so loudly that the lord was grieved;
     the blood shot for shame into his shining cheeks
                          and face.

> Like the wind he began to rave,
> as did all in that place.
> The King was always brave;
> nearer he stepped, a pace.

320

15   He said: "Sir, by heaven, thy request is silly;
    asking for folly, thou art fit to find it!
    I know of none aghast at thy great words.

325

    Give me now thy gisarm, for God's sake,
    and I shall grant the boon that thou hast begged."
    He runs lightly to him, laying hold of his hand,
    then fiercely the other man lights on his feet.
    Now Arthur has his axe; he grips the handle,

330

    and sternly swings it round as if to strike with it.
    The strong man before him stood at full height,
    above all in the house by a head or more.
    With a stern look he stood there; he stroked his beard,
    and with a calm countenance drew down his coat,

335

    no more daunted or dismayed for those mighty strokes
    than if some man on the bench had brought him a drink
> of wine.
> Gawain, sitting by the Queen,
> to the King did incline.

340

> "I beg—and it's clear-seen—
> this contest must be mine!

16   "If you, glorious Lord," said Gawain to the King,
    "would bid me rise from this bench and stand beside you,
    that without lacking manners I may leave this table,

345

    and if my liege lady were not to dislike it,
    I would give you counsel before this noble court.
    For I think it untoward, if the truth may be told,
    when such a thing is openly asked in your hall,
    that you take it on yourself—though you may wish to—

350

    while so many bold men sit about you on benches,

none under heaven, I trust, more high-spirited,
or better on the battle-field when strife breaks out.
I am the weakest, I know, the slowest witted,
and my life the least loss, if you like the truth.   355
But since you are my uncle I am worth praising
(with nothing good but your blood, I own, in my body),
since a deed so foolish should not fall to you,
and since I asked you first, let it fall to me.
If my request is unfitting, let this fine court decide,   360
                    without blame."
        The knights talked secretly,
        and they all said the same:
        let the crowned King go free
        and give Gawain the game.   365

17   Then the King commanded the knight to come;
he eagerly rose and turned round gracefully,
knelt before the King and caught up the weapon.
The gracious King let him have it, and with lifted hand
gave him God's blessing, and gladly bade him   370
be hardy of heart and of hand both.
"Cousin," said the King, "take care in cutting him;
by handling him right, I readily believe
thou wilt dare face the blow that he deals thee later."
With the gisarm in hand Gawain goes to the fellow   375
who boldly stands up to him, not one bit dismayed.
Then the knight in green says to Sir Gawain:
"Let us re-form our compact before we go further.
First I ask thee, Knight, what thy name is;
tell me truly so that I may trust thee."   380
"In faith," said the good knight, "Gawain I am called,
who will offer this buffet,—come what may afterwards—
and a twelvemonth from now will take one from thee
with what weapon thou wilt, and let no other warrior
                    be there."   385

This answer then he had:
"Sir Gawain, I swear,
that I am mighty glad
to take thy blow. I dare!"

"Bi-gosh!" said the Green Knight. "Sir Gawain, I'm delighted   390
to take from thy hand what I asked for here.
Thou hast readily rehearsed, by true reasoning,
clearly, the whole covenant I asked of the King,
except to pledge me, Knight, by a true promise,
to seek me thyself, wherever thou thinkest   395
I may be found on earth, and fetch such wages
as thou dealest me today before this daring band!"
"Where shall I hunt?" said Gawain. "Where is thy home?
I know not where thy mansion is, by Him that made me;
I know not thee, knight, nor thy court nor thy name.   400
But teach me truly, tell me what thou art called,
and I'll use all my wits to find my way there;
I swear so, in truth, on my certain honor."
"That's enough on New Year's, no more is needed,"
said the man in green to the courteous Gawain.   405
"If I tell thee truly, when I've taken thy rap
and thou hast neatly smitten, smartly I'll let thee know
of my house and home, and mine own name;
thou shalt then test my conduct, and keep thy covenant.
If I make no speeches thou shalt speed the better,   410
lingering in thine own land and looking no further.
Stop, ho!
Take thy grim tool to thee,
and let us see thy blow."
Said Gawain: "Sir, gladly!"   415
He strokes his axe edge—so!

19 The Green Knight quickly gets down on the ground,
bows his head a little and lays bare the flesh.
His long luscious locks he laid over his crown
and then bared his naked neck for this business. *420*
Gawain gripped his axe and swung it aloft;
setting his left foot before him on the floor
he let it fall lightly on the naked flesh,
so that the sharp edge shivered the bones,
passed through the white flesh and cut it apart *425*
till the bright steel blade bit into the ground.
The fair head, off its neck, then hit the earth;
many kicked it away as it rolled around.
Blood gurgled from the body and gleamed on the green.
For all that, the fellow neither faltered nor fell, *430*
but stoutly started forth on his stiff shanks
and roughly reached out to where the men stood,
caught up his lovely head and straightway lifted it.
Then he goes to his steed, snatches up the bridle,
steps into the steel bows and straddles aloft, *435*
holding his head by the hair in his hands.
The man sat as sedately there in his saddle
as though nothing ailed him; yet there he was
      with no head.
   He turned his trunk about, *440*
   the ugly body bled.
   Many felt fear and doubt
   by the time his say was said.

20 Then he held his head in his hands, high up,
turning the face to the lady, the loveliest on the dais. *445*
It lifted its eyelids, looked with a broad stare,
and spoke thus with its mouth, as you may now hear:
"Look, Gawain; be prompt to keep thy promise,
and loyally seek for me, Sir, till thou findest me;
thou hast pledged in this hall, in hearing of these knights. *450*

To the Green Chapel go, I charge thee, to get
such a dint as thou hast dealt—thou hast deserved it—
to be duly paid back at New Year's dawn.
Knight of the Green Chapel, so many men know me;
if thou tryest to find me thou shalt not fail.   *455*
Therefore come, or be fit to be called a recreant."
With a violent wrench he turned the reins
and swept out the hall door, his head in his hand,
while fire flew from the flint of his foal's hooves.
No-one knew to what region he then rode off;   *460*
no more could they say whence he came at first.
What then?
The King and Gawain grinned there,
at the Green Knight laughed again.
The tale spread, to declare   *465*
this marvel among men.

21   In his heart Arthur pondered, yet the polite King
let no sign be seen, but said aloud
with courteous words to the comely Queen:
"Dear Lady, today be not dismayed;   *470*
such tricks are becoming at Christmastide,
interludes played for laughing and singing,
between noble carols of knights and ladies.
Nonetheless, it's time now to turn to my dinner,
for I have seen a marvel; I cannot say otherwise!"   *475*
He glanced at Sir Gawain, and graciously said:
"Now, Sir, hang up thine axe; it has hewn enough."
It was put over the dais, to hang on the dosser
where all men might gaze on it as a marvel,
and tell of this wonder in a true account.   *480*
Then they pressed to the table, these princes together,
the King and the good knight, and gallant men served them
double portions of dainties in the noblest way possible,
with all manner of meats, and minstrelsy too.

They passed that day happily till darkness came 485
                    on the land.
            Now think well, Sir Gawain,
            lest thou shouldst fail to stand,
            or this adventure gain
            that thou hast taken in hand. 490

PART TWO

II

22 This adventure was a New Year's gift to Arthur
    when, in the young year, he yearned for a brave tale.
    Though words failed them when they went to their seats,
    they are facing hard work, their hands cram-full of it.
    Gawain was glad when games began in the hall; 495
    no wonder what must come weighed heavily on him!
    Though men's minds are merry when they have drunk much,
    a year flies by swiftly, yielding never the same;
    the beginning and end are seldom at one.
    This Yule-tide went by, and the year after it, 500
    and each season in order followed the other.
    After Christmas comes the crabbed Lent
    that tries flesh with fish and with simpler food.
    But then the world's weather struggles with winter,
    the cold melts away, clouds are uplifted, 505
    the rain shimmers down in warm showers
    and falls on the fair turf; flowers appear.
    The ground and groves too are clothed in green,
    birds are busy building and brightly sing

in the solace of the soft summer that swiftly flows over   *510*
       the land.
      Buds swell and open wide
      where the rich, thick hedges stand;
      bird-calls from every side
      are heard in the proud woodland.   *515*

23   Then comes the summer season with soft breezes,
    when the west wind sighs on seeds and herbs;
    very lovely the plants that are pushing upward,
    while the dripping dew drops down from the leaves,
    awaiting the blissful gleam of the bright sun.   *520*
    But autumn draws near and hardens all,
    gives warning to ripen before the winter;
    it strikes with drought till the dust rises
    from the face of the fields, flying high up.
    Wrathful winds in the sky wrestle with the sun,   *525*
    leaves loosen from the lime trees and light on the ground,
    and gray grows the grass that was once green.
    All that first arose now ripens and rots.
    Thus the year runs on with many yesterdays,
    and winter returns, as the world's way is,   *530*
          no fear,
      until the Michaelmas moon
      gave sign of winter near.
      Then Gawain must think soon
      of his own journey drear.   *535*

24   Yet till All-Hallows Day he lingers with Arthur,
    who then, for his sake, served a festal banquet
    with much high revelry of the Round Table.
    Courteous knights and comely ladies
    were all lost in grief for love of that man;   *540*
    nonetheless, they tried to talk mirthfully,
    joylessly jesting for the gentle knight's sake.

After meal-time he talked to his uncle, mournfully;
he spoke of his journey, and said plainly:
"Liege Lord of my life, I now ask your leave.   545
   You know how this case stands; I can keep no longer
   from telling you my troubles, though they are trifling,
   for I must face my blow without fail tomorrow,
   and search for the knight in green, as God guides me."
The best men of the castle then came together,   550
   Ywan and Eric, and many others,
   Sir Dodinel de Sauvage, the Duke of Clarence,
   Lancelot and Lionel, and the good Lucan,
   Sir Bors and Sir Bedivere, big men both,
   and many more worthies, with Mador de la Port.   555
All this courtly company came up to the King
   to counsel the Knight, with care-filled hearts.
Much heavy sorrow spread through the hall
   that one as worthy as Gawain should go on that errand,
   bear a dread blow, then no more swing his brand   560
                              on high.
               The Knight still made good cheer,
               and said: "Why whould I fly?
               Facing destiny's dark fear,
               what can a man do but try?"   565

25   All that day he lingers; at dawn he makes ready,
        asking early for his arms, that were all brought in.
     A Toulouse carpet first they spread on the floor,
        and plenty of gold gear glinted on it.
     The strong man steps onto it and handles the steel.   570
     They put on him a doublet of dear silk from Tharsia,
        then a well-cut cape closed tightly above it,
        fashioned inside with shining white fur.
     They fixed steel-toed shoes on the knight's feet;
        they wrapped elegant greaves around his legs,   575

with knee-pieces fitted on, polished clean
and tied about his knees with knots of gold.
Then came the plates that cunningly encased
his thick strong thighs, attached with thongs;
then the byrny woven of bright steel rings   580
enfolded the knight with its fine weaving,
with a well-burnished brace on both arms,
handsome elbow pieces, plated gloves
and all the good gear that would be a gain to him
                        in that ride: 585
            a rich heraldic shirt,
            gold spurs worn with pride,
            and a trusty sword, well girt
            by a silk sash to his side.

26   When he was cased in armor his harness looked costly;   590
the least lacings or loops all gleamed with gold.
So, harnessed as he was, he heard the mass
offered and celebrated at the high altar.
Then he comes to the King and his court-comrades,
taking leave graciously of the lords and ladies   595
who kissed and escorted him, trusting him to Christ.
Gryngolet was all ready, girded with a saddle
that gleamed gayly with many gold fringes,
new studs put in everywhere, prepared for the journey.
The bridle was barred and bound with bright gold;   600
the trimming on the straps and on the proud skirts,
on the crupper and the coverlet, accorded with the saddle-
            bows,
and everywhere, set on red, were rich gold nails,
till all glittered and glowed like gleams of sunlight.
Then he takes his helmet and hastily kisses it;   605
it was strongly stapled and stuffed within.
It sat high on his head, held fast behind

by a light linen band over the beaver,
embroidered and bound with the best gems
on broad silk borders, with birds on the seams,   *610*
such as painted parrots perching at intervals,
turtle-doves and true-love-knots twined in as thickly
as though many maidens had made it for seven winters
              right there.
     A circlet of great price   *615*
     was set upon his hair.
     Of diamonds its device;
     brilliant they were, and fair.

III

27   They showed him the shield bearing red-shining gules,
with the Pentangle painted on it in pure gold hues.   *620*
He caught it by the baldric and cast it round his neck;
it fitted the hero in handsome fashion.
Why the Pentangle suited that noble prince
I am set on telling you, though it slows me up.
It was a sign that Solomon set forth long ago   *625*
as a token of truth, by a title that it has:
it is a figure that holds five points,
and each line overlaps and locks in the other,
and so it is endless; the English call it
everywhere, as I hear, the Endless Knot.   *630*
It thus accords with this knight and his clear arms:
forever faithful in five ways, and five times each way,
Gawain's goodness was known, like gold refined,
free from all villainy, with courtly virtues
              made clean.   *635*
     Thus the Pentangle new
     on his shield and coat was seen,
     for a man of speech most true
     and knight of gentlest mien.

28   First, he was found faultless in his five wits,   640
then he never failed in his five fingers,
and all his faith on earth was in the five wounds
that Christ bore on the cross, as the Creed tells us.
And wherever he found himself facing warfare,
he thought steadily of this, over all things: 645
that his strength was found in the five joys
that heaven's courteous Queen had in her Child.
For this cause the Knight, in a comely fashion,
had her image painted on the broad part of his shield;
by a glance at her he heartened his courage.   650
The fifth set of five that I find him following
is: open free-handedness, fellowship beyond others,
cleanness and courtesy that were never corrupted,
and, best of all, pity; these perfect fives
were more deep-set in him than in other heroes.   655
Indeed, all these five traits were so fixed in this knight,
each so knit to the other, that none had an end;
and they formed into five points that never failed,
never overlapped, and were never sundered,
nowhere ending, I find, at any one place,   660
where the drawing began or drew to an end.
Therefore, on his bright shield this sign was shaped
royally, with red gold upon red gules,
the perfect Pentangle, as people called it
                        in their lore.   665
      Now he's ready, Gawain the fair;
      well-set, a lance he bore.
      He said goodbye right there,
      as he thought, forevermore.

29   His spur-pricked steed sprang forth on the way   670
so fast that stone-sparks were struck out after him.
Those who saw that gallant one sighed from their hearts,
and all the knights there said to each other,

in their care for the comely man: "By Christ, it's a shame
to lose thee, my Lord, and thy life so noble!   675
To find such on earth, in faith, is not easy.
It would have been wiser to go more warily,
and have yonder daring man dubbed a duke,
brilliant leader of men; that would be like him!
That were better than being broken to nothing,   680
beheaded by an elvish man through uppish pride.
Whoever knew a king to take such counsel
from knights' foolish goings-on in Christmas games?"
And then warm tears welled up in their eyes
when that handsome knight went away from home   685
     that day.
  No time he there abode,
  but swiftly went his way.
  By winding paths he rode;
  I heard the book so say.   690

30 Now the knight goes riding through the realms of Logres,
Sir Gawain, for God's sake, though he thought it no game!
Comradeless, he must linger alone at night,
never finding before him the food that he likes,
no companion but his horse in copses and downs,   695
no-one to parley with, on the pathways, but God,
till he draws very near to North Wales.
All the isles of Anglesey are there on his left;
he crosses the fords in the low fore-lands,
over at Holy Head, then holds to the mainland   700
in the wilderness of Wirral; few men were there
who loved either God or man with a good heart.
And ever, as he pressed on, he asked those he met
if they knew any gossip of a Green Knight,
or of a Green Chapel on the grounds nearby,   705
and all tossed back "no"; never in their lives

had they seen any man of such a color
as green.
The knight took roadways strange;
on many grim banks he's been.
710
His mood would often change
till that chapel he had seen.

31   He climbed over many cliffs in strange countries;
far-wandering he rides, a friendless stranger.
At each bank or water-course that the warrior passed   715
he found a foe facing him (strange if he failed to!)
so foul and fierce that he had to fight it.
The knight met so many marvels in the mountains
that it would be tiresome to tell of the tenth part.
Sometimes he wars with dragons, with wolves as well,   720
sometimes with wood-trolls that lurk in twisted crags,
with bulls and bears both, with boars at other times,
and with giants who puffed after him from high precipices.
Were he not brave and steady, serving the Lord,
he would doubtless have died, undone, more than once.   725
Though this warring was troublesome, winter was worse
as the clear cold water showered from the clouds
and froze as it fell on the faded earth.
Nearly slain by the sleet, he sleeps in his armor
more nights than enough, among naked rocks   730
where, clattering from the cliffs a cold brook runs down
and hangs high overhead in hard icicles.
Thus in peril and in pain, in a sore plight,
this knight roamed the country-side till Christmas-Eve,
alone.
735
Well did he, in that tide,
to Mary make his moan;
may she show him where to ride
and make some shelter known!

32   In the morning he rides merrily past a mountain   740
into a deep forest, fearsomely wild,
high hills on each hand with holtwood under them,
huge hoary oaks, hundreds together.
Hazel and hawthorn were here tangled up
with rough ragged moss rampant everywhere,   745
and many birds, unhappy on the bare twigs,
were piteously piping for pain of the cold.
The knight on Gryngolet goes straight on under them
through quagmires and marshes, a lonely man,
fearful for his duty, lest he should fail   750
to give service to the Lord who, that selfsame night,
had been born of a maid, to end our battling.
Thus, sighing, he said, "I beseech Thee, Lord,
and Mary, mildest of mothers so dear,
for some harbor where I may hear mass worthily,   755
and Thy Matins tomorrow; meekly I ask it.
And so I pray promptly my Pater and Ave
               and Creed."
          He rode on in his prayer,
          lamenting each misdeed.   760
          He signed himself often there:
          "May Christ's cross fill my need!"

I V

33   When the knight had crossed himself three times, no more,
he was aware of a dwelling by a moat in the woods
above a lawn on a hill, locked under the boughs   765
of mighty tree-trunks along the moat-side,
a castle, the handsomest that ever knight cared for,
placed there in a meadow, a park all around,
with a palisade set thick with pointed spikes
that enclosed many trees for more than two miles.   770
From the far side the knight gazed on that stronghold

as it gleamed and shone through the shimmering oaks.
He lowered his helm politely, heartily thanking
Jesus and Saint Julian who, with such gentility,
had both shown courtesy, harkening to his cry.   775
"Now, good hostel," said the knight, "I beseech you to
        grant!"
Then he pricked Gryngolet with his gilt heels,
and by chance made his way to the chief gate
that straightway brought him to the bridge's end,
                        at last.   780
            The bridge was stoutly made,
            upraised, the gates locked fast.
            The walls were well arrayed;
            it feared no storm-wind's blast.

34   The knight on his horse was held back at the banks   785
        of a double ditch drawn round the place;
        the wall reached into the water wondrously deep,
        before towering up to a huge height over it,
        all of hard-cut stone up to the cornices,
        with horn-work under battlements, in the best manner,
        with gay turrets geared between them   791
        and many lovely loops, interlocking cleanly.
        Safer defence the knight had never yet seen.
        Within, he beheld the high-standing hall,
        towers placed around it, with horn-like pinnacles,   795
        fair turrets, well-joined and fearfully high,
        with carved summits, all cleverly made.
        Chalk-white chimneys he picked out, plenty of them,
        on the roofs of the towers that twinkled whitely.
        Many painted pinnacles were powdered about   800
        in the castle embrasures, clustering so thickly
        that they seemed to be pared out of paper only.
        The gallant knight on his horse thought it good enough
        just to manage to come within that cloister,

find harbor in that hostel while the holy-days lasted,   *805*
     well-spent.
    He called, and soon there came
    a porter most pleasant;
    from the wall he asked his claim
    and hailed the knight-errant.   *810*

35 "Good Sir," said Gawain, "wilt thou go on my errand
  to the high lord of this house, and ask him to harbor me?"
"Yes, Peter!" said the porter, "and upon my word,
  you are welcome to linger, Sir, while you will."
The man went off, and again hurried back   *815*
with many ready folk to receive the knight.
They let down the great drawbridge and graciously went
   out,
getting down on their knees on the cold ground
to welcome this knight in the worthiest way.
They opened the broad gate for him, pulled it back wide;
bidding them rise, he rode over the bridge.   *821*
Several men seized his saddle as he dismounted,
then plenty of stalwarts stabled his steed.
The knights and squires then came downstairs
to bring this man into the hall with bliss.   *825*
When he lifted his helmet, many hurried
to take it from his hand, to serve the handsome one;
his sword and blazoned shield were both taken.
Then he greeted graciously each of those grooms,
while proud men pressed round to honor the prince.   *830*
Still clad in heavy armor he was brought to the hall;
a fair fire in the grate was fiercely burning.
The lord of those people came politely from his room
to meet the man standing there with the best manners.
He said: "You are welcome to do as you will;   *835*
what is here is all yours, every wish you may now
     fulfill."

"My thanks," said Gawain then,
"May Christ repay you still!"
In each other's arms these men   *840*
embraced with glad good will.

36   Gawain glanced at the one who greeted him well,
and thought what a bold man managed that castle,
a huge hero, in fact, at the height of his years.
Broad and bright was his beard, all beaver-hued,   *845*
a firm man, stiffly striding on stalwart shanks,
with a face fierce as fire, free of his speech,
well-suited, indeed (so it seemed to the knight)
to hold lordship over his fine liegemen.
The lord led him to a room and loudly commanded   *850*
that a man be assigned to serve him humbly.
Swiftly at his bidding there were servants enough
who brought him to a bright bower, with fine bedding
and curtains of clean silk with clear gold hems,
curious coverlets with lovely counterpanes   *855*
of bright fur on top, embroidered at the edges,
curtains running on ropes through red-gold rings,
tapestries on the walls from Toulouse and Tharsia,
underfoot on the floor carpets to fit them.
The man was disrobed amid mirthful talk,   *860*
freed from his byrny and his bright armor.
Readily the servants brought rich garments
to change and put on, choosing the best.
As soon as he took one and was apparelled in it,
one that fitted him well with wide-sailing skirts,   *865*
in his face was springtime, so it truly seemed
to each man who beheld him so many-hued;
so glowing and lovely were his limbs under it,
that a comelier knight Christ had never made,
                    they thought.   *870*

In the whole world, far or near,
he seemed to have been wrought
a prince without a peer
in the field where fierce men fought.

37   A chair before the chimney where charcoal burned   875
      was at once decked out for Sir Gawain, with drapes
      and cushions on the quilt covers cleverly made.
      Then the man was covered with a cheery mantle
      of brown silk fabric embroidered richly,
      fair, furred within with the finest skins,   880
      all adorned with ermine, his hood also.
      He settled in his seat so suitably rich
      and first warmed himself; then he felt more cheerful.
      Soon a table was set up on handsome trestles,
      covered with a clean cloth that shone clear white,   885
      with top-cloth, salt cellars and silver spoons.
      Willingly the knight washed and went to his meal.
      Waiters served him, with seemly politeness,
      several excellent stews with the best seasoning,
      double portions, as was fit, many kinds of fish,   890
      some baked in bread, some broiled on coals,
      some boiled, some in stew savored with spice,
      and all the cunning sauces that a man could crave.
      The knight called it a feast, freely and often,
      most courteously, till the household claimed that he was 895
                        well-bred.
              "All this your penance is;
               soon you'll be better fed!"
              The man made mirth at this
              as the wine went to his head.   900

38   They watched him, and asked in a tactful way,
      by private questions put to the prince himself,
      to tell them courteously of the court he came from,

the one that noble Arthur held as his own,
the splendid royal King of the Round Table,   905
and if Gawain himself was sitting in their home,
come just for Christmas, by chance in this case.
When the lord learned what a leader he had there
he laughed loudly, so delightful he thought it,
and all the men in the castle made it their pleasure   910
to appear in his presence, promptly this time,
since all worth and prowess and polished manners
pertain to his person; he is always praise-worthy,
and of all men on earth the most famous.
Each servant, very softly, said to his fellow: 915
"Now we shall see knightly conduct, surely,
and the impeccable terms of noble talk;
we may learn without asking how to speak effectively,
since we find here the father of fine-breeding.
Truly God has given grace in a goodly way   920
in granting to us such a guest as Gawain,
when men, for His birth's sake, shall blissfully sit
              and sing.
        Understanding of manners fine
        this man will surely bring;   925
        I know that those who hear
        will learn of love-talking."

39   When the dinner was over the dignitaries rose;
it was nearing the time when night settles down.
The chaplains then led the way to the chapel   930
and rang the bells (as they rightly do)
for the solemn even-song of the festal season.
The lord goes to it, and his lady also;
gracefully she enters her elegant pew.
Gawain follows eagerly and goes right there;   935
the lord catches his cloak, leads him to a seat
as one known familiarly, calls him by name,

saying he was more welcome than any man in the world.
The knight thanked him earnestly, they embraced each other
and soberly sat together throughout the service.   940
Then the lady was pleased to look at the knight
as she moved from her pew with many fair maidens.
She was fairest in skin, in features and face,
in form and in color and in fine manners;
much lovelier than Gwenevere—so the man thought.   945
He goes to the chancel to salute that gracious one.
Another lady led her by the left hand,
one older than she, very aged, it would seem,
highly reverenced, with retainers all round.
But the two ladies were unlike to look upon;   950
if the one was fresh the other was yellow!
On the one a rich red rioted everywhere;
rough wrinkled cheeks hung in rolls on the other.
The kerchiefs of one—set with many clear pearls
displayed bare on her breast and her bright throat—   955
shone brighter than snowdrifts shed on the hills;
the other had wound up her neck in a wimple,
and bound her black chin with chalkwhite veils.
Her forehead was muffled in folded silk,
adorned and tricked out with trifles all around   960
till nothing was bare but the lady's black brows,
the two eyes, the nose and the naked lips,
and these were sour to see, strangely bleared.
A grand lady indeed! Let men, before God,
              decide!   965

      Her body was thick and short,
      her hips were round and wide.
      But of more lovesome sort
      was the other at her side!

40   Gawain glanced at the pretty one looking graciously at
       him,   970

and went, with leave from the lord, to meet them.
He greets the elder, bowing gracefully low;
he takes the lovelier lightly in his arms
and kisses her handsomely, holding forth like a knight.
They crave his acquaintance, and at once he asks   975
to be their true servant, if it so please them.
They take him between them and lead him, talking,
to a seat by the chimney-side, then promptly send
for spices; men hurried to get them, unsparingly,
and joy-giving wine they got also, each time.   980
The courteous lord right often leaped up,
urged them to merriment, time and again,
snatched off his hood gaily, hung it on a spear
and waved it: a prize that they might win!
Mirth carried them away that Christmas-time.   985
"I'm bound, by my faith, to out-play the best of you
before I go hoodless, with the help of my friends!"
Thus with laughing words the lord makes merry,
to gladden Gawain with games in the hall
                         that night,   990
       until the time befell
       when the lord sent for a light.
       Sir Gawain said farewell,
       then off, with bed in sight.

41   On the morning when every man remembers the time   995
when Our Lord (who would die for our destiny) was born,
joy awoke in each home in the world for His sake.
So it did there, that day, with many dainties;
at each meal there were courses cleverly cooked
for the strong men dressed in their best on the dais.   1000
The ancient old lady had the place of honor,
the gracious lord stayed by her side, I am sure.
Gawain and the sweet lady sat together,
right in the middle where meats were first brought;

then through the big hall, as seemed best to them,   *1005*
each, by degrees, was served by a groom.
There was food, there was mirth, there was much joy;
it would be too troublesome to tell all about it,
and point out everything, even though I took pains!
Yet I know that Gawain and the graceful lady   *1010*
found such comfort in company together
(through delightful dalliance of dark-whispered words,
clean, courteous talk, free from all coarseness)
that their play, in truth, surpassed each prince there
                        in his game.   *1015*
        Trumpets, drums, loud airs,
        and the sound of piping came.
        Each minded his own affairs,
        and those two did the same.

42   Pleasure filled that day and the day after,   *1020*
and the third, just as pleasant, pressed hard upon them.
On Saint John's day the joy was delicious to hear;
it was their last playtime, so the people thought.
Some guests must go in the gray morning,
so they stayed awake wonderfully, drinking their wine *1025*
and dancing endlessly to delightful carols.
At last, when it grew late, they took their leave;
each strong worthy now must go on his way.
Gawain says good-bye; the good man takes hold of him,
leads him to his own chamber beside the chimney,   *1030*
there draws him apart and thanks him dearly
for the delicate favor that he had done for them:
to honor their house in that high season
and embellish their castle with his fair countenance.
"Be sure, Sir, while I live I shall be the better   *1035*
since Gawain was my guest at God's own feast."
"I am grateful," said Gawain, "in good faith, Sir, to you.
The honor goes to you; may the high King give it!

I am ready at your will, Sir, to fulfill your wishes,
as beholden to you, in high and in low,   *1040*
> by right."
> The lord then did his best
> to longer keep the knight.
> Gawain, to that request
> said by no means he might.   *1045*

43   Then the lord, in polite words, wanted to know
what dark deed had driven him in those festal days
so rashly from the King's court, to ride off alone
before all the holidays were over in town.
"Indeed," said the knight, "you have spoken the truth;   *1050*
a high errand drove me in haste from those dwellings.
For I have been summoned to seek out a place,
not knowing where to fare in the whole world to find it.
I would not miss arriving on New Year's morn
for all the land in Logres, so may Our Lord help me!   *1055*
For this, Sir, a request; I require of you here
to tell me, in truth, if you have heard tell
of the Green Chapel, of what ground it stands on,
of the knight that keeps it; he's colored green!
We established a covenant by statute between us,   *1060*
to meet that landmark, if I hope to live on.
There are but a few hours before that New Year,
and I would look on that fellow, if God lets me,
more gladly, by God's Son, than have other good things.
So, if you are willing, I must wander on.   *1065*
I have barely three days left now for this business,
and I had rather fall dead than fail in my errand."
The lord said, laughing: "You had better linger;
I shall guide you to your tryst before the time ends.
Stop fretting for the Green Chapel and its grounds.   *1070*
You shall lie in your bed, Sir, in lazy ease
for four days, then go forth on the first of the year,

reach that place at midmorn, for your pleasure in the woods
so dense.
Dwell here till New Year's day,   *1075*
then rise and set off thence.
We will put you on your way;
it is not two miles hence."

44 Then Gawain was glad and laughed gamely.
"I heartily thank you, and for other things too.   *1080*
Now luck is with me; I shall, at your will
stay here, and do whatsoever you say."
Then the lord seized him, made him sit down,
had the ladies fetched to furnish more pleasure.
They had a joyous time, just they themselves;   *1085*
the lord talked merrily, all for love's sake,
like a man with his wits lost, not minding what he does.
He called to the knight, crying out loudly:
"You are pledged to do whatever deed I bid.
Will you keep that promise, here, on one point?"   *1090*
"Yes, Sir, indeed," the trusty knight said.
"While I stay in your home I am at your service."
"You've been travelling," said the lord, "on a long journey,
then staying up late. You are not well restored
by food or by sleep, I know that for certain.   *1095*
You must linger in your room and lie at ease
tomorrow until mass-time, then go to your meal
when ready, with my wife, who remains with you
to cheer you with company, till I'm back at court.
You stay.   *1100*
Early, I'll rise from rest
and to hunting take my way."
Gawain grants this request
and bows in his graceful way.

45 "And further," said the host, "we'll form a bargain: *1105*
    Whatever I win in the woods will be yours,
    and what you achieve here, exchange with me.
    Sweet Sir, we shall swap—swear on it truly—
    whatever we win, man, for better or worse!"
  "By God," said good Gawain, "I grant all this.   *1110*
    What pleases you is a pleasure to me."
  "Bring beverages! The bargain is made!"
    So said the castle's lord; both of them laughed.
    They drank, they dallied, they dealt in small-talk,
    these lords and ladies, as long as they liked.   *1115*
    Then with frenchified politeness and fair speeches
    they stopped, stood together, and spoke in still voices,
    kissed each other lightly and took their leave.
    And many brisk grooms with gleaming torches
    brought each man at last to his bed   *1120*
                so soft.
        Yet before they went to bed
        they recalled their promise oft.
        The lord of that home-stead
        could well hold sport aloft.   *1125*

PART THREE

V

46 Right early, before day, the company rises.
    Guests who have to go call to their grooms
    who spring up promptly to saddle the horses.
    They prepare their outfits, pack up their bags,
    dress up in their richest riding array,

then leap up quickly and catch their bridles,
each off on the way that he wants to go.
The liege-lord of the land was not the last
arrayed for riding, with many attendants.
He has a hasty bite after hearing mass,   1135
then hurries—bugles blowing—to the hunting field.
By the time daylight had touched the earth
he and his men were on their tall horses.
The careful dog-trainers coupled their hounds,
opened the kennel door and called them out,   1140
blowing loud on their bugles three long notes.
When the brachets bayed and raised a bold noise,
they chastised and checked those that went chasing off,
a hundred hunters, so I heard tell—

> fine men.   1145

> To their stations keepers go,
> the dogs are unleashed then.
> For the good blasts they blow
> the forest rings again.

47   At the first questing cry the wild creatures quaked.   1150
Deer drove through the dales, foolish with dread;
they hurried to high places, but hastily then
they were stopped by the beaters, stoutly shouting.
These let go by the harts with their high heads,
the proud bucks also with broad palm-antlers;   1155
for the true lord had forbidden, in the time of closed season,
that any man should attack the male deer.
Hinds were hauled in with "Hey!" and "Look out!"
Does were driven with great din to the deep vales
where slanting arrows were seen slipping by;   1160
in each forest nook a feather whizzed through
and bit deep into brown hide with its broad head.
Ho! They bay and they bleed, they are dying on the banks,
and the rachets still follow, rushing in a rout,

while hunters with high horns hasten after them   *1165*
with cries that ring out as though cliffs were crumbling.
Any wild beast who dodged the shooting bow-men
was pulled down, torn to bits at the meeting place.
They were worried on the heights and harried to the waters,
so skillful the hunters in the hidden stations,   *1170*
so huge the greyhounds that soon got hold of them
and fetched them down as fast as the folk could look,
just right!

Bliss swept the lord away;
he would gallop, then alight.   *1175*
With joy he passed that day,
thus, until dark night.

48   So the lord is frolicking on the linden woods' fringe
while Gawain—good man—lies in a gorgeous bed,
lingering while the daylight dances on the walls   *1180*
under a fine coverlet, curtained about.
As he slid into slumber he heard, slily,
a little din at the door that opened deftly;
lifting his head from under the linen,
he caught up the corner of the curtain a little   *1185*
and looked out warily to see what it was.
It was the lady, so lovely to look at,
who closed the door after her secretly, quietly,
and came towards the bed; the man, embarrassed,
lay down slily and pretended to sleep.   *1190*
And she stepped stilly, and stole towards the bed,
drew back the curtain and crept within,
then sat down softly on the bedside,
and lingered strangely long to look for his waking.
The knight lay lurking for a long time,   *1195*
searching his conscience for what this case meant
or what it amounted to; he thought it a marvel,
but said to himself: "It would be more seemly

to find out, by speaking on the spot, what she wants."
So he wakened, twisted round and turned towards her,   *1200*
unlocked his lids and looked as if wondering,
and signed himself, to honor his Savior by his words,
                    aright.

> With chin and cheek most sweet,
> mingling red and white,   *1205*
> lovely was she to greet,
> with small lips laughing bright.

49   "Good morning, Sir Gawain," said the gracious lady.
"You are no wary sleeper, since one can slip in;
you are taken, right off! Unless we make truce   *1210*
I shall bind you in your bed, be sure of that!"
All in laughing, the lady made these light jests.
"Good morning, fair one," said Gawain, delighted.
"It shall be as you will, and I am well pleased;
I give in heartily and cry out for grace,   *1215*
and that is best, I think, for so it must be."
And thus he plays back to her, with blithe laughter.
"But if, lovely lady, you would give me leave,
set free your prisoner and pray him to rise,
I'd get out of this bed and clothe myself better;   *1220*
I would be more comfortable conversing with you."
"Indeed, no, fair Sir," said that sweet one.
"You shan't rise from your bed; I'll plan something better.
I shall hold you here safe, on the other side also,
then talk with my knight whom I have now caught.   *1225*
I guess it for a fact, you are Sir Gawain
whom all the world worships wherever he rides;
your honor, your courtly ways, are courteously praised
by lords, by ladies, by everyone living.
And now we are here, indeed, we two alone.   *1230*
My lord and his followers have gone afar,
other men are in bed, my maids also,

the door drawn and fastened with a firm bolt,
and since I have in this house he whom all like,
my time, while I have it, with good talking   *1235*
                    I'll fill.
          My body now is free
          to take at your own will;
          and I, perforce, will be
          your own servant still."   *1240*

50 "In good faith," said Gawain, "I seem to be gaining,
    though I am not the sort that you are speaking of;
    to deserve such reverence as you here render me
    I am unworthy, as I well know myself.
    By God, I would be glad, if you thought good,   *1245*
    in words or in service to set myself
    to giving you pleasure—that would be pure joy."
    "In good faith, Sir Gawain," said the gracious lady,
    "the worth and the prowess that please all others,
    if I lessened or belittled them I would lack good breeding.
    There are ladies enough who would far liefer   *1251*
    have thee in their hold, fair Sir, as I have,
    (to dally pleasantly with your polite words
    and so find comfort and relieve their cares)
    than all the goods or the gold that they have.   *1255*
    But, praise that same Lord who rules the skies,
    I have wholly in my hands him whom all desire,
                    through grace."
          She made great cheer, for sure,
          she, so fair of face.   *1260*
          The knight with speeches pure
          answered in every case.

51 "Madame," said he merrily, "Mary reward you!
    I have, in good faith, found your generosity noble.
    Folk fashion their deeds after other folk;   *1265*

the fine things they say of me are foolish, unmerited.
But your worshipful self thinks well of everything."
"By Mary," said the fine lady, "I find it otherwise.
Were I worth the host of all women now living,
with all the wealth of the world in my hands,   *1270*
forced to bargain and choose to buy me a lord,
from the nature I've seen, Knight, here in thee
—beauty, good breeding and blithe demeanor—
and from what I have heard and hold to be true,
no champion on earth should be chosen before you."   *1275*
"Noble lady," the man said, "you have made a better choice.
But I am proud of the price that you put on me;
soberly, I'm your servant, my sovereign I hold you,
and your knight I become. May Christ repay you!"
So they murmured this-and-that till past mid-morning,   *1280*
and the lady let on that she loved him much
while the man, on his guard, behaved gracefully.
"Were I the loveliest of women," so the lady was thinking,
"there's little love in his manner"—for he must face danger
                             with speed,   *1285*
        a blow to lay him low;
        he could not shun that deed.
        So the lady made to go
        and he at once agreed.

52   She gave him good-day, glanced at him, laughing,   *1290*
then, standing there, stunned him with strong words:
"May He who prospers speech repay you this sport!
But whether you are Gawain—a doubt goes through me."
"Why?" asked the knight, and he said it anxiously,
fearful of failing in speech-formality;   *1295*
but the woman blessed him and answered this way:
"One as good as Gawain is granted to be,
revealing courtesy so clearly in himself,
not lightly could linger so long near a lady

without craving a kiss in his great courtesy,   1300
at some trifling hint at the tale's ending!"
Then Gawain said: "Willingly; do as you want.
I shall kiss at your command, as becomes a knight
and more, lest he displease; so plead no further."
At that she comes nearer, catches him in her arms,   1305
bends down courteously and kisses the man.
Graciously they commend one another to Christ.
She goes out the door without more ado;
he hastens to rise and soon arrays himself,
calls to his chamberlain, chooses his robe,   1310
and when he is clothed comes forth blithely to mass.
Then he went to the meal that was waiting, worthy of him,
and made merry all day till the moon arose,
                          with game.
          Better no man could do: 1315
          on each side a noble dame,
          the old, the young one too.
          Among them, much joy came.

53   The lord of the land was still lingering in sport,
      hunting holt and heath for the barren hinds.   1320
      The number there slain, before the sun sloped down,
      of does and other deer, is too difficult to count.
      Fiercely the folk flocked in for the finish,
      and quickly made a quarry of the deer there killed.
      The nobles hurried in with men enough;   1325
      they gathered the fattest of the game there
      and cut it up carefully, as is the custom;
      they searched the flesh of some, to assay it,
      and in the poorest found it two fingers deep.
      They slit the throat-hollow, seized the stomach,   1330
      flayed it with a sharp knife, tied the white flesh,
      ripped the four limbs apart and rent off the hide.
      They broke the belly and took out the bowels,

throwing them away quickly, then the flesh-knot.
They gripped the throat, and thriftily divided   1335
the gullet from the wind-pipe and pulled out the guts,
then sheared off the shoulder-blades with sharp knives,
pulling them through a small hole, to leave whole the sides.
They sliced the breast and split it in two,
then they began again on the gullet   1340
and rapidly cut it right up to the fork,
threw out the waste part, and after that
fittingly slit the fillets by the ribs,
cleared them off neatly near the backbone
as far as the haunches, till all hung together,   1345
then heaved it up whole and hewed it off;
some parts, I know, are named numbles, and these
                    they find.
          At the forking of the thigh,
          loose skin they cut behind;   1350
          to hew it in two they try,
          and the backbone they unbind.

54   They then hewed off both the head and the neck,
       swiftly sundering the sides from the spine,
       and the "raven's fee" they flung into the bushes.   1355
       They ran a hole in each thick side through the ribs,
       and hung up both by the hocks of the haunches;
       each fellow had for his fee what was fitting.
       On the hide of a fair beast they fed their hounds
       with the liver, the lungs, and the paunch's lining; 1360
       bread soaked with blood was blended with it.
       Boldly they blew the prize-blast; the rachets bayed.
       They took their flesh-meat and turned towards home,
       sounding right stoutly many shrill notes.
       When daylight was gone all the company gathered   1365

in the noble castle where the knight waited,
>> all still,
with bliss and bright fires burning.
The lord drew near, until
Gawain and the one returning   *1370*
met with right good will.

55   The lord commanded that his household be called,
that both ladies come downstairs with their damsels.
Before the by-standers he bade his followers
bring all his venison before him at once.   *1375*
Making a game of it, he called Gawain,
told him the number of nimble beasts taken,
showed him how fair the fat flesh on the ribs.
"Are you pleased with this sport? Have I won praise?
Have I merited thanks by this skill of mine?"   *1380*
"Yes, indeed," said the other, "here are the best spoils
I've seen for seven years in the winter season."
"I leave it to you, Gawain," the lord answered.
"According to our covenant, you may claim it as yours."
"That is true," said the knight, "and I'll tell you, too,   *1385*
what I've worthily won within these walls;
yes, with as much good will it is yours."
He enfolds the man's fair neck in his arms,
kissing him as nicely as he knows how.
"There, take my winnings; I've won nothing more.   *1390*
I would give it freely were it even greater."
"That's good," said the fine man; "I give thanks for it.
Such a gift is the best; you had better tell me
where you won this same wealth by your own wits."
"That was not in our pact," said he. "Press me no further.
You have taken what's yours; trust that no more can be *1396*
>> your due."

They laughed and acted gay
with courtly jesting true,
then to supper went straightway   *1400*
with enough dainties new.

56 Then they sat in their chamber by the chimney side
where the waiters kept plying them with choice wine,
and, still making game, they agreed in the morning
to keep the same promise they had pledged before: *1405*
whatever chance befell, to make an exchange
of the new things gained when they met at night.
They accepted this covenant before the whole court;
beverages were brought in, jokes bandied about,
then with lordly manners they took leave at last,   *1410*
and each man went briskly off to his bed.
When the cock had crowed and called only three times
the lord leaped from his bed, his liegemen too.
They took their meal, heard mass properly,
and were ready for the woods before day had risen,   *1415*
                    for the chase.
          Huntsmen with loud horns
          in the fields' open space
          uncoupled among the thorns
          hounds ready for the race.   *1420*

VI

57 They cried the quest soon by the marsh-side;
hunters urged on the hounds that first held the scent,
hurling wild words at them with a horrible noise;
the hounds that heard them hurried up swiftly
and fell fast on the trail, forty at once.   *1425*
Then such clamor and uproar of gathered rachets
arose, that the rocks all about rang loudly;
hunters heartened them with their horns and voices.

Then all in a swarm they swayed on together
between a forest pool and a frightful crag;   *1430*
on a stone-pile by the cliff, at the swamp-side,
there where the rough rocks had ruggedly fallen,
they pressed on to the lair with the people following.
They raced round the crag and the rock-pile both,
these men, for they knew well that he was in there—
the beast for whom the blood-hounds were baying.   *1435*
They beat in the bushes and bade him rise up;
wildly he lunged at the men in his way.
The most splendid of wild swine swung out at them
   there;
long away from the herd, he was hoary with age.   *1440*
He was a brave one, the biggest of boars,
mighty grim when he growled; then many grieved,
for at one thrash he thrust three men to earth,
then hurtled forth speedily, doing no more harm.
The others hallooed: "Hi!", cried loudly: "Hey! Hey!"
Many merry voices of men and of horns   *1446*
cried after the boar with clamor and noise:
      now quell!
  Often he waits at bay
  and maims the pack who fell;   *1450*
  he hurts the hounds, and they
  right loudly yowl and yell.

58 A band then showed up to shoot at him,
  aimed with their arrows and hit him often.
The points failed on the skin protecting his shoulders   *1455*
and the barbs would not bite into his brows;
though the shaven shafts shivered into pieces,
the heads hopped off wherever they hit.
But, stunned by the blows of strong strokes
and brain-mad for the fray, he rushes at the folk,   *1460*
hurting them fiercely as he hurries on;

many, frightened at that, drew back in fear.
But the lord dashed after him on a light horse;
 like a bold hunter he blows his bugle,
sounds the rally, riding through rank shrubbery,   *1465*
chasing this wild swine till the sun shone high.
Thus they passed that whole day in these same doings,
while our lovable knight lies in his bed,
Gawain, comfortable at home, under bed-clothes rich
                      of hue.   *1470*
        The lady did not forget
        her greeting to renew.
        Right early she was set
        to move his mind anew.

59   She approaches the curtain and peeps at the knight.   *1475*
Sir Gawain welcomes her at once, worthily,
and she retorts, ready with her words,
settles softly beside him, laughs heartily,
and with loving looks speaks in low words:
"Sir, if you are Gawain, it seems wonderful   *1480*
that a man so well trained in polite ways
should not act in company with correct manners,
or, if you do know them, should drop them from mind.
You have totally forgotten what I taught you yesterday
in the plainest talk in which I could tell you."   *1485*
"What is that?" said the knight. "Surely, I know nothing.
If what you mention is true, the blame is all mine."
"I gave a lesson in kissing," said the fair lady,
"how to claim one quickly when the chance comes;
that becomes a knight who tries to be courteous!"   *1490*
"Stop such talk, my dear," the strong man answered.
"That I dare not do, lest I be denied;
if refused, I would be wrong for having requested."
"My faith!" said the merry lady. "You will not be refused;
you are strong and can use force, if you feel like it,

if one were so rude as to refuse you!"   *1496*
"Yes, by God," said Gawain. "What you say is good,
but force is unlucky in the land I live in,
so too a gift not given with good will.
I am at your command, to kiss when you like;   *1500*
you may start when you please and stop when you think well,
                              for a space."
                    Then the lady bent low
                    and sweetly kissed his face,
                    and long they talked on so   *1505*
                    of true love's grief and grace.

60 "I would know from you, Sir," that noble one said,
    "without rousing your anger, what is the reason
    why one young and fresh as you are at this time,
    so courteous, so knightly, as all know you to be—   *1510*
    for the choice parts of chivalry, the points most praised,
    are love's loyal sport and the true lore of arms;
    telling the struggles of these true knights,
    that is the title and text of such writings:
    how heroes for true love have ventured their lives, *1515*
    have endured for love's sake most doleful days,
    then avenged all and ended their cares by valor,
    bringing bliss into bowers by their bountifulness.
    And you are the noblest knight of your times;
    your renowned honor runs before you everywhere,   *1520*
    yet I have sat by you here twice already
    and have won from your mouth not a single word
    that savors of love, either less or more!
    And you, so polite, so deft with your promises,
    ought to yearn to show to such a young thing   *1525*
    some token of love's true craft, and teach her.
    Why! Are you ignorant, you whom all praise?
    Do you think me too dull to harken to dalliance?
                              For shame!

Alone I come and sit   1530
to learn from you this game;
come, teach me by your wit
while my lord's too far to blame."

61 "In good faith," said Gawain, "may God repay you!
It brings great gladness and right good cheer   1535
that one worthy as you are should want to come
and take pains with so poor a man, playing with your knight
with favorable demeanor; it delights me.
But to take up the task of expounding true love,
to touch on such themes and tales of arms   1540
to you who, I know well, are so much wiser
in that art, by a half, than a hundred such
as I am or shall be while I live on earth,
would be manifold folly, fair one, by my faith!
I shall do as you please with all my power,   1545
as I am bound to do; I will be evermore
your very servant; so may the Lord save me!"
Thus the fair lady tried him, and attempted often
to win him to wickedness, to what she wanted.
But his defence was so gracious that no fault was seen,   1550
no evil on either side, and they knew nothing
but bliss
Long they laughed and played;
at last she gave a kiss,
with fair goodbyes, and stayed   1555
no longer after this.

62 Then the man bestirs himself, rising for mass,
and their dinner was dished up and duly served.
The knight spent all day in sport with the ladies,
but the lord was galloping through the open lands   1560
for the unlucky boar that swung past the banks
and bit asunder the backs of the best brachets

while he waited at bay, till the bowmen broke in
and made him, despite himself, move onward,
so fierce flew the arrows where the folk gathered.   1565
Yet he forced the stoutest to stop sometimes,
till at last, so spent he could speed on no more,
he came with what haste he could to a hole
in a rise by a rock where the brook runs.
He gets the bank at his back, begins to scrape;   1570
the froth from his mouth's ugly corners foams out
as he whets his white tusks. They were all too tired,
the men so bold who were standing by,
to hurt him from afar; in such danger, none dared
                              draw near.   1575
          He had hurt so many before
          that all were full of fear
          that his tusks would tear them more
          so frenzied did he appear.

63   Then the knight came himself, urging his horse,   1580
seeing the boar at bay with the men beside him.
He alights gracefully and leaves his courser,
draws a bright brand and bravely strides on,
hurrying through the ford where the fierce thing waited.
The wild beast was aware of him, weapon in hand;
his hairs bristled up, hatefully he snorted   1586
till many feared for the man, lest the worst befall him.
Then the swine rushed out and set full on him,
till the knight and the boar were both in one heap
where the water ran rough. The boar had the worst of it,
for the man aimed a blow as they first met,   1591
set his sharp sword in the breast-bone, surely,
drove it up to the hilt till the heart split.
Snarling he gave way and, crossing the water,
                              he fled.   1595

A hundred hounds came fast,
and their fierce bites brought dread.
Men drove him forth at last
and the dogs killed him dead.

64 The capture was blown on bright-sounding horns   *1600*
with loud, high halooing from men lusty enough;
brachets bayed at the beast as their masters bade,
the leading huntsmen of that hard chase.
A man who was wise in woodland craft
zestfully begins the boar's dismembering.   *1605*
First he hews off the head and sets it on high,
then rends straight down the back very roughly,
tears out the bowels, burns them on the coals,
and with these mixed with bread rewards the brachets.
Then he slices the brawn into broad, bright slabs,   *1610*
pulls out edible entrails in the proper manner;
yet in one whole he puts the halves together,
then stoutly hangs them on a strong pole.
Now with this same swine they hasten homeward,
with the boar's head borne before the hero   *1615*
who had slain it with the force of his own strong hand
                    at the ford.
            He did not see Gawain
            for a long time in the hall,
            but, to claim rewards again,   *1620*
            the knight came at his call.

65 The lord called with loud words, laughing merrily
and talking joyously when he saw Sir Gawain.
The good ladies were called and the household gathered;
he shows them the sliced flesh, and tells the story
of the weight and the length of the wild swine   *1626*
and of the fierce war as he fled through the woods.
The knight courteously commended his deed

and praised it as proof of his great prowess,
for such brawn in a beast, the bold knight said,   *1630*
and such sides on a swine he had never seen.
Then they handled the huge head; the handsome man
    praised it
and let on to feel horror, to honor the lord.
"Now, Gawain," said the good man, "this game is your own,
by our fast-binding promise, as you know, faithfully."
"That is true," said the man, "and just as truthfully   *1636*
I shall again give you my gains, on my honor."
He clasps the knight's neck and delicately kisses him,
then at once served him in the same way again.
"Now we are even," said Gawain, "this evening-time,   *1640*
by all the covenants made since I came hither,
              so true!"
      The lord said: "By Saint Gile!
      No better man than you!
      You'll be rich in a short while   *1645*
      if such bargaining you do!"

66   Then they put up the tables on their trestles
and covered them with cloths; the clear light then
wakened on the walls from waxen torches;
the meal was set out and served through the hall.   *1650*
A happy clamor rang out from the crowd
around the hearth-fire, and in varied fashion
at supper and afterwards, many noble songs,
tunes for Christmastime, and new carols,
with all sorts of mirth that men tell of—   *1655*
our lovable knight always by the lady's side.
So gracious was her manner as she dealt with the man
with still, stolen glances to please that staunch one,
that he was bewildered and blamed himself.
But through good breeding he would not gainsay her;   *1660*

he dealt with her delicately, however the deed might turn
at last.
> After playing in the hall
> as long as the wish might last,
> from his room he heard the lord call;   *1665*
> to the chimney side they passed.

67　There they drank and played, and promised again
to observe the same terms on New Year's eve.
But the knight asked leave to be off in the morning;
that appointment was near to which he was pledged.   *1670*
The lord put him off and pressed him to linger,
saying: "As a man of honor, I assure thee in truth
thou shalt be at the Green Chapel to take thy chances,
Sir, with the New Year's light, long before prime.
So, lie in thy room and lounge at ease;   *1675*
I shall hunt in the woods, bring thee the winnings,
and change booty with thee when I come back,
for I have tested thee twice and found thee trustworthy.
Now, 'third throw the best!' Think of that in the morning;
make merry while we may and be mindful of joy,
for sorrow is met with whenever men wish."   *1681*
This was graciously granted, and Gawain lingered on;
cheering drinks were brought, then to bed they went
> with their light.
> Sir Gawain lies and sleeps   *1685*
> right still and soft all night;
> the lord to his purpose keeps,
> and early is clad aright.

68　After mass the lord and his men took a morsel.
Merry was the morning; he asked for his mount;   *1690*
all the hunters who were following him on horseback
were soon high on their steeds before the hall gate.
Very fair were the fields, for the frost clung;

ruddy-red through cloud-banks the sun was rising,
skirting the clouds into the clear sky.   *1695*
The hunters loosened their hounds by a holt side;
rocks rang in the covert with the cry of horns.
Some fell on the track where the fox lurked,
trailing back and forth with tricky wiles.
A small hound gives the cry, hunters call after him,   *1700*
the pack falls in line, panting fast,
running in a rabble right on his trail
while he scampers before them. They soon find him,
and when they catch sight of him swiftly pursue,
crying after him clearly, with a fierce clamor   *1705*
as he dodges and turns through many dense groves,
doubles back and harkens by a hedge, often.
At last, by a little ditch, he leaps a thorn hedge,
steals out stealthily by a skirting thicket,
trying to slip the hounds by a trick, through the woods. *1710*
Too late he found himself near a fine hunting-station
where three strong hounds at once harried him,
                    all gray
          Quick, he swerved again
          and staunchly ran astray;   *1715*
          driven by great pain
          in the wood he went away.

69   Then it was lively sport to listen to the hounds
when the whole pack met and mingled together;
at that sight they called down loud curses on his head,   *1720*
as if clustering cliffs had clattered into heaps.
Here he was halooed when the heroes met him,
loudly taunted with testy shouts;
there he was threatened, often called a thief,
and with trail-dogs at his tail he could not tarry.   *1725*
Often they ran at him when he rushed out
and as often reeled in again; so wily was Renard!

Yes, he led till they got left, the lord and his followers,
through the hills in this manner until mid-day,
while at home the noble knight wholesomely sleeps   *1730*
within handsome curtains through that cold morning.
But the lady's love would not let her sleep
or fail in the purpose fixed in her heart.
She arose swiftly and came straight there
in a gorgeous mantle that reached to the ground,   *1735*
all finely furred with well-finished skins,
on her head no bright colors, but well-cut gems
twisted through her hair in clusters of twenty;
her fair face and neck were left naked,
her breast bare in front and behind also.   *1740*
She comes through the chamber door, closes it after her,
casts up a window and calls to the knight,
promptly rallying him with pleasant words
             and cheer.
    "Ah, man! How canst thou sleep   *1745*
      when the morning is so clear?"
    He was drowsing deep,
      but then he began to hear.

70 In the moody gloom of a dream the noble man muttered
like a man mourning for many dire thoughts:
how destiny, that day, would deal him his Wyrd   *1751*
at the Green Chapel when he meets the champion
and waits for his buffet without more words.
When that fair one came he recovered his wits,
swung out of his dreams and speedily answered.   *1755*
Then the lovely lady, laughing sweetly,
bent down to his fair face and daintily kissed him.
He welcomes her worthily, with well-bred manners;
seeing her so glorious, so gayly attired,
so faultless in feature, with such fine coloring,   *1760*
joy ardently welled up, warming his heart.

With sly, gentle smiles they broke into merry speech;
all was blissful happiness between them, with joy
             alight.
      They bantered words so good   *1765*
      with much gladness bright;
      great peril between them stood,
      had not Mary watched her knight!

71   For that precious princess pressed him so strongly,
urged him so near the edge that he needs must   *1770*
either return her love or rudely refuse her.
He was careful of courtesy, lest he prove craven,
more careful of the mischief if she made him sin
and be traitor to the man who ruled that mansion.
"God shield us," said the knight, "that shall never be!"   *1775*
With a little love-laughter he lightly turned off
all the fond speeches that fell from her mouth.
Said the lady to the brave knight: "You are to blame
if you love not the person near whom you are lying,
who's more wounded in heart than anyone in the world,
unless you have a sweetheart who suits you better,   *1781*
and are pledged to some fair one by so fast a bond
that you don't want to break it; that I now believe.
Tell me so now, truly, I pray you;
by all the loves there are, let not the truth hide   *1785*
           under guile!"
      The knight said: "By Saint John!"
      And with a gracious smile:
      "In faith, I yet have none,
      nor will have, for a while."   *1790*

72   "That word," said the lady, "is the worst of all,
but it's a true answer, and troubles me sorely.
Now kiss me graciously and I'll go away;
I can but mourn on earth, as a maiden who loves much."

Sighing, she leaned down and kissed him sweetly,
then, before starting off, stood still, saying: 1796
"Now dear, at this parting, do me this favor:
give me some gift, thy glove perhaps,
to remember thee by, Sir, and so lessen my mourning."
"Indeed," said the knight, "I wish now I had here 1800
the best thing, for thy love, that I have in the land.
For you have earned, in truth, and most excellently,
more reward, by right, than I can reckon.
But to give you a love-token would avail little;
it would not honor you to own just now 1805
a glove for a keepsake, of Gawain's giving,
and I am here on an errand to an unknown land,
with no servants with trunks full of treasured things.
That troubles me, Lady, for love's sake, at this time.
Each man does his best; take it not amiss, 1810
    nor repine."
  "No, knight of honor true,"
   said that beauty, clad so fine,
  "though I have no gift from you,
   you shall have one of mine." 1815

73 She gave him a rich ring of red gold-work,
with a gleaming stone standing out on it
that shot blazing beams like the bright sun;
be sure it was worth a vast deal of wealth!
But the knight refused it, and firmly said: 1820
"No gifts for good and all, just now, gracious one.
I have none to offer, and none will I take."
She begged him earnestly; he refused her bidding
and swore hard, by his truth, that he would not touch it.
Sorry that he spurned it, she said at once:
"If you refuse my ring for seeming too rich, 1826
and you do not want to be so indebted,
I shall give you my girdle, a less gain to you!"

Lightly, she took a lace that lay round her waist,
fastened to her skirts under her fair mantle;   *1830*
it was made of green silk all set with gold,
bordered with nothing less, embroidered by hand.
She pressed it on the knight, light-heartedly pleading
that he would take it, though it was worthless.
And he swore that he would not, in any way, touch   *1835*
either gold or treasure, till God send him grace
to achieve the adventure he had undertaken.
"And therefore, I pray you, be not displeased;
give up your urging, for to grant this I'll never
                         agree.   *1840*
       I am dearly in your debt
       for your gracious ways to me.
       Come heat or cold, ever yet
       your servant true I'll be."

74 "Do you refuse this silk," said the fair lady then,   *1845*
"because it is so simple? So it seems indeed.
Look! it's so little, worth less than nothing!
But one who knew what qualities are knitted into it
would perhaps appraise it at a higher price.
If a man is girded with this green lace,   *1850*
while he has it fairly fastened about him
no hero under heaven can hew him down;
he cannot be slain by any sleights on earth."
The knight hesitated; it came into his heart
that this would be a jewel in the jeopardy ahead   *1855*
when he found himself at the Chapel to face his blow;
it would be a good way to get through alive!
So he listened to her pleading, letting her speak
as she pressed the belt on him and bade him take it,
until he agreed. She gave it with good will,   *1860*
asking him, for her sake, not to let it be seen,
but conceal it from her lord; the knight consented

that no-one, truly, save they two should know it
by right.
He thanked her heartily,   1865
and thought with all his might.
By that time, kisses three
she had given her brave knight.

75   Then she takes her leave and lets him be;
she could get no more pleasure out of that man.   *1870*
When she has gone, Sir Gawain soon gets ready,
rises and robes himself in noble array,
lays by the love-lace that the lady gave him,
hiding it carefully where he could find it.
His chief idea was to get to the chapel.   *1875*
He approached a priest privately, and there prayed him
to purify his life, and plainly teach him
how to save his soul when his end was in sight.
He confessed fully, declared his faults,
great and small, and sought for mercy,   *1880*
then implored absolution from the priest
who absolved him well and made him as clean
as if doomsday were due the next morning.
Then he makes merrier among the fair ladies
with lovely carols and all kinds of joy   *1885*
than ever before that day, till the dark night,
blissfully.
Each man was well treated there
by him, and said: "Just see!
He has shown no merrier air   *1890*
since he came, till now—surely!"

VII

76   Let him linger in that shelter; may love come his way!
The lord is abroad, still leading his men.

He has outstripped the fox that he followed so long,
springing over a thorn-hedge to spy out the rascal.   *1895*
When he heard the hounds pressing hard after him
Renard came racing through a rugged grove
with the whole rabble rushing right at his heels.
The man watched for the wild thing, waiting warily,
then drew out his bright brand and thrust at the beast   *1900*
who swerved from its sharp edge and tried to shunt.
A hound hurried up to him as he hastened off,
and right at the horses' feet they all fell on him
and worried that wily one with a wild noise.
The lord alights quickly and soon catches him,   *1905*
snatches him hastily from the mouths of the hounds,
holds him high over head, halooing loudly;
many bold hounds were baying up at him.
Hunters hurried in with their many horns,
sounding high the recall, till they saw the knight.   *1910*
When the gallant company had all gathered,
those who carried bugles blew them together
and the others halooed, those who had no horns.
It was the merriest hound-baying that ever men heard,
a mighty noise raised there for Renard's soul,   *1915*
> a din!
> Men pat and rub each head
> of the hounds who praises win;
> then they take Renard, dead,
> and strip him of his skin.   *1920*

77 Then they turn towards home, for night-time is near,
blowing right stoutly on their sturdy horns.
The lord alights at last at his loved home,
finds a fire on the hearth with the hero beside it,
good Sir Gawain, who was glad to be there   *1925*
among the ladies, enjoying their love-making.
He wore a blue robe that reached to the floor,

his softly furred surcoat fitted him well
and a hood to match it hung on his shoulders,
both adorned with white fur all around them.   *1930*
He met the good man in the middle of the hall
greeting him jokingly in just the right way:
"I shall now be the first to fulfill our pledge
that we luckily spoke of as we drank unsparingly."
He took hold of the knight and kissed him three times   *1935*
with relish, as soundly as he rightly could.
"By Christ," said that other, "you made a lucky catch
in getting these wares, if the bargain was good!"
"Yes, ask not the cost," said the other quickly,
"since plainly I have paid the price that I owe."   *1940*
"Mary!" said the other man. "My gift is much less,
for all day I have hunted, and I have nothing
but this foul fox's skin; the fiend take such goods!
That's a poor price to pay for such precious things
as you've heartily thrust on me, these three kisses   *1945*
                     so good."
               "Enough," said Sir Gawain,
               "I thank you, by the Rood."
               And how the fox was slain
               he was told, there where he stood.   *1950*

78   With mirth, with minstrelsy, with the meats they wanted,
they made as merry as any men might
while the ladies were laughing with light jests.
Both Gawain and the good man were glad as could be—
short of all going silly or getting drunk!   *1955*
Lord and retainers both bandied their jokes
till the time came when the two must part;
the knights were bound for their beds at last.
Then he humbly took leave of the lord first;
the well-bred knight thanked him warmly: *1960*

"For the happy sojourn I have had here,
  and your honor at this festival, the High King repay you!
  I give myself over as your man, if you like,
  for I must, as you know, move on tomorrow.
  Give me someone, as you promised, to guide my way   *1965*
  to the Green Chapel, that God may allow me
  to do on the New Year what my Wyrd dooms for me."
"By my faith," said the good man, "with good will
  I shall promptly do all that I promised you."
He assigned him a servant to set him on the way   *1970*
  leading over the downs, that nothing might daunt him
  riding in the woods by a path through the groves
                      most nigh.

        And now Gawain must thank
        for favors heaped so high.   *1975*
        To the ladies of proud rank
        the knight then said goodbye.

79 He kissed them sorrowfully and spoke to all,
  beseeching them to accept his earnest thanks,
  and they promptly said the same thing to him.   *1980*
  They commended him to Christ with cold sighing.
  He parted courteously from the household company,
  telling every man that he met of his thanks
  for the service, the kindness, the care each had taken
  to be always busy about serving him;   *1985*
  and the men were as pained to part from him there
  as though they had dwelt with that dauntless knight always.
  Then with servants and lights he was led to his chamber
  and brought cheerfully to bed, to be at rest.
  If he slept soundly, I dare not say so;   *1990*
  he had much to be mindful of about the next morning
                   in thought.

So let him lie there still
nearer to what he sought.
If you, for a while, keep still,   *1995*
I shall tell you what day brought.

PART FOUR

VIII

80   The New Year draws close now, the night passes,
day breaks through the dark as the Lord bids it;
but the world's wildest weather wakened outside,
clouds cast their coldness to earth, keenly,   *2000*
with sting enough from the north to pain the naked.
Snow shivered down sharply, snapping at the wild things;
the whistling winds whipped out of the sky
and drove each dale full of deep drifts.
The knight listened while he lay in his bed;   *2005*
though he locks his eye-lids, little can he sleep!
By each cock that crew he knew too well what called him.
He got up early before the dawn glimmered,
for light shone from a lamp lit in his chamber.
Calling to his chamberlain who quickly answered   *2010*
he said to bring his byrny and saddle his horse.
The other got up and fetched his garments,
then made Gawain ready in a great fashion.
First he put clothes on him to ward off the cold,
then his other harness that was handsomely kept,   *2015*
all the pieces of plate-armor polished clean,
rings rubbed clear of rust in his rich mail-shirt.
All was fresh as at first; he found words of thanks
            at need.

He then put on each piece,   *2020*
well shined up, fine indeed.
The most sprightly from here to Greece,
the man bade bring his steed.

81   He then garbed himself in his richest garments—
his coat with blazonry of the best needle-work   *2025*
stitched upon velvet, stones of high value
set in it, well-made with embroidered seams,
finely furred inside with a fair lining.
Yet the lace was not left out, the lady's gift;
Gawain could not forget it, for his own good!   *2030*
After belting his sword on his broad thighs
he twisted the love-token twice about him.
The knight folded it well round his neck with delight;
the girdle of green silk suited that fine man,
on the royal red cloth so rich to look at.   *2035*
Not for its great worth he wore this girdle,
nor for pride in its pendants, though they were polished
and glittering gold gleamed at their ends,
but to save himself when he needs must suffer,
waiting death with no struggle, with no sword or   *2040*
                    knife for defence.
When the bold man was dressed
quickly he parted thence.
To that famed court he expressed
his thanks in recompense.   *2045*

82   Then Gryngolet was made ready, a great, huge horse
comfortably stabled in secure fashion;
the proud steed was fit and eager to prance.
The knight comes up to look at his coat,   *2050*
and says soberly to himself, swearing by his honor:
"The servants in this castle are mindful of courtesy,
their lord well maintains them; may they have joy!

And the dear lady living here, may love come her way!
If for charity they so cherish a guest
with such perfect manners, may He repay them   2055
who owns heaven above—and all of you also!
If my life goes on a while longer in this world,
I shall somehow reward you, willingly, if I may."
He steps into the stirrups and springs aloft.
A man gives him his shield; he lays it on his shoulder   2060
and strikes spurs into Gryngolet with his gilt heels.
The steed kicks the stones; waiting no more, he starts
                          to prance.
              On horseback the knight sits, fit
              to bear his spear and lance.   2065
              "This castle to Christ I commit!"
              He wishes it good chance.

83   The bridge was drawn down, and the broad gates
      unbarred and borne open on both sides.
      The man blessed himself quickly and crossed the   2070
              boarding;
      he praised the porter kneeling before the prince
      wishing good-day and God-speed—may He save Gawain!
      He went on his way with only one waiting-man
      to tell him where to turn off for that terrible place
      where he has to meet a hideous onslaught.   2075
      They go on by banks where the boughs are bare;
      they climb along cliffs where the cold clings.
      Clouds hung high overhead; underneath it was ugly,
      mist drizzling on the moor and melting on the mountains.
      Each hill had a hat on, a huge mist-cloak;   2080
      brooks boiled and broke against their banks,
      brightly spattering the shores as they shot down.
      Very wandering was the way they must take through the
              woods,
      until soon came the hour for the sun to rise
                          that day.   2085

They were on a hill-top high,
around the white snow lay.
The man that rode so nigh
then bade his master stay.

84 "I have led you here, my Lord, at this time,   2090
  and you are not far from that famous place
  that you've searched for and sought so earnestly.
  I speak the truth now, since I know you,
  and you are the living man whom I love most:
  if you follow my thought you will fare better.   2095
  The place that you press toward is held to be perilous;
  a being dwells in that waste, the worst on earth,
  for he is staunch and stern and loves to strike out,
  huger than any man on this middle-earth,
  with a body bigger than the best four   2100
  who are in Arthur's house, Hector or any other.
  He offers this chance at the Green Chapel:
  if one passes that place, even though proudly armed,
  he dings him to death with one dash of the hand.
  He is a violent man who shows no mercy,   2105
  for whether churl or chaplain rides by that chapel,
  monk or mass-priest, or any man else,
  he's as pleased to slay them as to still live himself!
  So I say, as sure as you sit in that saddle,
  if you get there you'll die—if that knight deals   2110
          with you!
  Trust me truly in this, though you had twenty lives
                          to spend.
              He dwelt here long of yore,
              battling without end.
              Against his buffets sore   2115
              your life you can't defend.

85 "And so, good Sir Gawain, let him get on alone;
go by another way, for God's own sake!
Ride to some other country where Christ will help you.
I shall hurry home, and I hereupon promise   2120
to swear by God and all His good saints
—so help me God, holy relics, and other good oaths—
truly to keep your secret, and tell no tales
of you trying to make off, for any man I know."
"Many thanks," said Gawain, and added grudgingly: 2125
"Good luck to you, Sir, for wishing my good;
I am certain you would loyally keep my secret.
But though you hid it faithfully, if I passed on,
taking flight through fear in the fashion you speak of,
I would be a coward knight, never to be excused.   2130
I will go to the chapel and take what chance comes;
I will talk to that fellow and tell him what I like,
come well-being or woe, whatever Wyrd wills me
          to brave.
       Though he stands there fierce to fight   2135
       with his big stick—the knave!
       the Lord can shape things right;
       His servants He will save."

"Marry!" said the other, "if thou dost insist
on bringing thine own doom down on thyself,   2140
and on losing thy life, I will no longer hinder.
Here: put helmet on head and take spear in hand,
and ride down this road by yonder rock's side
till thou get to the bottom of that grim valley.
Look a little beyond the field on thy left hand   2145
and see in that valley the very chapel,
and on the ground the stout man who there keeps guard.
Now farewell, in God's name, Gawain the noble!
For all the gold in the world I would not go

through this forest in thy company one foot further."   *2150*
And there in the woods the man wields his bridle,
hits his horse with his heels as hard as he can,
leaps over the fields and leaves the knight
                              alone.
              "By God Himself," said Gawain,   *2155*
              "I will not grieve nor groan.
                  To God's will I bow again;
                  I give Him all I own."

87   Then he spurs Gryngolet, sets out on the path,
      goes in by a ridge at a grove's side   *2160*
      and rides by the rough bank right into the dale.
      Then he looks around and all appears wild to him,
      seeing no sign of refuge on any side,
      only banks high and steep in both directions
      with rough gnarled rocks and rugged stones;   *2165*
      the clouds seemed grazed by the jagged cliffs.
      Then he halted a moment, holding in his horse,
      and turned his face everywhere to find the chapel.
      He saw no such anywhere—he thought it strange—
      save a little off in a field what looked like a mound,   *2170*
      a bare barrow by the bank of a brimming stream
      near the falls of brook that was flowing there.
      The brook bubbled as though it were boiling.
      The knight urges his horse and comes to the hill,
      alights gracefully and fastens to a linden tree   *2175*
      the reins of his fine steed on a rough branch.
      Then he went to the mound and walked all around it,
      debating within himself what it might be.
      It had a hole in the end and on either side,
      overgrown with patches of grass everywhere,   *2180*
      and all was hollow within, only an old cave
      or a crevice of an old crag; which he could not guess
                              or say well.

"Ah, Lord!" said the gentle knight,
"is this the Green Chapel?   2185
  Here, at about midnight
  might the devil his Matins tell!

88 "Now indeed," said Gawain, "it is gruesome here;
this oratory is ugly, overgrown with weeds.
Well it suits that creature clothed all in green   2190
to do his devotions in the devil's way!
Now I feel it is the fiend, in my five wits,
who has arranged this meeting to undo me here.
It's a chapel of mischance; bad luck check-mate it!
It's the cursedest church that I ever came into."   2195
With helmet on head and lance in hand
he made for the rocks of that rough dwelling.
Then he heard from the high hill, on a hard rock
beyond the stream, on a bank, a strangely loud noise.
Ho! It clattered on the cliff as though to cleave it,   2200
like a scythe being ground upon a grind-stone.
Ho! It whirred and whirled like water at a mill.
Ho! It rushed and rang, nerve-wracking to hear!
"By God!" said Gawain. "That devise, I guess,
is meant to honor me, to meet me fitly   2205
                    on the spot.
  "Let God work, Ah, lo!
  Sighing will help me not.
  Though my life I forgo,
  noise scares me not a jot!"   2210

89 Then the knight called out, high and clear:
"Who is master of this place, to keep his promise?
For Gawain the Good has now got right here.
If anyone wants something, let him come at once
—now or never—to do what he needs to!"   2215
"Wait!" came from the bank above his head.

(256)

"Thou shalt soon have all I once promised thee."
Yet the noise went on rushing rapidly a while
as he kept on with his whetting before coming down.
He makes his way by a crag and comes through a hole,   *2220*
whirling out of the nook with a nasty weapon,
a Danish axe new-sharpened for dealing the blow,
with a huge head bending towards the handle,
filed on a grind-stone, four feet broad
—no smaller for the lace girdle that gleamed brightly!   *2225*
And the man in green, all geared as at first,
the face and the legs, the locks and the beard
(save that flat on the ground he walked on his feet),
set the handle on the stones and stalked nearer.
When he came to the water he would not wade,   *2230*
but hopped over on his axe and haughtily strode
over the broad field, fiercely angry,
               through snow.
      Sir Gawain went to meet
      the knight, not bowing low.   *2235*
      The other said: "Now, Sir Sweet,
      thou wilt keep thy word, I know!"

90 "Gawain," said the green man, "God must look after thee!
Thou art welcome indeed, Sir, to my estate;
thou hast timed thy travel as a true man should,   *2240*
knowing the covenant we came to between us:
this time a twelvemonth didst thou take what fell to thee,
and I, this New Year, will eagerly repay thee.
We are in this valley by ourselves, verily;
there are none to part us, struggle as we please!   *2245*
Take the helmet from thy head, and have here thy payment;
make no more resistance than I made then
when you whipped my head off at one whop."
"No," said Gawain. "By God who gave me a soul,
I begrudge not one grain of any grief that comes.   *2250*

Only stop after one stroke, and I shall stand still
and show no reluctance to doing what you like—
nowhere."
                He bent his neck down low
                till the white flesh lay bare,   2255
                as if no fear could show.
                He flinched for no dread there!

IX

91 The man dressed in green quickly drew himself up,
    lifting his grim tool as if to smite Gawain;
    With all the strength in his body he swung it aloft   2260
    and aimed as desperately as though to destroy him.
    Had it fallen down with the force he displayed
    the ever-brave man would have died of that blow.
    But Gawain glanced sidewise at that gisarm
    as it glided down to kill him on the ground;   2265
    his shoulders shrank a little from the sharp iron.
    The other with a swerve swept the bright blade aside,
    then reproved the prince with puffed-up words,
    "Thou art not Gawain," said he, "who is held so good,
    who never flinched from a host on hill or in vale;   2270
    now thou shrinkest for fear before feeling harm!
    Such cowardice in that knight I could not hear of.
    I swerved not, nor fled, Sir, when thou didst swing at me;
    I offered no cavilling in King Arthur's house.
    My head flew to my feet, yet I never fled,   2275
    and thou, before harm falls, shrinkest in heart.
    The better man it behooves me to be now called,
                therefore!"
                "I shrank once," Gawain said,
                "and so I will no more.   2280
                But once on the stones, my head
                I never can restore!

92 "Be quick, man, by my faith, and come to the point!
 Deal my destiny to me, and do it out of hand.
 I'll stand up to thy stroke and stagger no more   2285
 till thine axe has hit me; here is my word for it!"
 "Have at thee!" said the other, and heaved it aloft,
 glaring as crossly as if he were crazy.
 He swung mightily, but never cut the man,
 withholding his hand hastily before it could do hurt.   2290
 Gawain faithfully waited and flinched in no limb,
 but stood as still as a stone, or else a stump
 that grapples the rocky ground with a hundred roots.
 Then the man in green called out merrily:
 "So, now thou art whole-hearted, I must really hit.   2295
 Turn up that grand hood that Arthur gave thee,
 keep thy neck from this cut—if it can survive!"
 Then Gawain, in mighty anger, said grimly:
 "Why, thrash on, fierce man; thou threatenest too long;
 I think my heart is afraid of thine own self."   2300
 "Indeed," said the fellow, "for talking so fiercely
 I will dally no longer, nor delay thine errand
                              right now."

         Then he stands firm for the blow
         and puckers both lip and brow.   2305
         Not strange if the other feared so
         that he hoped for no rescue now!

93 Lightly lifting his blade he let it fall square
 with the barbed edge right on the bare neck;
 though he hammered hard he hurt him not at all,   2310
 but nicked him on one side and severed the skin.
 The sharp edge reached the flesh through the fair fat,
 till bright blood shot over his shoulders to the ground.
 When the knight saw blood gleaming on the snow,
 he sprang forth, feet together, more than a spear's length,

firmly seized his helmet, set it on his head,   2316
swung his fair shield around before his shoulders,
drew out his bright sword and spoke boldly.
Never since that man had been born of his mother
had he ever been half so happy in this world!   2320
"Cease thy blows, man, ask no more of me!
I have taken one stroke in this place without struggling.
If you give me more I shall gladly requite,
and toss them back readily—trust me for that—
                 as a foe!   2325
        But one stroke was to fall;
        the compact was made so,
        formed in Arthur's hall.
        Therefore, good Sir, now ho!"

94   The man turned away, resting on his axe,   2330
set the shaft on the brook-shore and leaned on the
       sharp edge,
looking at the knight who had come to his land.
He saw him stand firm, fearless, undreading,
armed and dauntless; it did his heart good!
Then he speaks merrily in a mighty voice,   2335
telling the knight in roaring tones:
"Bold Sir, in these fields be not so fierce;
no man has mistreated thee with bad manners here,
nor acted but by contract made at the King's court.
I pledged one stroke—thou hast it; think thee well-paid. 2340
I release thee from the rest of all other rights.
Had I been brisker I could have dealt a buffet
more wrathfully, perhaps, and done thee real harm.
I threatened thee first with a feigned one, merrily,
not rending with a sore gash; I treated thee rightly,   2345
for the bargain that we framed on that first night.
For truly thou wert faithful and found trustworthy,
giving me all thy gains, as a good man should.

The second feint I made, Sir, for the morning
thou didst kiss my fair wife; those kisses thou gavest me.
For these I tried thee with but two bare feints,   *2351*
           no blow!
     A true man takes his due
     and then needs dread no woe.
     The third time thou wast not true;   *2355*
     one tap thou must take—so!

95 "That's my garment thou art wearing, that same woven
     girdle;
my own wife wove it, as indeed I know well!
I know well, too, thy kisses, and all thy ways,
and my wife's wooing—I worked that myself!   *2360*
I sent her to try thee; thou art, I think truly,
the most faultless man who walks on his feet!
As a pearl is more precious than a white pea,
so is Gawain, in good faith, than other fine knights.
But you were a little lacking, Sir, wanting in loyalty,   *2365*
not for underhand doings or for wooing, either,
but for love of your life—the less I blame you!"
The strong knight stood a long while in a study,
so grievously ashamed that he groaned within;
all his heart's blood burned in his face   *2370*
and he shrank while the man talked on, for shame.
Then the first word that the knight uttered was:
"Cursed be cowardice and covetousness, both!
In you is villainy, and vice that spoils virtue."
He caught at the knot, loosening the clasp,   *2375*
and fiercely flung his belt at the bold man himself.
"See! There goes falseness; may evil go with it!
For fear of thy blow, cowardice forced me
to accord with covetousness, to forsake what becomes me:
liberality and loyalty that belong to knights.   *2380*
Now I am faulty and false, who have always feared

treachery and untruth—may trouble take them,
                    and care!
          I acknowledge, Knight, here still
          faultily did I fare;   2385
          let me now do thy will
          and after I shall beware."

96   Then the other man laughed, and said amiably:
    "I hold it all healed, the harm that I met with.
    Thou hast confessed so clean, declaring thy faults,   2390
    openly doing penance at the point of my axe-edge,
    I hold thee purged of offence, purified as clean
    as if thou hadst not failed since thou was first born.
    And I give thee, Sir, this gold-hemmed girdle;
    it's as green as my gown. Sir Gawain, may you ever   2395
    remember this contest as thou ridest out
    among famous princes; it is a fair token
    of the Green Chapel's adventure between chivalrous knights.
    And you must come again, this New Year, to my castle,
    to revel for the rest of this regal feast,   2400
                    pleasantly."
          He pressed him hard, the lord:
          "With my wife you will be
          again in good accord,
          though she was your enemy."   2405

97   "No, indeed!" said the knight; he seized his helmet,
    lifted it gracefully and thanked the lord.
    "I have sojourned long enough. May joy be with you;
    may He who rewards courtesy repay you freely!
    Comend me to that courtly one, your comely wife,   2410
    to both one and the other of mine honored ladies
    who contrived to beguile their knight by a trick.
    But it is no marvel if a fool go mad,
    and through woman's wiles be won, to his sorrow!

So Adam in the garden was beguiled by one,   *2415*
and Solomon by several, and Samson after him—
Delilah dealt him his doom—and then David
was deluded by Bathsheba and bore much misery.
Since guile ruined such, it would be a gain
to love women and not trust them, if a knight only would!
These were noblest in former times, favored by fortune *2421*
more happily than other men who have been, under heaven,
                                        bemused.
   All these by wiles were caught
   by women whom they used.   *2425*
   Though now beguiled, I ought
   to hold myself excused.

98 "But your girdle," added Gawain, "may God reward you!
That I'll wear with good will, not for the fair gold,
for the sash or the silk or the side-pendants,   *2430*
not for wealth or honor or the proud workmanship,
but in sign of my ill-doing; I shall see it often
when I ride about, famous, and feel remorseful
for the faultiness and weakness of perverse flesh—
how fit it is to incur the stain of filth!   *2435*
Thus when pride pricks me for prowess in arms,
a look at this love-lace will bring my heart low.
But one thing, I pray you—be not displeased—
since you're lord of the land yonder where I lived
with you so worshipfully—may He reward you   *2440*
who upholds the heavens and reigns on high—
by what name you are rightly called, then no more?"
"That I shall tell thee," retorted the other.
"Bercilak de Hautdesert I am here called,
 by the might of Morgan le Faye, who dwells in my   *2445*
   mansion,
 by her skillful lore and well-learned tricks.
Many magic arts she once took from Merlin,

for she had pleasant love-affairs in times long past
with that notable wizard, as your knights at home
                    all know.   2450
        Morgan the goddess, she;
        that's her name—just so!
        There is none of high degree
        that she cannot lay low.

99 "She sent me in this garb to your glorious hall   2455
    to test its pride, and so prove true
    what is rumored, the renown of the Round Table.
    She worked this wonder on me to shake your wits,
    to so daunt Gwenevere as to make her die
    of dismay at that fellow who spoke like a phantom   2460
    with his head in his hands before the high table.
    She's the one now at home, that ancient lady;
    she is thy very aunt, Arthur's half-sister,
    daughter of Tintagel's Duchess, on whom trusty Uther
    begot Arthur, now so nobly renowned.   2465
    Therefore I urge thee, Knight, come to thine aunt,
    make merry in my house. My menials love thee,
    and Sir, I wish thee as well, by my faith,
    as any one under God, for thy great loyalty."
    He answered: No! He would not by any means.   2470
    They embrace and kiss, and commend one another
    to the Prince of paradise, and part right there
                    in the snow.
        Gawain on his horse is keen
        to be off to the King's court so.   2475
        And then the knight, bright green,
        goes where he wants to go.

100 Gawain rides through the world by wild ways now
     on Gryngolet, his life given back by grace.
     He lodged often in houses, and often outdoors,   2480

met adventures in the valleys and always vanquished;
I cannot tell everything in my tale at this time.
The hurt that he had in his neck was healing,
and around it he bore the glittering belt,
aslant like a baldric bound to his side,   *2485*
the lace in a knot tied under his left arm
as a token that he had been caught in a fault.
Thus the knight came back, safe and sound, to court.
Joy woke in that castle when the great King knew
that good Gawain had come; good news to him!   *2490*
The King kissed the knight, the Queen also,
then many goodly knights sought to greet him;
they asked how he fared, and he told them—fantastic!
He made known the grim troubles he had gone through:
what happened at the chapel, the knight's behavior,   *2495*
the love of the lady, and the lace at last.
He showed them the nick in his bare neck
that he got for disloyalty at the lord's hands,
                in blame.
       He grieved at his disgrace,   *2500*
       he groaned and took the blame;
       the blood rushed to his face
       when he told it, to his shame.

101 "See, Lord," said the knight as he handled the lace,
  "I bear this band round my neck, to blame me   *2505*
for the injury and the loss that I underwent,
for the cowardice and covetousness in which I was caught.
It's a token of the untruth in which I was taken;
I must wear it as long as my life lasts.
No one may hide a wrong, or ever remove it,   *2510*
for once fixed on him it cannot be unfastened."
The King comforted the knight, and the court also
laughed loudly at all this; they courteously agreed
—those lords and ladies who belonged to the Table—

that each of the brotherhood should have a baldric 2515
of bright green bound obliquely about him,
and for that knight's sake should wear the same.
That was agreed on, for the good of the Round Table,
and anyone wearing it was honored ever after,
as written in the best of the books of romance. 2520
Thus in Arthur's times this adventure took place,
and all the Brut books bear witness to it.
Since the bold Brutus first abode here
after the seige and the assault had ceased at Troy,
              I know 2525
      such adventures here-to-fore
      have befallen, long ago.
      May He who a thorn-crown wore
      to His own bliss bring us so!

                Amen
HONY SOYT QUI MAL PENCE.

PEARL

I

1 Pearl, pleasing in a Prince's way
when he sets her in gold, clean-cut, clear!
Oriental; I make bold to say
I never found a more precious, her peer.
So round, so perfect to display,   5
so small, so smooth her contours were,
that, whenever judging a gem's clear ray,
I set her apart, singularly dear.
But Oh! In a garden I lost her. Here
it slipped to the ground in a grassy plot.   10
I waste away, wounded by Love's fear
for the pearl, all mine, with no spot.

2 Since then, in the spot where it sprang from me
I keep watch, longing for that rich thing
that once, when I grieved, could set me free,   15
lift me up, hold me in well-being.
It bruises my heart now, heavily,
swells in my breast with a burning sting.

Yet a sweeter song could never be
that what, in a still hour, came stealing;   20
then more songs drifted, echoing,
as I thought of her color blurred by earth's clot.
Mould! Thou art marring a jewel-like thing,
the pearl, all mine, with no spot.

3   With spice that spot should be overspread;   25
     where such richness ran to rot, undone,
     blossoms pale and blue and red
     shine now, brilliant against the sun.
     Where it fell, no flowers or fruits will shed
     their colors on that soil dank and dun;   30
     all grass must grow from grain that is dead,
     or—no wheat for homes, no harvest won!
     From a good thing another is thus begun;
     so fair a seed could fail us not,
     nor springing spices ever have done   35
     from that precious pearl with no spot.

4   Once, in that same spot, as I say,
     I entered the garden, freshly green
     in August, on a great feast day,
     when scythes sweep the corn down, cutting clean.   40
     One mound, where the pearl had rolled away,
     was shadowed by spice-plants of glinting sheen,
     gilly-flowers, ginger and gromwell, gay
     with peonies scattered in between.
     If the place was beautiful, so seen,   45
     scents no less lovely drifted there;
     it has a worthy home, I mean
     my pearl of no spot, precious, rare.

5   By that spot I clasped my hands, aware
     of a chilling sorrow that held me caught;   50

in my heart, deep-hid, lay desolate care,
though reason could bring me peace, long-sought.
I mourned for my pearl imprisoned there,
I struggled with my restless thought;
though in Christ's own being my comfort were,   55
my wretched will, in woe, still fought.
I fell on the turf, flower-enwrought;
such fragrance made my senses whirl
that I slipped away, at sleep's onslaught,
over my precious, spotless pearl.   60

I I

6 From that spot my spirit sprang, in a trace;
on the bank my body lay dreamily.
My soul had gone, by God's grace,
adventuring where marvels be.
In the whole world I knew no such place;   65
I found cliffs around me, cleft sharply.
Towards a forest I turned my face,
where those rich rocks appeared to me.
Such light no man could hope to see,
such glory, gleaming and glowing there!   70
No fabric, man-woven, could ever be
half so richly adorned and rare.

7 Adorned like this was each hill-side
with crystal cliffs, clear-shining, high;
around, a bright wood stretching wide   75
with tree-trunks blue as indigo dye.
Like burnished silver the leaves slide
and quiver; thick on the boughs they lie.
When gleams from the open sky there glide
they shimmer with piercing light on high.   80
The gravel I crunched on the ground thereby

was precious pearls of orient ware;
sunbeams seem dark and dim to vie
with those adornments shining there.

8   The adornment of the precious hill   *85*
made my sad soul forget its state.
Like fresh fruit flavors it could fill
pleasantly, as good foods sate.
Flocks flew through the forest still,
in flaming colors, birds small and great;   *90*
lute and guitar, though played with skill,
for mirth so buoyant are no mate.
Those birds beating their wings, elate,
sang out in sweetest harmony.
What joy more welcome could await   *95*
in lands so adorned, than just hear and see!

9   All adorned in this lavish wise
was that forest where Fortune guided me;
its splendor no man could devise,
for no-one could have a tongue worthy.   *100*
I walked straight on in glad surprise—
no hill so high as to hinder me.
The farther, the fairer to my eyes
were the plain, the spice-plants, each pear tree,
hedgerows, water-lands lush to see;   *105*
like fine-spun gold the banks shone there.
I came where a stream swept by, swiftly.
Lord, its adornments were so rare!

10   Adorning the rich stream were its steep
banks, splendid with beryls, bright.   *110*
Singing sweetly, the waters sweep
with whispering sounds in unswerving flight.
Brilliant stones shine up from the deep;

they glint as through glass that glows alight,
as gleaming stars, when earth-men sleep,   *115*
stare down from the sky on a winter night.
In the pool every pebble in plain sight
was emerald, sapphire, or gem as rare,
till all the water glanced with light,
its adornments were so richly fair.   *120*

III

11   The rich adornments of hill and dale,
of wood and water and proud plain,
made bliss over woe at last prevail,
quieting sorrow, calming pain.
By a stream whose waters never fail   *125*
I roamed in bliss; brimfull my brain!
The further I followed that watered vale
my heart's joy sang a stronger strain.
For when Fortune tests, she may wax or wane,
she may send solace or make hearts sore,   *130*
but the man to whom she grants some gain
is likely to have still more, then more.

12   There was more joy in this same wise
than I could tell, though time delayed;
for an earthly heart cannot suffice   *135*
for a tithe of that joy with no shade.
And so I thought that Paradise
there, beyond those broad banks, stayed,
and I thought the water some device
for pleasure-gardens where streams played.   *140*
Beyond the brook, by hill or glade,
I looked for some walled town on the shore.
But the water was deep, I dared not wade
and still I longed; yes, more and more.

13 More and more, and yet still more   145
    I longed to see past the brook's strand,
    for if the place where I walked was fair,
    far lovelier was the distant land.
    I could but stumble around and stare,
    and hurry to find some ford at hand,   150
    but more perils, indeed, were there,
    the further I stole on by the strand.
    I knew I should not shrink, but stand
    where there was beauteous wealth to find.
    Then a new marvel came to hand;   155
    more and still more it stirred my mind.

14 Marvelling more, my thoughts went wild.
    Beyond that bright stream I could see
    a shimmering crystal cliff, high-piled;
    light-rays shone from it royally.   160
    At its foot there sat a child,
    a maiden of courteous dignity;
    her white mantle gleamed undefiled.
    She—seen before—was well-known to me.
    Like glistening gold worked artfully,   165
    so shone that fair one on the shore.
    I looked upon her lingeringly,
    and still I knew her, more and more.

15 The more I searched her lovely face
    and slendor form, trying to know,   170
    a gladdening glory came to embrace
    me then, unfelt a while ago.
    I longed to call her—my thoughts a-race—
    but amazement dealt my heart a blow;
    to see her in so strange a place!   175
    The shock might well lay my heart low.
    She lifted her fair brow, to show

a face white as polished ivory.
It stung my heart, and stunned it so
that, the longer, the more it was so with me.   *180*

I V

16   More than I wished my dread arose;
I stood stock still and dared not call.
With eyes open and mouth held close
I stood quiet, like a hawk in a hall.
Some mystic meaning, I knew, would unclose.   *185*
I dreaded what might then befall
lest she escape me whom I there chose
before I could hold her by my call.
Fair, gracious, with no fault at all,
so smooth, so small, so fitly slight,   *190*
she rises up—her array royal—
a precious thing in pearls set right.

17   Pearls of great price, set royally,
a man so favored could have seen
when she, fresh as a fleur-de-lys,   *195*
came straight down the bank between.
She was dressed in dazzling linen, free
at open sides, and bordered clean
with marjory-gems, as gay as could be,
the loveliest I have ever seen.   *200*
Ample her long sleeves must have been,
adorned by double pearls, made fair,
her skirts were of the same rich sheen
with precious pearls set everywhere.

18   A well-set crown she wore, that girl,   *205*
of no other stones than marjory,
high-pinnacled, of clear white pearl

in figured flowers formed perfectly,
and no other headpiece save this furl.
her hair enclosed her, hanging free   210
round a face grave as a duke or earl,
of complexion whiter than ivory.
Hair, shining like spun gold brilliantly,
unbound on her shoulders lightly lay.
Her clear color matched fittingly   215
the rare pearls set in her array.

19 In her cuffs and hems were stones, set right
at hands and sides and openings, pure
with no other gems than pearls all white,
and glittering white was her vesture.   220
But a wondrous pearl, unblemished, bright,
lay on her breast, set there secure;
a man would be baffled to judge it right
and value it by a true measure.
No tongue, I think, ever could be sure   225
to find words fit for that vision yet,
so clean it was, and clear and pure—
that precious pearl where it was set!

20 Set in pearls, that precious piece
overstream drew closer than before.   230
No gladder man from here to Greece
than I, when she stood thus on the shore.
She was nearer to me than aunt or niece,
and so, when she spoke to me, the more
that rare spice made my joy increase.   235
Inclining low, with womanly lore,
she took off the treasure-crown she wore
and hailed me with a welcoming air.
This (happy me!) was I born for,
to answer that pearl-set sweet one there.   240

V

21 "O Pearl," said I, "in pearls set bright,
    art thou my Pearl for whom I mourn,
    grieving all alone at night?
    I hid my longing for thee, pain-worn,
    when, through the grass, thou wast lost to sight.   *245*
    I am pensive, broken, quite forlorn—
    and thou in a life of joyous light
    in paradise, by pain unworn!
    While I so suffered, what Wyrd had borne
    my jewel here, while I ached for her?   *250*
    Since parting—from one another torn—
    I have been a joyless jeweler!"

22 That Jewel, with other fine gems blent,
    lifted her face with eyes of gray,
    put on her crown from the Orient   *255*
    and then, gravely, began to say:
    "Sir, your tale has a wrong intent,
    saying your pearl has gone away
    when it lies in a fine-made coffer, pent
    in this very garden, graciously gay,   *260*
    here to linger forever, and play
    where no loss or mourning come to her.
    Here would thy treasure-chest be, I say,
    wert thou a gracious jeweler.

23 "But, gracious jeweler, if thou wilt lose   *265*
    thy joy for a gem once dear to thee,
    now thou art mad, I think, to choose
    a passing thing, unreasonably.
    What thou hast lost is but a rose
    that flowered and failed; so it must be!   *270*
    But a chest of this kind may enclose

a priceless pearl; test it and see!
Thou hast called thy Wyrd a thief, but He
makes something from nothing—that is clear.
Thou blamest the cure of thy misery;   275
thou art not truly a jeweler!"

24   A jewel was she to me—my guest;
     fair jewels the words I heard her say.
   "In truth," said I, "dearest and best,
     thou hast driven my anguish far away.   280
     So, pray excuse me, I request;
     I thought my pearl lost from light of day.
     Now I have found it; I am twice blest!
     With it, in these bright woods I stay,
     praising my Lord and His law; today   285
     He has brought my bliss so very near!
     Were I with you, over this water-way,
     I would be a joyful jeweler!"

25 "Jeweler," said that Gem, bright-clean,
     "Why do men jest? They speak madly!   290
     Thou hast said three things; they have been
     ill-advised, in truth, all three.
     Thou hast no notion what they mean;
     thy words before thy wits still flee!
     Thou believest because thine eyes have seen   295
     here in this valley—even me!
     Again thou sayest: in this country
     thyself wilt dwell with me, right here.
     Third: over this bright stream thou wilt be.
     Not so—for a joyful jeweler!   300

V I

26 "I give that jeweler little praise
     who believes by seeing with his own eye;

blameworthy, of discourteous ways,
he thinks Our Lord would tell a lie,
when He gave His loyal pledge to raise   305
your life, though Fortune made you die!
You set His words contrariways
to believe but what you can descry.
It is a sign of pride too high,
unbefitting what good men know,   310
to think no tale true till they try
with their own minds to judge it so.

27 "Judge now: what a flippant thing to say,
a man throwing words at God, freely!
Thou sayest in this realm thou wilt stay.   315
Thou shouldst first ask leave, it seems to me,
and leave might not to be given today.
Then, over this water thou wouldst flee.
Thou must first submit to Another's way;
cold, deep in clay, will thy body be.   320
It was hurt in paradise-groves where he,
our first-father, ruined it.
Through death must a man go, painfully,
till beyond this stream God judge him fit."

28 "Wilt thou judge me," said I, "Sweet One,   325
to grief again? I am brought low!
Now that my loss has been re-won
why must I once more let it go?
Why hold then miss it, till life has run?
My precious Pearl brings me great woe.   330
What good a treasure that a man has won
but to lose again? His tears must flow!
Now I care not if, cast below,
far from this land I am driven again.
When I am parted from my Pearl so,   335
to what am I judged but endless pain?"

29 "Thou canst only judge of dire distress,"
 the maiden said. "Why dost thou so?
 In noisy grief, though the loss be less,
 some greater good men may forego.   340
 Better: thou thyself shouldst bless
 and praise God always, in joy or woe,
 for anger gains thee not a cress.
 He who must suffer should not rage so!
 Though thou dance about like any doe,   345
 writhe, and bray out thine agony,
 thou canst no more go to and fro,
 thou must take the judgment passed on thee.

30 "Judge the Lord! Question His right!
 He will not stir one foot from the way.   350
 Thou art no better off, by one mite,
 if thou in gloom so choose to stay!
 Stop thy striving, cease to fight;
 now seek His favor with no delay.
 At thy prayer His pity will alight,   355
 His mercy hold thee in its sway.
 His comfort, lifting thy care away,
 will lightly drive all grief from thee.
 Blunder, go mad, mourn, hide from day—
 with Him it lies to judge and decree!"   360

VII

31 I answered that fair maid, judging:
 "Let it not offend my Lord
 if, raving, I stumbled at this thing.
 In my heart a sense of loss was stored
 like water welling from a spring.   365
 I yield; His mercy is my reward.
 Rebuke me not with words that sting

although I stray, my dear Adored.
Be kind, be pitying, afford
me comfort, while you think of this: 370
you made sorrow and me accord,
you—once the ground of all my bliss!

32 "My bliss, my woe—you were both for me,
but still more you made me moan;
when, from these perils, thou wert set free,   375
I never knew where my Pearl had flown.
My loss is less now that I see.
Once we were one, now each alone,
so God forbid we should be angry.
We meet so seldom by stock or stone!   380
Though courteously you still speak on,
I am but dust; my ways are amiss.
But Christ's mercy, and Mary and John,
these are the ground of all my bliss.

33 "In bliss I see you set anew,   385
I—crushed and in a mournful state!
You, it seems, will have little to do
with this, while in burning grief I wait.
But now I am present, here with you,
and I beseech you, without debate,   390
that you would tell me straight and true
what life you lead, early and late.
For I am happy that your estate
is changed to honor and wealth like this;
it is a highway, leading straight   395
to joy, the ground of all my bliss."

34 "And bliss, Sir, now is on thy side!"
said she, her form and face so clear!
"Be welcome, walk here and abide,

for now to me thy speech is dear.   *400*
Masterful moods and high pride,
I assure thee, are heartily hated here.
My Lord is not the one to chide;
the meek dwell with Him, very near.
When in His home thou shalt appear,   *405*
show deep devotion, be meek like this.
My Lord the Lamb well loves such cheer;
He is the ground of all my bliss.

35 "Thou sayest: a blissful life I've led,
and thou wouldst know its every stage.   *410*
Thou knowest well, when thy pearl fled
I was still young, of tender age.
But my Lord the Lamb, through His godhead,
took me to Himself in marriage,
crowned me His queen, blissfully wed   *415*
for length of days, He keeps His gage,
and possessed of all His heritage
is His beloved. I am wholly His!
His worth and His noble lineage
are the root and ground of all my bliss."   *420*

VIII

36 "Blissful," said I, "can this be true?
Be not displeased if I speak error.
Art thou the Queen of heaven's blue
to whom the whole world gives honor?
We believe in Mary from whom grace grew,   *425*
who bore a Child, a virgin-flower.
Who could uncrown her, save one who
was higher than she in some favor?
Yet, for the peerless sweetness of her,

we call her Phoenix of Araby 430
who, flawless, flew from her Maker,
the very Queen of courtesy."

37 "Courteous Queen!" that fair one said
while, kneeling down, she hid her face.
"Matchless mother, happiest maid, 435
blessed fountain of every grace!"
Then she arose and, lingering, stayed,
speaking to me across that space:
"Sir, here many strive to be well paid,
but no supplanters are in this place. 440
She is an Empress; she can embrace
all heaven, with earth and hell in fee.
From his heritage she will displace
no-one, as Queen of courtesy.

38 "The kingly court of the God of life 445
has this property of its own being:
each one of all those who arrive,
over that whole realm is queen or king.
Yet no-one ever would deprive
another, but (glad of his having) 450
wishes his crown were but worth five,
if possible were its enhancing.
My Lady, who is our Jesus-spring,
holds power over this company,
and that grieves none of our gathering, 455
for she is the Queen of courtesy.

39 "By courtesy, as Saint Paul said,
members of Jesus Christ are we,
as leg or arm, navel or head,
joined to His body unbreakably. 460
Just so, each Christian soul is bred

a limb of that Master of mystery.
Then how could hate or spite instead
be twined among limbs knit so closely!
Thy head feels no grief, spitefully,   465
if, on arm or finger, a ring is seen;
so we live in love, each one happy,
by courtesy a king or queen."

40 "Courtesy, I believe," said I,
and charity unite your throng.   470
But—twist not my words awry—
I think what thou hast said is wrong.
In heaven thou risest up too high
to make thyself queen—thou so young!
For what higher honor could one try   475
who in this world endured, strong
to live in penance his whole life long
and buy bliss, suffering bodily?
What greater worship could belong
to such, then be king by courtesy?   480

IX

41 "That courtesy is too off-hand,
if that be true—what thou dost say.
Thou didst not live two years in our land,
unable to please God or pray,
or Pater and Creed to understand—   485
and made a queen on the first day!
I cannot think—on God's witness-stand—
that He would work in so wrong a way.
A countess, my fair child—no withsay—
is in heaven a good enough degree,   490
or a lady entitled to less array.
But a queen! An end too high for thee!"

42 "No end to His goodness; it can surpass
    all limits," said that maid so bright.
    "All rings true that He brings to pass;   *495*
    He can do nothing but what is right.
    As Matthew tells us in the mass
    (true gospel of the Lord of might
    set in a parable it was)
    He likens it to heaven's light.   *500*
    'My kingdom,' He says, 'set on a height,
    is like a lord with a vineyard fair.'
    When the year's best season comes in sight
    his end is to dress the vines with care.

43 "His household know the year's end, too.   *505*
    The lord at early dawn arose
    to hire for his vineyard workmen new
    and fit for his purpose; these he chose.
    They all agree; they will be true
    for a penny a day. Then each one goes   *510*
    to toil at the painful work they do
    cutting the clusters, binding them close.
    Once more, near noon, the master goes
    to market; men idle time away.
    'Why stand here idle?' he says to those.   *515*
    'Don't you know what end is set for today?'

44 " 'We're here for that end!' So from all
    together came the answer sought.
    'Since sunrise we have stood on call;
    no man has bidden us do aught.'   *520*
    'In my vineyard take what may befall,'
    said the lord; and so the bargain caught.
    'A reasonable wage, before nightfall,
    I shall pay to each, in deed and thought.'
    They worked that vineyard as they ought;   *525*

all the day the lord went on his way
and still into his vineyard brought
new men, till near the end of day.

45   "Day's end drew near; at evensong
    one hour before the sun had flown,   530
    he saw men idle still, though strong,
    and said to them in a serious tone:
    'Why stand here idle all day long?'
    'Unhired,' they said, 'we're left alone.'
    'Go to my vineyard, yeomen young,   535
    and work, each one as he is shown.'
    It was late; soon all the world had grown
    dark as the sun went down at last.
    He called each man to claim his own,
    for now the end of the day had passed.   540

X

46   "At the day's end the lord will go
    and call his foreman: 'Hand out the pay!
    Give all of them the money I owe
    and—lest they murmur—do it this way:
    just stand them all up in a row,   545
    give each alike his penny-a-day;
    begin with the late ones who stand low
    and end with the first to come today.'
    Bitterly, the first complain and say
    they have endured toil long and sore.   550
    'These but one hour have labored away;
    we think that we should get still more!

47   "'We have served more (as we should know
    who suffered from the heat all day)
    than those who worked two hours or so,   555

yet you treat us all in the same way!'
The lord then said to one man: 'No!
My friend, I have not lowered thy pay;
just take what is thine own and go.
I hired for a round sum, a penny a day. 560
Why threaten and grow angry? Stay:
didst thou agree to a penny before?
With a contract there's no more to say;
so why shouldst thou still ask for more?

48 " 'Still more, is my gift my lawful right? 565
May I do with my own as it pleases me?
Or has thine eye an evil sight
when I am kind, treating none falsely?'
'And thus,' said Christ, 'I plan aright:
the last who come are first, and he 570
who was first is last, for all his might;
of those called, few are chosen by me.'
Poor men gather their portion free,
though they come late with little in store,
and should their toil turn out meagrely 575
the mercy of God is much the more.

49 "I have more bliss and joy herein,
more life's bloom, full and womanly,
than all men in the world could win
if they claimed earnings rightfully. 580
Though it was late when I could begin
(at evening the vineyard welcomed me)
my Lord remembers my hire therein;
I am paid at once the whole wage, free.
Others, who spent more time maybe, 585
who toiled and sweated long of yore,
may take home nothing of their fee,
nor will, perhaps for years, earn more."

50   Then I said more, and spoke frankly:
    "I think thy tale unreasonable.   590
    God's justice is firm, fixed lastingly,
    or Holy Writ is but a fable.
    A verse of the Psalms speaks openly
    and lays down a point determinable:
    'Thou wilt pay what each man earns of Thee,   595
    High-King of will pre-ordainable.'
    If one stood all day, firmly stable,
    and thou for payment cut in before,
    then those working less get more, are able
    to do always less and be payed more."   600

XI

51 "With more or less, where God's rule sways,"
    said she, "there is no unfair play.
    Each man alike He there repays
    though small or great the sum may be.
    Our courteous Lord has no niggard ways.   605
    Pleasant or hard things pour out, free
    as a gushing dyke; He gives always
    like wells overflowing ceaselessly.
    Free gifts come to him who daringly
    goes to the One who saves from sin;   610
    no bliss is held back from such as he,
    for great enough God's grace has been.

52 "Enough! This move is my checkmate:
    wrongly I took my penny! I dare,
    thou sayest (I who came too late),   615
    to claim, unworthy, a fee so rare.
    But is there a man who does not abate,
    though ever so holy in his prayer,

who does not forfeit his estate
sometimes, with less of heavenly share?   620
The oftener the more years they bear
men leave the right for something base.
May gracious mercy guide them there,
for great enough is God's grace!

53 "But grace enough have the innocent.   625
    When they are born they go straightway
    through baptismal waters; their descent
    opens the vineyard wide that day.
    At last the light with dark is blent;
    the night of death then turns those away   630
    who did no wrong before they went.
    The courteous Lord will surely pay,
    for His own are with Him; they obey.
    Why cannot He allow for their case,
    yes, pay them fully, as He may?   635
    For great enough is God's grace.

54 "Man's noble race (enough to tell)
    for perfect bliss was formed aright;
    but from it our first-father fell
    because of an apple he chose to bite.   640
    For that food all were damned as well,
    to die in anguish, far from delight,
    then go down into burning hell
    and live on there with no respite.
    But soon the right cure met our sight;   645
    rich blood ran down the cross so rough,
    and beauteous water. In that plight
    the grace of God grew great enough.

55 "Enough came flowing from that well
    of blood and water, the broad wound.   650

The blood bought us from the pains of hell,
from a second death, all safe and sound!
The water is baptism, truth to tell;
it followed the lance-point sharply ground,
and washed us from the guilt that fell   655
on all whom Adam in death once drowned.
There is nothing now in the whole world round
to block our bliss; what He withdrew
is, in a happy hour, refound.
Great enough is God's grace anew.   660

XII

56 "Grace enough that man may have
who sins again, if he repent;
this with keen sorrow he must crave,
and bear whatever pain is lent.
But reason by right will always save,   665
unerringly, the innocent.
There is one doom God never gave:
a guiltless soul to perdition sent!
The guilty, on contrition bent,
is drawn by mercy to grace, secure,   670
and one who towards evil never went
through innocence is rightly sure!

57 "I know right well that in this case
two men are saved; they each fulfill
His plan: the just shall see His face,   675
and the sinless one come to Him still.
A Psalm has put it, in brief space:
'Lord, who shall climb Thy high hill
or rest within Thy holy place?'
His answer comes with ready will: 680
'The one whose hands have done no ill,

the one whose heart is clean and light;
there shall his steps at last stand still.'
The innocent is saved by right.

58 "The righteous man shall—once again—   685
approach His palace of royal style;
he does not spend his life in vain
or cheat his neighbor with any guile.
Of the just man Solomon says plain
that Wisdom pays him honor, while   690
by straight ways still she must constrain;
she shows him the realm of God awhile
and says: 'Behold! That lovely isle!
Thou canst win it, if thou art brave.'
But more surely, with no such trial,   695
the innocent, rightly, He will save.

59 "And thus of righteous men speaks one
—David, whose Psalms are not belied—
'Lord, judge not Thy servant for deeds done
for no living man is justified.'   700
So, when an entrance has been won
to the court where all causes must be tried,
pleading thy rights thou couldst be undone
by those same words that I implied.
But He who bled on the cross, and died   705
with hands pierced through in a painful plight,
may let thee pass when thou art tried
by innocence and not by right.

60 "One reading rightly, to understand,
may look in the Book, where it says clear   710
that Jesus walked in an ancient land
where people brought their little ones near,
for joy and health came from His hand.

They prayed Him: 'Touch our children here!'
Disciples, fault-finding, bade them stand;   715
their stern rebukes made many fear.
But Jesus sweetly brought good cheer:
'Not so! Let the children come to me;
to such will heaven's realm appear.'
The innocent are saved rightly.   720

XIII

61 "Jesus called to Him the mild,
saying His realm no man could win
unless he came there like a child;
never, else, would he come therein.
If blameless, true and undefiled,   725
with no spot or speck of staining sin,
one knocks at that home thus unbeguiled,
the doors swing wide to let him in.
Unfading bliss is found within.
This, of all gems, the jeweler sought,   730
and sold all, woolen and fine linen,
for a spotless pearl which he thus bought.

62 "The spotless pearl thus bought so dear
(the jeweler gave his goods gladly)
is heaven's kingdom, shining clear;   735
so said the Father of land and sea.
For it is stainless, a clean sphere,
well-rounded, holding serenity,
common to all the righteous here.
Upon my breast it now lies. See!   740
My Lord the Lamb, who shed blood for me,
in token of peace has placed it there.
Leave this mad world, I counsel thee,
and buy thy pearl, spotlessly fair."

63 "O spotless Pearl, in pearls so pure,   745
    wearing that priceless pearl I see,
    who was it fashioned thy fair figure?
    Who made thy robe? Most wise was he!
    Thy beauty came not from nature,
    Pygmalion never painted thee,   750
    Aristotle, who wrote so sure,
    spoke nowhere of such rare property.
    Thy color defies the fleur-de-lys,
    thy angel-bearing, exquisite, clean.
    Tell me, Bright One, what role has she   755
    who wears that pearl of spotless sheen?"

64 "My spotless Lamb, making all complete,"
    said she, "for my high destiny
    chose me as bride, although unmeet
    such a union once seemed to be;   760
    When I left your world, cold with sleet,
    to His own blessedness He called me,
    'Come here to me, my true love sweet;
    no spot or stain is found in thee.'
    He gave me strength and rare beauty;   765
    in His blood He washed my robes, and here
    crowned me in clean virginity
    and set me with pearls, spotlessly clear."

65 "Why, spotless bride now flaming bright
    with full refulgent royalty,   770
    does thy Lamb act thus? Was He right
    when, as His wife, He wedded thee?
    Thou hast climbed over others to this height,
    living with Him as a fine lady.
    There are many well-robed ones who might   775
    have striven for Christ's sake valiantly.
    Thou hast driven away those more worthy,

deprived them of such a marriage; grown
(thou only) strong enough to be
a matchless, spotless maid—alone!"   780

XIV

66 "Spotless," said that happy queen,
    "unblemished, I, from all stains free,
    and this is honorable, I mean;
    but 'peerless queen' I claim not to be.
    In bliss the Lamb's brides we have been,   785
    one hundred forty-four thousand we,
    as in the Apocalypse is seen.
    Saint John saw them all in company
    on Sion's mountain of great beauty.
    The apostle, in mystic dream, saw them   790
    on the hill-top, in wedding panoply
    in the new city, Jerusalem.

67 "About Jerusalem let me tell.
    If thou ask of what kind He may be
    (my Lamb, my Lord, my dear Jewel,   795
    my Joy, my Bliss, my Loved One, He!),
    the Prophet Isaiah once spoke well
    of His gentleness, compassionately:
    'That glorious Innocent they will quell
    with no proved cause of felony;   800
    like a sheep led off for butchery,
    like a lamb the shearer takes in hand,
    He closed His mouth at each query
    in Jerusalem, on the judgment-stand.'

68 "In Jerusalem was my Loved One slain,   805
    torn on the cross by ruffians bold.
    Eager to carry all our pain,

He took up the woes that strike us cold.
His face was marred by blow and stain,
that face once beautiful to behold!   810
For sin, He held His life as vain,
while of Him no sin was ever told.
He let them scourge Him, let them hold
and stretch Him on the rugged cross;
a meek Lamb uncomplaining, sold   815
in Jerusalem, He died for us.

69 "In Jerusalem, Jordan, and Galilee
the good Saint John baptized alone;
he spoke as Isaiah had, when he
saw Jesus walking; this was shown   820
to him as in a prophecy:
'See! God's Lamb, as true as stone,
who roots out sin with which, heavily,
the whole world now is overgrown.
He who sinned not makes His own   825
the sins of all men, claiming them.
His generation who has known?
He died for us in Jerusalem.'

70 "In Jerusalem my sweet Loved One
thus with a lamb could twice compare   830
(as true tales of both Prophets run)
for His meek heart and ways so fair.
A third time He is still so known,
as told in the Apocalypse, where
among saints seated near the throne   835
the Apostle saw Him clearly. There
He loosed the Book with its leaves cut square
from the seven signets clasping them.
At the sight each strong bowed, aware,
in hell, on earth, in Jerusalem.   840

XV

71 "This Lamb in Jerusalem had no stain,
and no color save sparkling white
where never spot nor speck had lain,
the white wool was so thick and bright.
So is each soul that can remain 845
spotless: the Lamb's honored wife.
Though daily He brings more again,
among us is no wrangling strife.
We wish each single one were five—
the more the merrier! Such will God bless. 850
Great company makes our love thrive
in honor more, and never less.

72 "A lesser bliss no-one can bring
to us, with this pearl on our breast;
we never think of quarreling 855
who wear these spotless pearls as crest.
Though our clay bodies lie shrivelling
and you weep, grieving without rest,
throughout, we understand this thing;
by one Death alone our hope is blessed. 860
The Lamb delights us; how be distressed?
His feast brims over with joyfulness.
The bliss of each is full—the best!
Yet no-one's honor is the less.

73 "If now thou canst less understand 865
my tale, the Apocalypse is true:
'There I saw,' says John,' the Lamb stand
on Sion's mount, strong, fair to view
with His maidens, one hundred thousand and
forty-four thousand—not a few! 870
Marked on each forehead in that band

I saw the Lamb's name, His Father's too.
From heaven I heard a sound; it grew
like full floods rushing on with power,
like thunder in dark hills, rolling through;   *875*
no less the sound heard in that hour.

74 " 'No less—although that sound might ring
on high, and loud those voices were—
a song all new I heard them sing,
lovely to listen to. And there,   *880*
like harpers harping on each string,
they sang that new song clear and fair
in ringing tones—an exquisite thing;
its modes were linked in unison rare.
And right before God's high throne, where   *885*
the four Beasts bend in humbleness
and the Elders also, with grave care,
they sang their new song nonetheless.

75 " 'But nonetheless, no men have skill,
for all the arts they ever knew,   *890*
to sing one note of that song, until
they join the Lamb's close followers, who
are brought, removed from earth; they still
are first-fruits to God's service due;
knit to the gentle Lamb, they will   *895*
be very like Him in speech and hue.
For never a lie or a tale untrue
has touched their tongue under any stress.
That pure household never withdrew
from their all-pure Master, nonetheless.' "   *900*

76 "Yet no less may my thanks be told,
my Pearl," said I, "although I pose
questions to test thy wisdom, bold

before the bride whom Christ so chose!
I am made up of dust and mould, 905
and thou so fair and fresh a rose
beside this stream where bliss, untold
in life, comes never to a close!
Lady, thy simplicity grows.
I ask one thing, in all frankness— 910
I, a churl blundering as he goes;
let my prayer avail now, nonetheless.

XVI

77 "Nonetheless, on you I surely call,
—if it please you to do your share!
Thou art so glorious, with no fault at all, 915
do not say no to my wistful prayer!
Have you no home, no castle wall,
no manor to gather and dwell in there?
Thou hast named Jerusalem's royal hall
where David ruled from his kingly chair. 920
It is not in these groves anywhere,
that fine home, but in Judah's land.
As under the moon you walk, spotless, fair,
spotless, too, should your dwelling stand.

78 "For this spotless band where, thou wouldst say, 925
thousands are crowding in a rout,
a great city where many stay
you needs must have, beyond a doubt.
Such a cluster of jewels, brightly gay,
should not be left lying without, 930
and near these banks where I roam today
I see no dwellings scattered about.
You walk alone, winding in and out
by this stream splendid to gaze upon.

If your stately home stands hereabout,   935
   to that happy spot now lead me on."

79 "That spot thou hast named, in Judah's land,"
    so that rare spice answered me,
  "a city that saw the Lamb once stand
   and suffer for mankind's sake, sorely,   940
  was the old Jerusalem, understand,
   that wiped out the old sin, finally.
  The new, come down by God's command,
   Saint John's Apocalypse shows clearly.
  To it the Lamb, from dark stains free,   945
   has led His company so fair;
  and, as His flock unflecked must be,
   so without spot is His city there.

80 "To speak clearly: two spots are seen;
   Jerusalem is their name apiece.   950
  Nothing more can that name mean
   than 'City of God' or 'Sight of Peace.'
  In one, our lives were made serene
   when the Lamb chose pain for our release;
  the other holds only peace to glean   955
   everlastingly, without cease.
  We press on towards that city's peace,
   for, when our flesh is laid to rot,
  there bliss and glory still increase
   for that company without a spot."   960

81 "Mild, spotless maid, who speaks humbly,"
   so I answered that lovely flower,
  "open thy pleasant home to me
   and let me see thy blissful bower."
  She said: "God will not let that be;   965
   thou canst not enter His own tower.

But I have asked the Lamb for thee
a favor: to glimpse it in this hour,
to see from without my cloister dower;
but put in one foot—thou mayest not!   *970*
To walk those streets thou hast no power
unless thou be clean, with no spot.

XVII

82 "This very spot shall open wide.
Go up, where the river rises free;
I will follow on the other side   *975*
until a hill-top opens to thee."
At that, I could no longer bide;
under full-leaved boughs I moved quietly
until I saw on a mountain-side,
while I pressed on, that brave city   *980*
beyond the brook, half-hid from me,
that brighter than shafted sunlight shone.
The Apocalypse draws it so, clearly
pictured by the Apostle John.

83 What John the Apostle once could see   *985*
I saw: a city of great renown,
Jerusalem, new-made royally
as though from heaven coming down.
Golden it burned, that bright city
that gleamed like glass, burnished gold-brown,   *990*
with noble gems ranged skilfully,
with twelve bantels well fastened down
on twelve foundations, in a rich crown.
Like a different jewel each storey shone.
He splendidly pictured this same town   *995*
in his Apocalypse, the Apostle John.

84   Every stone John's writings trace;
     I knew each that he named for me.
     Jasper, the first gem, found a place
     in the lowest wall that I could see;   1000
     it glinted green on its surface.
     Sapphire held the second degree;
     chalcedony, with flawless face
     there on the third tier shone palely.
     Emerald, the fourth, was green to see,   1005
     sardonyx then was the fifth stone,
     ruby the sixth; so they must be,
     from the Apocalypse of Saint John.

85   To these John joined the chrysolite,
     seventh in the wall-stones, where   1010
     the eighth was beryl, clear and white;
     twin-toned topaz in the ninth stair.
     Chrysopras, the tenth, is set right,
     jacynth, the eleventh gem, is rare;
     the twelfth, with power for any plight,   1015
     was amethyst, purple with blue blent fair.
     The walls set firm on the bantels were
     jasper; like dazzling glass they shone.
     I knew them by description, there
     in the Apocalypse of the Apostle John.   1020

86   What John pictured was really there:
     those twelve tiers broad and steep, upright.
     The city stood above, four-square,
     the same in length and breadth and height,
     with streets of gold, like glass laid bare   1025
     and walls of jasper glinting white.
     Its dwellings were adorned, all fair
     with endless precious jewels alight.
     The estate's square sides stretched far in sight,

for full twelve furlongs running on,   *1030*
equal in length and breadth and height;
he saw it measured, the Apostle John.

XVIII

87   More of what John wrote I could see:
on each side was a triple gate,
twelve in the circling wall. Richly   *1035*
those portals were set with precious plate,
each formed from a single marjory,
a pearl keeping its perfect state.
On each was written a name, clearly,
Israel's children in ordered rate,   *1040*
that is, according to birth-date,
the eldest first; so it was done.
A light gleamed from those streets, so great
they needed neither moon nor sun.

88   Of sun or moon they had no need   *1045*
when God Himself was their lamplight,
the Lamb their lantern, He indeed;
by Him that city gleamed so bright.
Through walls and homes my look pierced, freed
by that piercingly clear light.   *1050*
There is the high throne, if you heed,
with all its adornments in full sight
(as John the Apostle was bidden write)
for the high God to sit upon.
From the throne a river rushed with might;   *1055*
brighter than sun or moon it shone.

89   No lovelier shone the moon or sun
than the plentiful, outwelling flood,
strongly, through each street, rushing on,

bearing no dirt or slime or mud.   1060
There is no church to look upon
where no chapel has ever stood;
their church: the Almighty, a perfect one;
the Lamb, their sacrifice, their food.
None closed those gates, nor ever would;   1065
the roads lie open to everyone,
though none could seek refuge there who should
show any spot under moon or sun.

90   The moon gains nothing from that sight,
she is too pocked, her face too grim;   1070
and here, where it is never night,
why should the moon attempt to trim
her course, when a more glorious light
is shining back from the brook's brim?
The planets are in too poor a plight,   1075
the sun itself is far too dim.
Trees near the stream, with light a-brim,
bear twelve fruits of life, ripening soon
twelve times a year on each full limb,
renewed afresh at every moon.   1080

91   Marvels under the moon may fail;
no fleshly heart can long endure.
I gazed on that home to no avail,
so amazing, patterned so sure!
I stood as still as a dazed quail   1085
in wonder at its fine contour.
I felt no rest, nor yet travail,
I was so ravished, it gleamed so pure!
In all conscience I can insure:
a man in his body, given that boon,   1090
though the wisest men all tried his cure,
would lose his life beneath the moon.

XIX

92   Just as the strong full moon will rise
before the day-gleam dies away,
suddenly, in a wondrous wise   *1095*
I saw a procession wind its way.
This noble city of famed size
filled swiftly (how, I cannot say)
with virgins clad in the same guise
as my Blissful in her crown that day.   *1100*
And all wore crowns in the same way
adorned with pearls, in robes of white.
On the breast of each was placed to stay
the pearl of bliss, to their great delight.

93   As one they moved in great delight   *1105*
through streets with gold paved brilliantly,
a hundred thousand, counted right,
and all alike their livery;
no telling which the happiest sight!
The Lamb went before them; proud was He   *1110*
in His seven horns, red-gold and bright;
His robes, like pearls, gleamed lustrously.
To the throne all moved on solemnly
and, though many, they pressed no-one.
Like maidens at mass, most modestly   *1115*
in great delight they still moved on.

94   He came. I saw delight befall,
far too great for me to tell.
As He approached, those Elders all
prostrate at His feet then fell,   *1120*
while legions of angels, at His call,
scattered their incense of sweet smell.
Fresh glory and joy poured forth, while all
sang out to praise their bright Jewel.

Such sounds could ring through earth to hell 1125
from heaven's host at that glad sight.
In the throngs that praised the Lamb so well
I too was caught, with great delight.

95   Delight filled my whole mind: to gaze
upon the Lamb so openly. 1130
The best, the happiest, beyond praise
He was; no fit words came to me,
so white His robes, so simple His ways,
so gracious in His bearing, He!
But a wound showed, wide and wet always 1135
near His heart, through skin torn cruelly;
from His white side the blood poured free.
Oh! thought I, who had such spite?
Burning with grief should his heart be
if such a thing could bring delight! 1140

96   The Lamb's delight! This He must mean,
though hurt by the wide wound He had,
for on His face no pain was seen,
so glorious were His eyes, so glad!
I looked where His fair band had been, 1145
on whom fulness of life was laid;
and there I saw my little queen
whom I thought near me in the glade.
Lord! How great the mirth she made
among her comrades, all in white! 1150
The sight stirred me; I longed to wade
that stream, with love and great delight.

XX

97   Delight assailed me, ear and eye;
near mad, my mortal mind was tried.
I saw my fair one; I must fly 1155

beyond the water, though she should chide.
I thought nothing hindered, and that I
could gather strength, then spring and stride
into that river. I would try
to swim the rest, although I died!   *1160*
But my desire was soon denied.
Just as I reached the stream, astray,
my rush was checked and turned aside.
I could not please my Prince that way.

98 He was not pleased that I thus flew   *1165*
past the strange stream, madly unafraid—
a thing most rash and rude to do!
And so, abruptly, I was stayed.
My violence tore me, as I drew
near to the bank, from my dream-glade.   *1170*
In the lovely garden I woke anew;
my head on that same hill was laid
where, to the ground, my Pearl once strayed.
Startled, I felt a great dismay
and, sighing, to myself I said: *1175*
"May all please my Prince now, in His way!"

99 I was ill-pleased, driven out again
from that fair realm so suddenly,
in sight of life's vivid, happy reign!
Longing, I sank down heavily;   *1180*
grieving, I cried out in my pain:
"O Pearl," I said, "now famed widely,
what thou hast taught is precious gain,
in this real vision given me!
If it be so, and if really   *1185*
in a gay garland thou art set,
in grief's dungeon all is well with me:
thou pleasest the Prince in His way yet!"

100   Had I but pleased the Prince that way,
     yearned but for what was given me,   *1190*
     in His will truly glad to stay
     (as my happy Pearl prayed earnestly),
     into God's presence drawn away
     I would have pierced His mystery!
     But men will seize, as best they may,   *1195*
     more happiness than comes rightly.
     Soon, then, my joy was torn from me,
     cast from that land of endless life.
     Lord, mad are they who struggle with Thee
     or offer Thee displeasing strife.   *1200*

101   How to please their Prince most peacefully
     good Christians may easily design.
     By day and night He proves to be
     a God, a Lord, a Friend of mine.
     On that hill I took my destiny   *1205*
     where, mourning my Pearl, I lay supine.
     To God I gave it, willingly,
     with Christ's dear blessing and with mine—
     He whom, in form of bread and wine,
     the priest shows to us every day.   *1210*
     May He make us, His home-servants, shine:
     precious pearls, pleasing in His way!
                    Amen, Amen.

SAINT ERKENWALD

I

At London, in England, not so very long after
Christ suffered on the cross and established
     Christendom,
there was a bishop in that city, blessed and consecrated;
Saint Erkenwald, I believe, that holy man was called.

In his time, the greatest of all temples in that town   *5*
was dragged down—one part of it—to be re-dedicated;
for it had been heathen in the days of Hengist
whom the hostile Saxons had sent over here.

They beat out the Britons and brought them into Wales,
perverting all the people who dwelt in that place.   *10*
This realm was renegade for many wretched years,
till Saint Augustine was sent into Sandwich by the Pope.

Then he preached the pure faith here, planted the truth,
and converted all communities to Christendom once more.
He changed over the temples then attached to devils,   *15*
cleansed them in Christ's name and called them churches.

He hurled out their idols and had saints brought in,
changing their names first and fitting them out better.
One that was Apollo's is now Saint Peter's;
Mahomet's became Saint Margaret's, or else Madeleine's.   *20*

The synagogue of the sun was assigned to Our Lady;
Jupiter's and Juno's went to Jesus or James.
He so dedicated all in honor of dear saints,
places held once by Satan in Saxon times.

What is now London was then named New Troy,   *25*
maintained as metropolis and master-town since then.
A mighty devil owned the great minster there,
and his name was the title that the temple bore.

He was the lord most honored of all idols there praised,
his sacrifice the most solemn in all Saxon lands,   *30*
his temple third highest of Triapolitanus,
for within Britain's boundaries were but two such others.

I I

Now Erkenwald is a bishop of Augustine's province,
in beloved London-town, and he teaches law;
he worthily holds the seat of Saint Paul's minster,   *35*
the Triapolitan temple, as I told you before.

This, destroyed and beaten down, was built up anew,
a noble place, to be sure, called the New Work;
many a merry mason was made to work on it,
shaping the hard stones with sharp-edged tools.   *40*

Many grubbed in the gravel, searching the ground,
that the first-laid foundations might be a foot-hold.
As they shovelled and undermined they uncovered a marvel
which is still recorded in trusty chronicles.

For while they dug and delved deep in the earth,   45
they found a strangely fair tomb formed in the floor;
it was a coffin of thick stones, skillfully hewn,
thickly garnished with gargoyles, all of gray marble.

Three bars of the tomb, crossing above it,
were made of fine marble and finished handsomely;   50
the border was embellished with bright gold letters,
but rune-like was the writing that ran around it.

Very life-like the figures, as many onlookers saw—
all too bemused to say what they might mean;
many clerics in that cloister, with high-shaven crowns,   55
were trying in vain to translate them into words.

When tidings spread through town of that tomb-wonder,
hundreds of noblemen hurried over at once.
Burgesses came there, beadles and others,
and the master-craftsmen of many more trades.   60

Boys left their work, bounding towards the spot,
running in a wild rout while the noise rang high;
so many, of all kinds, were keen to be there
that all the world seemed to have turned out at once.

When the mayor with his officers saw that marvel,   65
with the sexton's consent they guarded the sanctuary.
He bade them unlock the lid and lay it aside;
they were longing to see what might lie in the coffer.

After that, spry workmen went straight at it;
they put levers to it and pushed them under,   70
they caught it by the corners with crowbars of iron
and, though the lid was large, they soon laid it aside.

But a great wonder then gripped the by-standers;
they could not make out this strange marvel.
The open space was gorgeous, all painted gold,   75
and a blissful body lay on the bottom,

richly arrayed in royal garments.
His gown was trimmed with glistening gold
with many rich pearls set upon it,
a golden girdle gripped his waist.   80

a full mantle covered him, furred with miniver,
of clean camel's-hair cloth with comely borders;
and on his head rested a very rich crown,
while a fine sceptre was set in his hand.

His robes were spotless, without a stain,   85
neither mouldy nor musty nor moth-eaten,
and as bright with colors of brilliant shade
as if fresh-made yesterday in that very church-yard.

Fresh was his face—like the naked flesh
of the ears and hands that showed openly   90
and the two red lips—with a rich rose-color,
as if suddenly, in sound health, he had fallen asleep.

It was useless to waste time asking each other
whose might be the body that was buried there,
or how long he had thus lain, his lineaments unchanged   95
and his robes free from mould. So every man wondered:

"Surely such a man must have been long remembered;
he was king of this country—that seems clear,
since he lies so deep down. It would be a dire wonder
if no-one could say that he had once seen him."   *100*

But all this meant nothing, for no man could claim
from any sign or inscription, or from any story
rumored in the city or set down in a book,
that such a man was remembered—nothing more, nothing
    less.

Word of this was brought to the Bishop at once,   *105*
all the baffling wonder of the buried body.
The Primate with his prelates had departed from home;
Sir Erkenwald was in Essex visiting an Abbey.

Men told him the tale—how the people were troubled;
such an outcry for a corpse, carried on and on!   *110*
The Bishop sent word to stop, by beadles and letters,
and, mounting his horse, hurried straight off.

When he came to the church that is called Saint Paul's
many met him on horseback to tell him the marvel.
He passed on to his palace, bade them hold their peace,   *115*
kept away from the dead man and shut the door after him.

The dark night passed over, the dawn-bell rang;
Sir Erkenwald was up in the early morning.
Almost all night he had said his Office,
beseeching his Sovereign, by His sweet grace,   *120*
to vouchsafe to reveal this, by a vision or otherwise.

"Though I be unworthy," he said weeping
in his noble graciousness, "grant this, my Lord,
confirming Thy Christian faith: help me to find out
the mystery of this marvel that men wonder about."   *125*

So long did he plead for grace that it was granted,
an answer from the Holy Ghost; dawn came after that.
The minster doors were flung open when Matins had been
    sung;
the Bishop solemnly robed to sing high mass.

Soon the Prelate was attired in his pontificals;   *130*
becomingly, with his ministers, he begins the mass
Spiritus Domini, for aid, with deep intent.
The choir burst into bright song, weaving skillful tunes.

Many fine great lords were gathered to listen
—the most elegant of the realm often repaired there—   *135*
till the service was over, said through to the end;
the illustrious company then turned from the altar.

The Prelate crossed the level space while the lords bowed to
    him;
richly vested as he was, he went on to the tomb.
The cloister was unclosed for him with a cluster of keys,   *140*
but the great crowd was anxious as it pushed after him.

The Bishop came to the tomb, his barons beside him,
the Mayor with his top men and mace-bearers before him.
The Dean of that famous place then first described
the finding of the marvel; he pointed with his finger.   *145*

"See, Lords," said that man, "here has lain a body
 thus locked down below, no-one knows how long,
 yet his color and his clothing have caught no defect,
 nor his face, nor the coffer where he is enclosed.

"There is no-one who has lived for such a long time   *150*
 that he can hold in mind when such a man reigned,
 or can tell us of his name or of his renown,
 though many a poorer man here put in his grave
 is marked in our martyrology, to his memory forever.

"We have looked through our library these seven long   *155*
       days,
 but no chronicle of this king could we ever find.
 For one to lie so long—to look at it naturally—
 as to pass out of memory, is surely a marvel."

"Thou hast spoken truly," said the consecrated Bishop.
"What is marvelous to man amounts to little   *160*
 in the providence of that Prince who rules paradise,
 when pleased to unlock the least of His powers.

"When man's might is check-mated, his mind overcome,
 when reason is torn to shreds and he stands resourceless,
 then little hinders God from lifting with His finger   *165*
 what all the hands under heaven could never hold.
 When the creature's skill swerves away from wisdom,
 The Creator's comfort will have to cure him.

"Let us now do our deed, divining no further;
 you see it does no good to seek truth by ourselves.
 But let us call on God, and ask grace of Him   *170*
 who sends with no cost His counsel and comfort.

"So, to strengthen your faith and your certain belief,
I shall now proclaim to you His power so truly
that you will at last believe He is Lord almighty,   *175*
glad to fulfill your wish if you trust Him as a friend."

III

Then he turns towards the tomb and talks to the body;
lifting up his eyes, he utters these words:
"Now, body thus lying, be silent no longer!
Since Jesus has seen fit to show His joy today,   *180*

"be obedient to His word, I bid on His behalf.
As He was bound to a beam when He shed His blood
(as thou knowest well and we ourselves believe)
answer at my command: conceal not the truth.

"We know not who thou art; inform us thyself   *185*
who thou wert in this world, why thou art lying thus,
how long thou hast lain there, what law thou didst follow,
whether thou art in joy or adjudged to pain."

When he had so spoken and given a sigh,
the bright body in the grave then moved a bit,   *190*
and with a doleful sound stammered a few words,
given life through some spirit by Him who governs all.

"Bishop," said the body, "thy bidding is dear to me;
I cannot but answer thee—not for both my eyes.
The name thou hast spoken, by which thou hast
          summoned me,   *195*
all heaven and hell bow to, and the earth between.

"To at once tell the truth as to who I was:
the most hapless of men who ever moved on earth;
not a king nor an emperor, not even a knight,
but a man of the law, as followed in this land.   200

"I was here commissioned and made a magistrate
to sit on serious cases; I governed this city
under a prince of rank, of the pagan creed,
and all his followers believed the same faith.

"The time I've lain here is of incredible length,   205
too long for any man to add up rightly:
since Brutus built this city in the beginning,
eight hundred years, less by eighteen,

"before your Christ was born, by Christian accounts,
three hundred and thirty more, and then thrice eight,   210
I was then heir, in New Troy, of the Court of Oyer,
in the reign of the rich king that ruled us then,

"the bold Breton, Sir Berlin; Sir Bering was his brother,
and many the insults offered between them
in ruinous warfare, while their wrath lasted!   215
Then I was named judge here, under gentile law."

While he in the crypt spoke, there sprang from the people
no word for all the world, no voice was wakened;
but as still as stones they stood and listened,
wrung with great wonder, and many wept.   220

The Bishop bids the body: "Lay bare the reason
why thou who wert no king art wearing a crown.
Why does thou hold high that sceptre in thy hand,
without land or liegemen, or power over life and limb?"

"Dear Sir," said the dead body, "I intend to say all.   *225*
  It was never my will that this was so done.
  I was deputy and doomsman under a noble duke,
  and this place was put fully into my power.

"I did justice in this fair town in a noble fashion,
  according to my good faith, for forty winters.   *230*
  The people were fierce and false, froward to rule over;
  I suffered much harm in holding them to right.

"But for no ill- or well-being, for no anger or dread,
  no mastery or bribery or fear of any man,
  swerved I ever from the right, as my reason saw it,   *235*
  or passed a wrong doom, not one day of my life.

"My conscience never yielded, through earthly covetousness,
  to make treacherous judgments or to play tricks,
  out of reverence for any man, no matter how rich,
  not for any man's menace, not for malice or pity.   *240*

"None drew me from the highroad, to dodge justice,
  in so far as my faith and my heart conformed;
  had a wretch murdered my father I would not wrong him,
  nor favor my father falsely, though he should be hanged.

"Since I was righteous and straight, and ready in the law,   *245*
  when I died all Troy resounded dolorously.
  All mourned my death, the mighty and the lowly,
  and in reward they buried my body in gold.

"They clothed me as most courteous of the men who held
     court,
  in a mantle, as meek and merciful on the bench;   *250*
  they girded me as governor, the most gifted man in Troy,
  in fur, fit sign of the faith within me.

"In honor of my honesty, so openly renowned,
  they crowned me king of all clever justices
  who had held sway in Troy, or would ever so do;   *255*
  and for giving fair rewards they gave me a sceptre."

Again the Bishop asked him, in anguish of heart:
  though men had so honored him, how might it be
  that his clothes were so clean. "Into clouts, it seems,
  they should have long since rotted and been rent in rags. *260*

"Thy body may be embalmed; I am not abashed
  that no rot has eaten it, and no rank worms.
  But thy color and thy clothes! I cannot tell
  how, by man's learning, they could last, lying here."

"No, Bishop," said that body, "I was never embalmed,   *265*
  nor by any man's counsel have my clothes kept unspoiled,
  but by the high King of reason who upholds what is right
  and loyally loves all laws that belong to the truth.

"He honors a man more for remembering righteousness
  than for all the works of merit that men do on earth;   *270*
  and if for my righteousness men so arrayed me,
  He who loves right most has allowed me to last."

"Yes, but speak of thy soul," the Bishop then said.
"In what state is it placed, if thou didst live strictly?
  He who rewards a man according to righteousness   *275*
  could not fail to give thee some offshoot of His grace.

"For, as He says in His truthful Psalmbook:
  'The righteous and the innocent ascend ever to me.'
  Then say something of thy soul, where it stays in bliss,
  and the glorious reward that our Lord gave it."   *280*

The man lying there murmured and moved his head,
and gave a great groan; he said to God:
"Strong Maker of men, great is Thy might!
How could Thy mercy come at any time to me?

"Was I not a dull pagan who never knew Thy pledge,   *285*
nor the measure of Thy mercy, nor Thy mighty power,
but a faithless fellow who fell short of the law
which Thou, Lord, art praised by? Alas, those hard times!

"I had no place among those bought with thy pain,
with the blood of Thy body on the black rood!   *290*
When Thou didst harry hell's pit, thence drawing out
Thy remnant from Limbo, Thou didst leave me there.

"There sits my soul; she can see no farther,
languishing in the dark death where our father led us,
Adam, our ancestor, who ate that apple   *295*
that poisoned forever a people unpledged to Thee.

"You were poisoned by those teeth, you took in that venom,
but, healed by that medicine, you are made to live:
baptism at the font, with faithful belief,
that we missed beyond mercy, myself and my soul.   *300*

"What won we by well-doing, we, ever righteous,
when dolorously we are doomed to the deep lake,
so exiled from that supper, that solemn feast
where richly are those refreshed who hungered for the right?

"There my soul must sit sorrowing, with cold sighs,   *305*
in the dimness of dark death where no morning dawns,
hungry in hell's pit, hankering for food.
Long till she sees that supper, till she is summoned!"

Thus dolefully the dead body unburdened its sorrow,
till all who heard those words wept in their grief.   *310*
The Bishop sadly bent down his eyes
and could say nothing, so heavily he sobbed,

till he paused for a time, looking at the tomb
and the body there lying, while his tears flowed long.
"May our Lord grant," he said, "that life be thine   *315*
long enough, by God's leave, for me to get water

to pour on thy fair body, pronouncing these words:
'I baptize thee in the Father's name, in His noble Son's,
and the gracious Holy Ghost's,' not a moment more granted.
Then, if thou shouldst drop dead, I would dread it less." *320*

As he said those words, water from his eyes
trickled down in tears and splashed on the tomb.
One fell on the face, and the man first sighed
then said, in solemn tones: "May our Savior be praised!

"Now be honored, high God, and Thy gracious Mother,   *325*
blessed be the blissful hour in which she bore Thee!
And blessed be Thou, Bishop, who brought healing to
        sorrow,
relief from the loathsome loss that my soul lived in!

"For the words thou hast spoken, and the water that
        poured
in a bright stream from thine eyes, have become my   *330*
        baptism.
The first drop that fell on me did away with my woe;
my soul sits, even now, at that supper table.

"With those words and the water that washes pain away,
a gleam flashed lightly through the low abyss,
and my spirit leaped swiftly, with joy unleashed,   *335*
to the Cenacle where those saved share the festal supper.

"There a marshal met her with courteous manners,
and with reverence opened her own home forever.
So I thank my high God, and thee too, O Bishop,
who brought us from pain to bliss; blessed be thou!"   *340*

With this the voice ceased; he said no more.
Suddenly his fair face faded and crumbled,
while the color of his body grew black as mould,
as rotten as rubble that rises up in powder.

For as soon as the soul had seized hold of its bliss,   *345*
corrupt were the elements that covered those bones;
for life everlasting that shall never end,
undoes the vainglory that avails so little.

Then praise to our Lord rose from uplifted hands;
much mourning and mirth were intermingled.   *350*
They passed forth in procession; the people followed,
while all the bells in town boomed out together.

APPENDICES

APPENDIX I

THE MANUSCRIPT

Transcription

The scribe of MS Cotton Nero A.X. used Anglo-Norman scribal devices, the most striking of which is the character 3 which represents two letters: *z* when final or initial (even when sometimes unvoiced), and *yogh*, representing various sounds of *g* (*y*, *w*, *gh*).

Editorial cruxes have arisen from several causes: blots occurring when the pages were turned too soon (some of the letters have been restored by mirror-offsets); dropping of final *e* in instances where it may have been pronounced, due to the time lag between the poem and the manuscript; scribal carelessness.

The final scribe should not be blamed for all these errors. It is probable that each of the four poems was first copied by a different scribe, that *Pearl* and *Sir Gawain* were then recopied by a fifth, and that a sixth recopied his work and added *Cleanness*. The man who then copied these and added *Patience* would be the seventh transcriber, working on texts extending over possibly forty years. His hand, or that of still another scribe, then made many corrections. (See Oakdon, *op. cit.*, appendix III.)

Divisions

Pearl (folios 39b–56a) opens the MS with a sixteen-line capital *P*. There is one four-line capital where the dream begins at l. 61: three-line letters open all the other pentads, and an extra one was made by mistake at l. 961. Each stanza is marked by a small check in the margin.

Cleanness (folios 57a–82b) opens with an eight-line capital *C*. Two four-line letters mark the major divisions at ll. 557 and 1157; ten three-line letters subdivide these into thirteen sections. The quatrain division is marked by the same small check seen in *Pearl*, but in two passages errors occur, when two stanzas of five lines are finally corrected by a couplet (ll. 1541-92, and ll. 1575-1792).

Patience (folios 83a-90a) opens with an eight-line capital *P*, and the divisions at ll. 61, 24, 305, 409 are marked by three-line letters. The quatrains are checked.

Sir Gawain and the Green Knight (folios 91a-126b) opens with an eight-line initial. Two six-line letters (at ll. 491 and 1126) and one four-line letter (at l. 1998) extend their flourishes right across the page and mark the four parts of the poem. Earlier editors have observed these divisions only. But five three-line letters (at ll. 619, 763, 1421, 1893, 2258) further subdivide the poem into nine sections, which are recognized in the present version. Each of the nine capitals is important as marking a turning point in the suspenseful action of the poem. (See L. L. Hill, "Madden's Divisions of Sir Gawain and the Large Initial Capitals of Cotton Nero A.X." *Speculum*, XXI [1946], 67-71.)

The Pictures

Pearl is preceded by four pictures that are grouped together. In the first the narrator, in a red gown and blue hood, lies on a flowery mound; his eyes are half-closed while a breeze blows his scarf into the shrubbery. In the second he stands with uplifted hands by a stream where large fishes sport. In the third he points to his white-clad Pearl on the opposite shore. In the last he lifts imploring hands to where Pearl stands behind the battlements of the New Jerusalem; with one hand she beckons, with the other she points to a mansion—perhaps his heavenly home-to-be.

Cleanness is preceded by two pictures. The first shows the ark, of rowboat size, perched on top of a wave. Seven persons are crowded into it, while a blank space shows where the head of the eighth should be. They stare in unconcern at the fishes clustering around Noah's oar, where one small fish is vanishing down the throat of a larger one. In the second picture Daniel is kneeling before the high table where the terrified Belshazzar stares at the handwriting on the wall.

Patience is preceded by a half-page picture of a tiny well-clinked boat riding a bulging wave. It holds two sailors, one smiling calmly while the other throws Jonah overboard; the Prophet's head is entering the jaws of a shark-like whale. On the reverse is a full-page picture of Jonah in Nineveh (whose walls and towers resemble those of the New Jerusalem in *Pearl*). He is preaching to supplicating Ninevites: a man, a woman, and an idiot in fool's garb.

Sir Gawain and the Green Knight is preceded by a picture showing two moments of the beheading scene: Arthur stands at the high table, bread knife in hand, the frightened Queen clinging to him; Sir Agravayne, well armed, is on his left. To his right Sir Gawain is begging the boon. Below, the Green Knight, on horseback, holds out his severed head to Gawain who, axe in hand, looks straight at the reader in triumph. Following the poem is a picture of Bercilak's wife tickling the chin of the sleeping Gawain in his curtained bed. Above is written (in another hand):

> My mind is much on one who, for me, will not amend.
> Once she was true as stone, and could from shame defend.

The badly blurred picture on the reverse side shows Gawain riding up to the Chapel while the Green Knight waits, ready with his axe, beyond a flower-bordered stream (there is snow on the ground in the poem!). On the last folio the King and Queen, with an unknown knight, welcome Gawain home. He appears to be dancing but is really trying to kneel.

APPENDIX II

LANGUAGE

Accidence

1. Articles: Indefinite: *a; an* or *on* before vowels and *h*.
   Definite: *þe; þo* sometimes in pl.
2. Demonstratives, adjective and pronoun: sing. *þat*, pl. *þose*.
3. Personal pronouns:

		Singular			Plural
1st.	nom.	I			we
	dat. acc.	me			us
	poss. adj.	my, myn			oure
2nd.	nom.	þu, þou			ȝe
	dat.	þe			yow
	acc.	þu			yow
	poss. adi.	þyn			ȝoure, youre

		Masculine	Feminine	Neuter	
3rd.	nom.	he	ho, scho	hit, hyt	þay
	dat. acc.	him, hym	hir, hyr, her	hit, hyt	hom, hem, him
	poss. adj.	his	hir, hyr, her	his	her, hor, þayr

4. Indefinite pronouns: *mon, men, who, quo, what, quatso.*
5. Relative pronouns: *whom, wham, quom.*
6. Nouns:

(326)

	Singular			Plural		
nom. acc.	-e,	—,		-ȝ,	-s,	-esse
gen.	-ȝ,	-e		-ȝ,	-s	

A few mutated forms are used.

7. Adjectives: no case or gender; pl. in -e, often dropped.
8. Verbs: Infinitive: -en, -e (often dropped), y sometimes, strong and weak verbs identical.

Participles: pres. *ande*, *yng* sometimes; past, -en, -n, -e (strong verbs)
    -d, -t (weak verbs)

Pres. Ind.   *Singular*   *Plural*

1st. -e, -eȝ or none	-en, -e, -eȝ, -tȝ
2nd. -eȝ	
3rd. -ȝ, -s, -tȝ	

Past Ind. Strong verbs: sing. no ending; pl. -on, -e; show mutation

Weak verbs: *Singular*   *Plural*

1st. -de/te	-(e)d/(e)t
2nd. des/tes	
3rd. -de/te	

Imperative: -e or no ending; pl. -eȝ, -es.

Proportion of Norse words

Patience,	9.4%	e.g.	*mysse*, offence
Cleanness,	7.6%		*heþing*, scorn, contempt
Sir Gawain,	10.3%		*droupyng*, deep gloom
Pearl,	9.2%		*caste*, purpose

Near synonyms

e.g. words for "man" with differing connotations:
mon, burne, freke, gome, knight, haþel, wyȝe, lorde, lede, tulke.

Specimen passages

"I am an Ebru," quoþ he, "of Israyl borne;
þat wyȝe þat I worchup, Iwysse, þat wroȝt alle þynges,
all þe worlde with þe welkyn, þe wynde and þe sternes,
and alle þat woneȝ wlthInne, at a worde one.

Alle þis meschef for me is made at þis tyme:
for I haf greued my God and gulty am founden;
for-thy bereȝ me to þe borde, and baþes me þer-oute,
er gete ȝe no happe, I hope for soþe."

Patience, 205–12.

And þer ar tres by þat terne of traytores,
and þay borgouneȝ and beres blomeȝ ful fayre,
and þe fayrest fryt þat may on folde growe,
as orenge and oþer fryt and apples garnade,

also red and so ripe and rychely hwed
as any dom myȝt device of daynteȝ oute;
bot quen hit is brused, oþer broken, oþer byten in twynne,
no worldeȝ good hit wythinne, bot wyndowande askes.

Cleanness, 1041–48

APPENDIX III

PROSODY

Teutonic system

1 The line: unrhymed (usually), alliterative, non-stanzaic, divided into two hemistiches with caesura between them, each hemistich with two stresses. A resolved stress frequently rested upon two syllables.
2. Alliteration was always on a stressed syllable, the first syllable of the second hemistich holding the key letter, echoed by first, second, or both stresses in first hemistich, and sometimes by the last stress in the line. Consonants alliterate with themselves (as *do sc, sp, st*), while vowels alliterate with another vowel or diphthong.
3. The scansion unit is the hemistich, each of which has two stressed syllables and a fluid number of unstressed syllables. The lifts and dips thus formed fall into five patterns, which could be freely intermixed in a pattern:

Pattern A, trochaic:	wŭndrum̆/scínan̆
Pattern B, iambic:	þur̆h déaþ/es nyd
Pattern C, iambic-trochaic: (clashing stress)	on̆ lýft/láedan̆
Pattern D, monosyllabic-trisyllabic:	feóht/eórneste

Pattern E, trisyllabic-
monosyllabic: hléo bòlstĕr oň/feńg
(the last two employ
secondary stress)

When the Old English system was applied to Middle English poetry
certain changes followed the changes in vocabulary. Alliteration
became heavier; rules relaxed. The number of light syllables increased,
giving greater speed and length to the line. It is difficult to know when
metrical value should be given to a final -e which was unpronounced in
many positions.

Illustrative passages

Sir Gawain shows the combination of the alliterative long line with
the French syllabic meter with rhyme used in the last five lines. *Pearl*
can be scanned in the syllabic meter, dominantly iambic, but the light
caesura, the frequent (though not regular) alliteration, and the changing cadence due to inversion suggest the Old English beat.

B	Day bóȝen bi bónkkeȝ/þer bóȝeȝ ar báre;	B
B	þay clómben bi clyffeȝ/þer cléngeȝ þe cólde;	B
B	þe heúen watȝ vp hált,/bot vgly þer-únder;	B
B	mist múged on þe mór,/malt on þe móunteȝ,	A
B	vch hílle hade a hátte,/a mýst-hàkel húge.	E
E	Brókeȝ býled and bréke/bi bónkkeȝ aboúte,	B
E	schyre schàterande on schóreȝ,/þer þay dóun schówued.	C
B	Wela wýlle watȝ þe wáy/þer þay bi wód schúlden,	C
C	til it watȝ sóne sésoun/þat þe súnne rýses	C
	þat týde.	a
	Day wére on a híll ful hýȝe,	b
	þe qúyte snaw láy bisýde;	a
	þe búrne þat róde hym by	b
	báde his máyster abíde.	a

Sir Gawain, 2077–90

The dúbbeménte of þo dérworth dépe	a
wern bónkeȝ béne of béryl brýȝt.	b
Swángwande swéte þe wáter con swépe,	a
wyth a równande róurde ráyknade arýȝt.	b

In þe foúnce þer stónden stónez stépe,   a
as glénte þurȝ glás þat glówed and glýȝt,   b
as strémande stérneȝ, quen stróþe-men slépe, a
stáren in wélkyn in wýnter nýȝt;   b
for v́che póbbel in póle þer pýȝt   b
watȝ émerad, sáffer, oþer gémme génte, c
þat álle þe lóȝe lémed of lýȝt,   b
so dére watȝ hít addúbbement.   c

Pearl, 109–20

SELECT
BIBLIOGRAPHY

The Manuscript

Pearl, Patience, Cleanness, and Sir Gawain, Facsimile of MS Cotton Nero A.X., ed. Sir Israel Gollancz, EETS, #162, 1923.

Hill, L. "Madden's Divisions of *Sir Gawain* and the Large Initial Capitals of Cotton Nero A.X.," *Speculum*, XXI (1946), 67–71.

Oakden, J. P. *Alliterative Poetry in Middle English*, Manchester, 1931, Vol. I. Appendix III, "The Scribes of the Poems of the MS Cotton Nero A.X."

———. "The Scribal Errors in MS Cotton Nero A.X.," *Library*, XIV (1933), 353–58.

The Alliterative Movement: language, style, and meter

Brunner, K. "Middle English Metrical Romances and their Audiences," *Studies in Medieval Literature in Honor of Albert Croll Baugh*, ed. M. Leach, Philadelphia: University of Pennsylvania Press, 1961.

Brown, A. C. L. "On the Origin of Stanza-Linking in English Alliterative Verse," *Romanic Review*, VII (1916), 271–83.

Day, M. "Strophic Division in Middle English Alliterative Verse," *Englische Studien*, LXVI (1931), 245–48.

Elliot, R. W. V. "Landscape and Rhetoric in Middle English Poetry," *Melbourne Critical Review*, IV (1961), 65–76.

Everett, D. *Essays on Middle English Literature*, ed. Patricia Kane. Oxford: Clarendon Press, 1959.

Greg, W. W. "Continuity of the Alliterative Tradition," *MLR*, XXVII (1932), 453–54.

Hulbert, J. R. "A Hypothesis Concerning the Alliterative Revival," *MP*, XXVIII (1931), 405–22.

———. "Quatrains in Middle English Alliterative Poems," *MP*, XLVIII (1950), 73–81.

Medary, M. and Brown, A. C. L. "Articles on Stanza-Linking," *Romanic Review*, VII (1961), 243, 271.

Oakden, J. P. *Alliterative Poetry in Middle English*, Manchester: University of Manchester Press, 1931, 1935, 2 vols.

Serjeantson, M. S. "The Dialects of the West Midlands in Middle English," *RES*, III (1927), 54–67, 188–203, 319–31.

Speirs, J. *Middle English Poetry: the non-Chaucerian Tradition*, London: Faber and Faber, 1957.

Waldron, R. A. "Oral-Formulaic Technique in Middle English Alliterative Poetry," *Speculum*, XXXII (1957), 792–804.

The Author

Cargill, O. and Slauch, M. "The Pearl and its Jeweler," *PMLA*, XLIII (1928), 105–23.

Chapman, C. O. "The Authorship of *The Pearl*," *PMLA*, XLVII (1932), 346–53.

———. "Chaucer and the Gawain-Poet; a Conjecture," *MLN*, LXVIII (1953), 521–24.

———. "Musical Training of the Pearl-Poet," *PMLA*, XLVI (1931), 177–81.

———. "Virgil and the Gawain-Poet," *PMLA*, LX (1945), 16–23.

Ebbs, J. D. "Stylistic Mannerisms of the Gawain-Poet," *JEGP*, LVII (1958), 522–25.

Gerould, G. H. "The Gawain-Poet and Dante: a Conjecture," *PMLA*, LI (1936), 31–36.

McChracken, H. N. "Concerning Huchown," *PMLA*, XXV (1910), 507–34.

Savage, H. L. *The Gawain-Poet: Studies in his Personality and Background*, Chapel Hill: University of North Carolina Press, 1956.

Collected Works

Chapman, C. O. *An Index of Names in Pearl, Patience, Purity and Sir Gawain*, Ithaca: Cornell University Press, 1951. Cornell Studies in English, XXXVIII.

The Complete Works of the Gawain-Poet, tr. John Gardner. Chicago: Chicago University Press, 1965.

Concordance to Five Middle English Poems. ed. Kotter, B., Markman, A. Pittsburgh: University of Pittsburgh Press, 1966.

Cuffe, Rev. Edwin, "An Interpretation of *Patience, Cleanness* and *Pearl* from the Point of View of Imagery," Doctoral Dissertation, University of North Carolina, 1951.

Early English Alliterative Poems, ed R. Morris, EETS #1, 1867. (contains *Pearl, Cleanness* and *Patience*)

Luttrell, C. A. "The Gawain-Group: Cruxes, Etymologies, Interpretations," *Neophilologus*, XXXIX (1955), 207–17.

———. "A Gawain-Group Miscellany," *Notes and Queries*, CCVII (1962), 447–50.

Medieval English Verse and Prose, ed. R. S. Loomis and R. Willard. New York: Appleton-Century-Crofts, 1948. (contains translations of *Pearl, Sir Gawain, Saint Erkenwald*)

Pearl, and Sir Gawain and The Green Knight, ed. A. C. Cawley, New York: Everyman's Library, 1962.

Zavadil, J. B. "A Study of Meaning in *Patience* and *Cleanness,*" Doctoral Dissertation, Stanford University, 1962. Ann Arbor, University Microfilms 62-2372.

Patience

EDITIONS

Patience, ed. I. Gollancz, London, 1924.

Patience, a West Midland Poem of the Fourteenth Century, ed. Henry Bateson. Manchester: Manchester University Press, rev. ed. 1918.

CRITICAL STUDIES

Berlin, N. "Patience, a Study in Poetic Elaboration," *Studia Neophilologica,* XXXIII (1961), 80–85.

Emerson, O. F. "A Parallel between the Middle English Poem *Patience* and an Early Latin Poem Attributed to Tertullian," *PMLA,* X (1895), 242–48.

Moorman, C. A. "Role of the Narrator in *Patience,*" *MP,* LXI (1963), 90–95.

Cleanness

EDITIONS

Cleanness, ed. I. Gollancz. London: Oxford University Press, 1921.

Purity, a Middle English Poem, ed. J. R. Menner, Yale Studies in English, 61. New Haven: Yale University Press, 1920.

CRITICAL STUDIES

Bateson, H. "The Text of *Cleanness,*" *MLR,* XIII (1918), 377–86.

Brown, C. F. "Note on the Dependence of *Cleanness* on *The Book of Mandeville,*" *PMLA,* XIX (1904), 149–53.

Emerson, O. F. "Legends of Cain, Especially in Old and Middle English," *PMLA,* XXI (1906), 831–49.

———."Middle English *Clannesse,*" *PMLA,* XXXIV (1919), 494–522.

———. "A Note on Middle English *Cleanness,*" *MLR,* X (1915), 373–74.

Gollancz, I. "The Text of *Cleanness*," *MLR*, XIV (1919), 152–62.

Luttrell, C. A. "Baiting of Bulls and Bears in the Middle English *Cleanness*," *Notes and Queries*, CXCVII (1952), 23–24.

———. "*Cleanness* and the Knight of the Tour Landry," *Medium Aevum*, XXIX (1960), 187–89.

Sir Gawain and the Green Knight

EDITIONS AND TRANSLATIONS

Gawain and the Green Knight, ed. R. Morris. EETS, #2, 1864.

Sir Gawain and the Green Knight, ed. J. R. R. Tolkien and E. V. Gordon. Oxford: Clarendon Press, 1925 (rev. ed. 1946).

Sir Gawain and the Green Knight, ed. I. Gollancz, M. Day, and M. Serjeantson. EETS, #210, 1940.

Sir Gawain and the Green Knight, tr. E. H. Banks. New York: Appleton-Century-Crofts, 1929.

Sir Gawain and the Green Knight, tr. O. Greenwood. London: Lion and Unicorn Press, 1956.

Sir Gawain and the Green Knight, tr. Brian Stone, New York: Penguin Books, 1959.

CRITICAL STUDIES

Ackerman, R. W. "Gawain's Shield: Penitential Doctrine," *Anglia*, LXXVI (1958), 254–65.

Barnet, S. "A Note on the Structure of *Sir Gawain and the Green Knight*," *MLN*, LXXI (1956), 319.

Baughan, E. "The Role of Morgan le Fay in *Sir Gawain and the Green Knight*," *ELH*, XVII (1950), 241–52.

Benson, L. D. "Source of the Beheading Episode in *Sir Gawain and the Green Knight*," *MP*, LIX (1961), 1–12.

———. *Art and Tradition in Sir Gawain and the Green Knight*. New Brunswick: Rutgers University Press, 1966.

Bercovitch, S. "Romance and Anti-Romance in *Gawain and the Green Knight*," *PQ*, XLIV (1965), 30–37.

Berry, F. "Sir Gawain and the Green Knight," *Age of Chaucer*, ed. B. Ford, New York: Penguin Books, 1954.

———. "The Sublime Ballet: an Essay on *Sir Gawain and the Green Knight*," *Wind and Rain* (Winter, 1949–50), 165–74.

Bloomfield, M. W. "*Sir Gawain and the Green Knight*: an Appraisal," *PMLA*, LXXVI (1961), 7–19.

Borroff, M. *Sir Gawain and the Green Knight: a Stylistic and Metrical Study*. Yale Studies in English, 152. New Haven: Yale University Press, 1962.

Bowers, R. H. "Gawain and the Green Knight as Entertainment," *MLQ*, XXIV (1963), 333–41.

Braddy, H. "Sir Gawain and Ralph Holmes," *MLN*, LXVII (1952), 240–42.

Buchanan, A. "The Irish Framework of *Gawain and the Green Knight*," *PMLA*, XLVII (1932), 315–38.

Burrow, J. "The Two Confession Scenes in *Sir Gawain and the Green Knight*," *MP*, LVII (1959), 73–79.

Carson, Mother Angela. "The Green Chapel: its Meaning and its Function," *Studies in Philology*, LX (1963), 598–605.

———. "Morgan la Fee as the Principle of Unity in *Gawain and the Green Knight*," *MLQ*, XXIII (1962), 3–16.

Colgrave, B. "Gawain's Green Chapel," *Antiquity*, XII (1938), 351–53.

Cook, R. G. "The Play-Element in *Sir Gawain and the Green Knight*," Tulane Studies in English, XIII. New Orleans: Tulane University Press, 1963.

Coomeraswamy, A. "*Sir Gawain and the Green Knight*: Indra and Namuci," *Speculum*, XIX (1944), 105–25.

D'Ardenne, S. "The Green Count and *Sir Gawain and the Green Knight*," *RES*, N.S. X (1959), 113–26.

Eagan, J. F. "The Import of Color Symbolism in *Sir Gawain and the Green Knight*," *St. Louis University Studies*, Series A, I (1949), 12–86.

Engelhardt, G. J. "The Predicament of Gawain," *MLQ*, XVI (1955), 218–25.

Friedman, A. B. "Morgan la Fee in *Sir Gawain and the Green Knight*," *Speculum*, XXXV (1960), 260–74.

Goldhurst, W. "The Green and the Gold: the Major Theme of *Sir Gawain and the Green Knight*," *College English*, XX (1958–59), 61–65.

Green, R. H. "Gawain's Shield and the Quest for Perfection," *ELH*, XXIX (1962), 121–39.

Highfield, J. R. L. "The Green Squire," *Medium Aevum*, XXII (1953), 18–23.

Hills, D. F. "Gawain's Fault in *Gawain and the Green Knight*," *RES*, N.S. XIV (1963), 124–31.

Howard, D. R. "Structure and Symmetry in *Sir Gawain*," *Speculum*, XXXIX (1964), 425–33.

Hulbert, J. R. "Sir Gawain and the Green Knight," *MP*, XIII (1915–16), 689–730, 433–62.

Kiteley, J. F. "The *De Arte Honeste Amandi* of Andreas Capellanus and the Concept of Courtesy in *Sir Gawain and the Green Knight*," *Anglia*, LXXIX (1961), 7–16.

———. "The Knight Who Cared for His Life," *Anglia*, LXXIX (1961), 131–37.

Krappe, A. H. "Who Was the Green Knight?" *Speculum*, XIII (1938), 206–15.

Loomis, L. H. "Gawain and the Green Knight," *Arthurian Literature in the Middle Ages,* ed. R. S. Loomis, New York: Oxford Press, 1959.

Loomis, R. S. "Gawain in the Squire's Tale," *MLN,* LII (1937), 414–16.

———. "More Celtic Elements in Gawain and the Green Knight," *JEGP,* XL (1943), 149–84.

Markman, A. M. "The Meaning of *Sir Gawain and the Green Knight,*" *PMLA,* LXXII (1957), 574–86.

Moorman, C. "Myth and Medieval Literature: *Sir Gawain and the Green Knight,*" *Medieval Studies,* XVIII (1956), 158–72.

Nitze, W. A. "Is the Green Knight Story a Vegetation Myth?" *MP,* XXXIII (1935–36), 351–66.

Pearsall, D. A. "Rhetorical *Descriptio* in *Sir Gawain and the Green Knight,*" *MLR,* L (1955), 129–34.

Randall, D. B. J. "A Note on the Structure of *Sir Gawain and the Green Knight,*" *MLN,* LXXII (1957), 161–63.

Renoir, A. "An Echo to the Sense; the Patterns of Sound in *Gawain and the Green Knight,*" *English Miscellany,* XIII (1962), 9–12.

———. "Descriptive Techniques in *Gawain and the Green Knight,*" *Orbis Litterarum,* XIII (1958), 126–32.

———. "Progressive Magnification: an Instance of Psychological Description in *The Green Knight,*" *Moderna Sprak,* LIV (1960), 245–53.

Saperstein, J. "Some Observations on *Sir Gawain and the Green Knight,*" *English Studies in Africa,* V (1962), 29–36.

Savage, H. L. "The Feast of Fools in *Sir Gawain and the Green Knight,*" *JEGP,* LI (1952), 537–44.

———. *The Gawain Poet: Studies in his Personality and Background.* Chapel Hill: University of North Carolina Press, 1956.

Schnyder, H. "Aspects of Kingship in *Sir Gawain and the Green Knight,*" *English Studies,* XL (1959), 289–94.

———. *Sir Gawain and the Green Knight: an Essay in Interpretation.* Cooper Monographs 6. Bern: Frank Verlag, 1961.

Smith, R. "Guinbresil and the Green Knight," *JEGP,* XLV (1946), 1–25.

Speirs, J. "Sir Gawain and the Green Knight," *Scrutiny,* XXVI (1949), 270–300.

Whiting, B. J. "Gawain: his Reputation, his Courtesy, his Appearance in Chaucer's Squire's Tale," *Medieval Studies,* IX (1947), 189–234.

Wright, E. M. "Sir Gawain and the Green Knight," *JEGP,* XXXIV (1935), 157–79, 339–50.

Zimmer, H. "Sir Gawain and the Green Knight," *The King and the Corpse,* ed. J. Campbell. New York: Pantheon Books, 1948.

Pearl

EDITIONS AND TRANSLATIONS

Pearl, an English Poem of the Fourteenth Century, ed. and tr. I. Gollancz, with Boccaccio's *Olympia,* London: Chatto and Windus, 1921. (rev. ed.)

The Pearl, a Middle English Poem, C. G. Osgood. Boston: Heath, 1906.

The Pearl: Medieval Text with a Literal Translation and Interpretation, ed. Sister Mary Vincent Hillman. Convent Station, N.J.: College of St. Elizabeth Press, 1961.

Pearl, ed. E. V. Gordon. Oxford: Clarendon Press, 1953.

CRITICAL STUDIES

Ackerman, R. W. "The Pearl-Maiden and the Penny," *Romance Philology,* XVII (1964), 615–23.

Bishop, I. "The Significance of the 'Garlande Gay' in the Allegory of *Pearl,*" *RES,* VIII (1957), 12–21.

Brown, C. "The Author of *The Pearl* Considered in the Light of his Theological Opinions," *PMLA,* XIX (1904), 115–53.

Campbell, J. M. "Patristic Studies and the Literature of Medieval England," *Speculum,* VIII (1933), 465–78.

Chapman, C. O. "Numerical Symbolism in Dante and *The Pearl,*" *MLN,* LIV (1939), 256–59.

Conley, J. "*Pearl* and a Lost Tradition," *JEGP,* LIV (1955), 332–47.

Coulton, G. G. "In Defence of *Pearl,*" *MLR,* II (1906), 39–43.

Elliot, R. W. V. "*Pearl* and the Medieval Garden," *Les Langues Modernes,* XLV (1951), 85–98.

Emerson, O. F. "Imperfect Lines in *Pearl* and the Rimed Parts of *Sir Gawain and the Green Knight,*" *MP,* XIX (1921), 131–41.

———. "Some Notes on *The Pearl,*" *PMLA,* XXXVII (1922), 52–93.

———. "More Notes on *The Pearl,*" *PMLA,* LXII (1927), 807–31.

Everett, D. and Hurnand, N. "Legal Phraseology in a Passage in *Pearl,*" *Medium Aevum,* XVI (1947), 9–15.

Farnham, A. E. "The Principles of Allegory and Symbolism Illustrated by the Middle English Poem *Pearl,*" Doctoral Dissertation, Harvard University, 1964.

Fletcher, J. B. "The Allegory of *The Pearl,*" *JEGP,* XX (1921), 1–21.

Garrett, R. M. *The Pearl: an Interpretation,* Seattle: University of Washington Publications, Vol. LV, no. 1, 1918.

Gordon, E. V. and Onions, C. T. "Notes on the Interpretation of *Pearl*," *Medium Aevum* I (1932), 126–36, and II (1933), 165–88.

Greene, W. K. "*The Pearl*: a New Interpretation," *PMLA*, XL (1925), 814–27.

Hamilton, M. "Notes on *Pearl*," *JEGP*, LVII (1958), 177–91.

———. "The Meaning of Middle English *Pearl*," *PMLA*, LXX (1955), 805–24.

Hart, E. "The Heaven of Virgins," *MLN*, XLII (1947), 113–16.

Heiserman, A. R. "The Plot of *Pearl*," *PMLA*, LXXX (1965), 164–71.

Hoffman, S. de V. "*Pearl*: Notes for an Interpretation," *MP*, LVIII (1960), 73–80.

Johnson, W. S. "The Imagery and Diction of *The Pearl*: towards an Interpretation," *ELH*, XX (1953), 161–80.

Knightley, W. J. "*Pearl*: the 'hyg seysoun'," *MLN*, LXXVI (1961), 97–102.

———. "Symbolic Imagery in *Pearl*," Doctoral Dissertation, Princeton University, 1956. University Microfilms no. 20–124.

Luttrell, C. A. "The Medieval Tradition of the Pearl Virginity," *Medium Aevum*, XXXI (1962), 194–200.

Madeleva, Sister. *Pearl: a Study in Spiritual Dryness*. New York: Appleton, 1925.

Moorman, C. "The Role of the Narrator in *Pearl*," *MP*, LIII (1955), 73–81.

Northup C. S. "The Metrical Structure of *Pearl*," *PMLA*, XII (1897), 326–40.

Oiji, Takero, "The Middle English *Pearl* and its Theology," *Studies in English Literature*, English Literary Society of Japan, English Number, 1960, 39–57.

Richardson, F. E. "*The Pearl*: a Poem and its Audience," *Neophilologus*, XLVI (1962), 308–16.

Robertson, D. W. "The 'Heresy' of *The Pearl*," *MLN*, LXV (1950), 152–55.

———. "The Pearl as a Symbol," *MLN*, LXV (1950), 155–61.

Schofield, W. H. "Nature and Fabric of *The Pearl*," *PMLA*, XIX (1904), 154–215.

———. "Symbolism, Allegory and Autobiography in *The Pearl*," *PMLA*, XXIX (1909), 585–675.

Schroeder, Sister Margaret Ann. *Pearl: A Study of Style in the Light of Literary Traditions and the Poet's own Genius*. Doctoral Dissertation, University of Cincinnati. University Microfilms no. 60–3299.

Sledd, J. "Three Textual Notes on Fourteenth Century Poetry," *MLN*, LV (1940), 381.

Spearing, A. C. "Symbolic and Dramatic Development in *Pearl*," *MP*, LX (1962), 1–12.

Stern, M. R. "An Approach to *Pearl*," *JEGP*, LIV (1955), 684–92.

Wellek, R. *"The Pearl:* an Interpretation of the Middle English Poem," *Studies in English,* IV, Prague: Charles University, 1933.

Wright, E. M. "Notes on *Pearl,*" (erroneously entitled "Additional Notes on *Sir Gawain and the Green Knight*"), *JEGP,* XXXVIII (1939), 1–22.

————. "Additional Notes on *Pearl,*" *JEGP,* XXXIX (1940), 315–18.

Saint Erkenwald

EDITIONS

Saint Erkenwald, ed. I. Gollancz. London, 1922.

Saint Erkenwald, a Middle English Poem, ed. H. L. Savage. Yale Studies in English, LXXII, New Haven: Yale University Press, 1926.

CRITICAL STUDIES

Benson, L. D. "The Authorship of *St. Erkenwald,*" *JEGP,* LXIV (1965), 393–405.

Chambers, R. W. "Long Will, Dante and the Righteous Heathen," *Essays and Studies of the English Association,* IX, 1923.

Hibbard, L. "Erkenbald the Belgian," *MP,* XVI (1920), 669–78.

Hulbert, J. R. "Sources of *St. Erkenwald,*" *MP,* XVI (1919), 485–89.

Analogues and Background Works

Alliterative Poems: *Alexander and Dindemus,* EETS, E.S. #31.
 Death and Life, ed. I. Gollancz, London: 1930.
 Destruction of Troy, EETS, #56.
 Joseph of Arimathie, EETS, #44.
 Morte Arthur, EETS, #8.
 Parlement of the Three Ages, EETS, E.S. #246.
 Pistel of Susan, EETS, #117.
 Wars of Alexander, EETS, #47.
 William of Palerne, EETS, E.S. #1.

Andreas Capellanus. *The Art of Courtly Love,* tr. J. J. Parry. New York: Columbia University Press, 1941.

Atkins, J. H. W. *English Literary Criticism: the Medieval Phase.* New York: Peter Smith, 1952.

Augustine Aurelianus, St. *On Christian Doctrine,* tr. D. W. Robertson. New York: Liberal Arts Press, 1958.

Baldwin, C. *Medieval Rhetoric and Poetic.* New York: Macmillan, 1928.

Boethius, Manlius Severinus. *Consolations of Philosophy*, tr. R. Green. New York: Library of Liberal Arts, 1962.

Book of the Knight of the Tour Landry, EETS, #33.

Chaucer, Geoffrey. *Book of the Duchess* and *Legend of Good Women*, in *Works*, ed. F. N. Robinson. Boston: Houghton Mifflin, 1961.

Cursor Mundi, EETS, #57–59, 62, 66, 68, 99, 101.

Dante Alighieri. *Divine Comedy*, tr. D. Sayers, New York: Penguin Books, L 6, 46, 105.

English Medieval Lapidaries, EETS, #190.

Faral, E. *Les Arts Poétiques du XII et XIII Siècles*. Paris: 1958.

Mandevilles's Travels, EETS, #153, 154.

The Romance of the Rose, tr. H. W. Robbins. New York: Dutton, 1962.

Spearing, A. C. *Criticism and Medieval Poetry*. London: Everett Arnold, 1964.

Usk, Thomas, *Testament of Love*, in Supplement to *Complete Works of Chaucer*, ed. W. W. Skeat. Oxford: Clarendon Press, 1894.

FOOTNOTES

THE BOOK AND ITS MAKER

The Past in the Present

[1] *Four Quartets*, "Burnt Norton."
[2] "Tradition and the Individual Talent."

The Manuscript

[1] "Salamon and Saturn."
[2] *Philobiblon*, tr. E. C. Thomas (London, 1903), III, VII, XVII.
[3] "The Book Moth," Anglo-Saxon Riddle.
[4] See Appendix I.
[5] H. L. Savage, *The Gawain-Poet: Studies in his Personality and Background* (Chapel Hill: University of North Carolina Press, 1956), chap. I.

The Language

[1] See Appendix II.
[2] G. H. Gerould, "The Gawain-Poet and Dante: a Conjecture," *PMLA*, LI (1936), 31-36.

The Alliterative Movement

[1] See Appendix III.
[2] W. W. Greg, "Continuity of the Alliterative Tradition," *MLR*, XXVII (1932), 453-54, and J. R. Hulbert, "A Hypothesis Concerning the Alliterative Revival," *MP*, XXVIII (1931), 405-22.

[3] J. P. Oakden, *Alliterative Poetry in Middle English* (Manchester, 1931, 1935), 2 vols.

The Author

[1] H. N. McChracken, "Concerning Huchown," *PMLA*, XXV (1910), 507–34.

[2] C. F. Brown, "Note on the Question of Strode's Authorship of *The Pearl*," *PMLA*, XIX (1904), 146–48.

[3] C. O. Chapman, "The Authorship of *The Pearl*," *PMLA*, XLVII (1932), 346–53.

[4] O. Greenwood, in his introduction to his translation of *Sir Gawain and the Green Knight* (London: Lion and Unicorn Press, 1956).

[5] O. Cargill and M. Slauch, "The Pearl and its Jeweler," *PMLA*, XLIII (1928), 105–23.

[6] Savage, *op. cit.*, p. 49 ff.

[7] C. O. Chapman, "Musical Training of the Pearl-Poet," *PMLA*, XLVII (1931), 177–81.

[8] D. Everett and N. Hurnand, "Legal Phraseology in a Passage in *Pearl*," *Medium Aevum*, XVI (1947), 9–15.

[9] Savage, *op. cit.*, p. 23.

[10] For arguments against this assumption see articles by J. W. Clarke, e.g., "Observations on Certain Differences in Vocabulary between *Cleanness* and *Sir Gawain*," *Philological Quarterly*, XXVIII (1949), 261–73, L. D. Benson, "The Authorship of St. Erkenwald," *JEGP*, LXIV (1965), 373–405.

[11] E. M. Wright, "Sir Gawain and the Green Knight," *JEGP*, XXXIV (1935), p. 162.

[12] See Appendix II.

[13] See Appendix III.

[14] Savage, *op. cit.*, p. 24.

[15] D. R. Howard, "Chaucer the Man," *PMLA*, LXXX (1965), p. 343.

BACKGROUND OF THE POEMS

Critical Approach

[1] R. Baldwin, *The Unity of the Canterbury Tales* (Copenhagen, 1955), p. 11.

[2] R. O. Payne, *The Key of Remembrance* (New Haven: Yale University Press, 1963), p. 173.

[3] Quoted in C. Baldwin, *Medieval Rhetoric and Poetic* (New York: Macmillan, 1959), p. 175.

[4] *On Christian Doctrine*, tr. D. W. Robertson (New York: Liberal Arts Press, 1958), pp. 54, 18.

[5] *Ibid.*, p. 93.

[6] *Ibid.*, p. 3.

[7] *Ibid.*, p. 75.

[8] *Poetics*, XXII.

[9] Tr. W. H. Stahl (New York: Columbia University Press, 1952), p. 85.
[10] *Summa Theologica*, I, QI.a.9.
[11] *Didascalion*, II, 9.

The Homilies

[1] Preface to the *Catholic Homilies*.
[2] J. B. Zavadil, "A Study of Meaning in *Patience* and *Cleanness*," Doctoral Dissertation, Stanford University, 1962, p. 240. Ann Arbor: University Microfilms 62–2372.
[3] C. A. Moorman, "Role of the Narrator in *Patience*," *MP*, LXI (1963), 90–95.
[4] *Patience*, ed. I. Gollancz (London, 1924), p. 9.
[5] N. Berlin, "*Patience*, a Study in Poetic Elaboration," *Studia Neophilologica*, XXXIII (1961), p. 85.
[6] Moorman, *loc. cit.*, p. 95.
[7] E. Cuffe, "An Interpretation of *Patience, Cleanness* and *Pearl* from the Viewpoint of Imagery," Doctoral Dissertation, University of North Carolina, 1951.
[8] Moorman, *loc. cit.*, p. 95.
[9] EETS, 153, p. 66.
[10] *Ibid.*, p. 140.
[11] EETS, 33, p. 1. Subsequent quotations from *The Book of the Knight of the Tour Landry* are taken from the French version given in Gollancz, *Cleanness*, vol. II.
[12] O. F. Emerson, "Legends of Cain, Especially in Old and Middle English," *PMLA*, XXI (1906), 831–49.
[13] C. A. Luttrell, "Baiting of Bulls and Bears in the Midle English *Cleanness*," *Notes and Queries*, CXCVII (1952).
[14] Zavadil, *op. cit.*, chap. III.

Sir Gawain and the Green Knight

[1] F. Berry, "Sir Gawain and the Green Knight," *Age of Chaucer*, ed. B. Ford (New York: Penguin Books, 1954), p. 150.
[2] R. W. V. Elliot, "Landscape and Rhetoric in Middle English Poetry," *Melbourne Critical Review*, IV (1961), 65–76, and D. A. Pearsall, "Rhetorical Description in *Sir Gawain and the Green Knight*," *MLR*, L (1953), 129–34, and D. Mehl, "Point of View in Middle English Romances," *Neueren Sprachen*, XIV (1964), 35–46.
[3] A. Renoir, "Progressive Magnification: an Instance of Psychological Description," *Moderna Sprak*, LIV (1960), 245–53, and "Descriptive Techniques in *Gawain and the Green Knight*," *Orbis Litterarum*, XIII (1958), 126–32.
[4] L. Loomis, "Sir Gawain and the Green Knight," *Arthurian Literature in the Middle Ages*, ed. R. S. Loomis (Oxford University Press, 1959), p. 528.
[5] F. Berry, "The Sublime Ballet: an Essay on *Sir Gawain and the Green Knight*," *Wind and Rain*, V (1950), 165–74.
[6] M. H. Bloomfield, "*Sir Gawain and the Green Knight*: an Appraisal," *PMLA*, LXXVI (1961), p. 18.

[7] G. L. Kittredge, *A Study of Sir Gawain and the Green Knight* (Cambridge: Harvard University Press, 1916), p. 11.

[8] *Ibid.*, p. 43.

[9] *The High History of the Holy Grail*, ed. S. Evans (New York: Dutton, 1936), p. 105.

[10] Kittredge, *op. cit.*, p. 7.

[11] A. H. Krappe, "Who was the Green Knight?" *Speculum*, XIII (1938), p. 215.

[12] J. Speirs, "Sir Gawain and the Green Knight," *Scrutiny*, XXVI (1949), p. 282.

[13] J. R. L. Highfield, "The Green Squire," *Medium Aevum*, XXII (1953), 18-23.

[14] H. Braddy, "Sir Gawain and Ralph Holmes," *MLN*, LXVII (1952), 240-42.

[15] S. D'Ardenne, "The Green Count and *Sir Gawain and the Green Knight*," *RES*, N.S. X (1959), 113-26.

[16] D. E. Baughan, "The Role of Morgan le Fee in *Sir Gawain and the Green Knight*," *ELH*, XVII (1950), 241-51, and A. B. Friedman, "Morgan la Fee in *Sir Gawain and the Green Knight*," *Speculum*, XXXV (1960), 26-74.

[17] A. Carson, "Morgan la Fee as the Principle of Unity in *Gawain and the Green Knight*," *MLQ*, XXIII (1962), 3-16.

[18] Malory, *Morte Dartur*, IX, 1.

[19] *Chronicle of the Kings of England*, ed. J. A. Giles (London, 1847), p. 315.

[20] Geoffrey of Monmouth, *History of the Kings of Britain*, X, 10.

[21] B. J. Whiting, "Gawain: his Reputation, his Courtesy, his Appearance in Chaucer's Squire's Tale," *Medieval Studies*, IX (1947), 189-234.

[22] *Morte Dartur*, XIII, 7.

[23] R. H. Bowers, "*Gawain and the Green Knight* as Entertainment," *MLQ*, XXIV (1963), 333-41, and R. G. Cook, "The Play Element in *Sir Gawain and the Green Knight*," Tulane Studies in English, XIII (New Orleans, 1963).

[24] Andreas Capellanus, *The Art of Courtly Love*, tr. J. J. Parry, (New York: Columbia University Press, 1941), p. 86.

[25] J. F. Kiteley, "The *De Arte Honesti Amandi* of Andreas Capellanus and the Concept of Courtesy in *Sir Gawain and the Green Knight*," *Anglia*, LXXIX (1961), 7-16.

[26] Andreas Capellanus, *op. cit.*, p. 187.

[27] A. M. Markman, "The Meaning of *Sir Gawain and the Green Knight*," *PMLA*, LXXII (1957), p. 575.

[28] D. F. Hills, "Gawain's Fault in *Gawain and the Green Knight*," *RES*, N.S. XIV (1963), 124-31.

[29] D. E. Baughan, "The Role of Morgan le Fee in *Sir Gawain and the Green Knight*," *ELH*, XVII (1950), 241-51, and J. F. Eagan, "The Import of the Color Symbolism in *Sir Gawain and the Green Knight*," St. Louis University Studies, Series A, Vol. I, 1949.

[30] H. Schnyder, "Aspects of Kingship in *Sir Gawain and the Green Knight*," *English Studies*, XL (1959), 289-94.

[31] J. Saperstein, "Some Observations on *Sir Gawain and the Green Knight*," *English Studies in Africa*, V (1962), 29-36.

[32] M. W. Bloomfield, "*Sir Gawain and the Green Knight*: an Appraisal," LXXVI (1961), p. 19.

[33] F. Berry, *The Age of Chaucer*, p. 155.

[34] W. A. Nitze, "Is the Green Knight Story a Vegetation Myth?" *MP*, XXXIII (1936), 351–66.

[35] H. Zimmer, "Sir Gawain and the Green Knight," *The King and the Corpse* (New York: Pantheon Books, 1948).

[36] W. Goldhurst, "The Green and the Gold: the Major Theme of *Sir Gawain and the Green Knight*," *College English*, XX (1958), 61–65.

[37] J. Speirs, "Sir Gawain and the Green Knight," *Scrutiny*, XXVI (1949), p. 279.

[38] Derry, *op. cit.*, p. 158.

[39] A. Coomeraswamy, "Sir Gawain and the Green Knight: Indra and Namuci," *Speculum*, XIX (1944), 104–25.

[40] J. Weston, from *Ritual to Romance*, (Garden City: Doubleday, 1957), p. 176.

[41] C. Moorman, "Myth and Medieval Literature: *Sir Gawain and the Green Knight*," *Medieval Studies*, XVIII (1956), 158–72.

[42] F. Berry, "The Sublime Ballet," *Wind and Rain* (Winter, 1949–50), p. 174.

[43] J. F. Eagan, "The Import of Color Symbolism in *Sir Gawain and the Green Knight*," St. Louis University Studies, Series A, I (1949), 12–86.

[44] H. L. Savage: See Chapter II for this allegorical interpretation.

[45] H. Schnyder, *Sir Gawain and the Green Knight: an Essay in Interpretation* (Cooper Monographs, 6, Bern, 1961), p. 15.

[46] H. Schnyder, *op. cit.*, p. 74.

Pearl

[1] All quotations from the *Divine Comedy* are taken from Dorothy Sayers' translation, Penguin Books, L 6, 46, 105.

[2] M. Medary and A. C. L. Brown, "Stanza Linking in Middle English Verse," *Romanic Review*, VII (1916), pp. 243, 271.

[3] C. L. Wrenn, "On Rereading Spenser's *Shephearde's Calendar*," *English Studies*, XXIX (1949).

[4] J. M. Campbell, "Patristic Studies and the Literature of Medieval England," *Speculum*, VIII (1933), 465–78.

[5] Quoted in W. J. Knightley, "*Pearl:* the 'hyg sesoun,'" *MLN*, LXXVI (1961), 97–102.

[6] C. Brown, "The Author of the *Pearl* Considered in the Light of his Theological Opinions," *PMLA*, XIX (1904), 115–53.

[7] See articles in the bibliography by J. B. Fletcher, R. Wellek, D. W. Robertson, J. Sledd, M. Hamilton, Sister Mary Vincent Hillman, and Takero Oiji.

[8] Sermo LXXXVII.

[9] Quoted in Sister Madeleva, *Pearl, a Study in Spiritual Dryness* (New York: Appleton, 1925), p. 199.

[10] From the translation given by I. Gollancz in his edition of *Pearl* (London, 1921).

[11] *Nicene and Post-Nicene Fathers*, Second Series, Vol. XIII (New York, 1898), p. 293.

[12] C. A. Luttrell, "The Medieval Tradition of the Pearl Virginity," *Medium Aevum*, XXXI (1962), 194–200.

[13] *Early English Alliterative Poems*, ed. R. Morris, EETS 1, p. IX.

[14] B. Ten Brink, *History of English Literature* (New York, 1889), p. 348.

[15] I. Gollancz, *loc. cit.*, p. xiii.

[16] *Pearl*, ed. C. G. Osgood (Boston: Heath, 1906).

[17] B. Ten Brink, *op. cit.*

[18] H. Schofield, "Nature and Fabric of *The Pearl*," *PMLA*, XIX (1904), 154–215 and "Symbolism, Allegory and Autobiography in *The Pearl*," *PMLA*, XXIV (1904), 585–675.

[19] R. M. Garrett, *The Pearl: an Interpretation*, University of Washington Publications, vol. LV, no. 1 (Seattle, 1918).

[20] J. B. Fletcher, "The Allegory of *The Pearl*," *JEGP*, XX (1921), 1–21.

[21] Sister Madeleva, *op. cit.*, pp. 90, 132.

[22] W. K. Greene, "*The Pearl*: a New Interpretation," *PMLA*, XL (1925), p. 826.

[23] R. Wellek, "*The Pearl*, an Interpretation of the Middle English Poem," Charles University, Studies in English IV (Prague, 1933).

[24] *The Pearl*, ed. and tr. Sister Mary Virginia Hillman (Convent Station, N.J.: College of St. Elizabeth Press, 1961).

[25] M. Hamilton, "The Meaning of the Middle English *Pearl*," *PMLA*, LXX (1955), pp. 810, 823.

[26] W. S. Johnson, "The Image and Diction of *The Pearl*: towards an Interpretation," *ELH*, XX (1953), 161–80.

[27] S. de V. Hoffman, "*Pearl*: Notes for an Interpretation," *MP*, LVIII (1960), 73–80.

[28] E. Cuffe, *op. cit.*

[29] F. E. Richardson, "*The Pearl*: a Poem and its Audience," *Neophilologus*, XLVI (1962), 308–16.

[30] A. C. Spearing, "Symbolic and Dramatic Development in *Pearl*," *MP*, LX (1962), 1–12.

[31] C. Moorman, "The Role of the Narrator in *Pearl*," *MP*, LIII (1955), 73–81.

[32] A. R. Heiserman, "The Plot of *Pearl*," *PMLA*, LXXX (1965), 164–71.

[33] A. Farnham, "*Pearl* in the Light of its Allegorical Significance," Doctoral Dissertation, Harvard University, 1963.

Saint Erkenwald

[1] Quoted in *Saint Erkenwald, a Middle English Poem*, ed. H. L. Savage, Yale Studies in English, LXXII (New Haven: Yale University Press, 1926), p. lxxvi.

[2] *Ibid.*, p. xxi.

[3] See I Pet. III, 18–20, Phil. II: 10, Col. II: 15.

Synthesis

[1] *Philebus*, 51.

[2] *Phaedrus*, 249.

[3] *Poetics*, VII, 4.

[4] *Enneads*, I, 6.

[5] *Divine Names*, IV.

[6] *Confessions*, X, 38.

[7] E. Chapman, *Saint Augustine's Philosophy of Beauty* (New York: Sheed and Ward, 1939), p. 54.

[8] *Soliloquies*, I.

[9] *Summa Theologica*, I, 39, 8.

[10] *Commentarium in Libro de Divinis Nominibus*, lect. 6.

[11] See Scotus Erigena, *De Divisione Naturae*.

[12] "Poetry and Drama."

[13] Ephrem the Syrian, *op. cit.*, p. 295.

[14] *Par.* III, 85.

[15] *Vitis Mystica*, III.

[16] *Summa Theologica*, I–II, 27, 3.

THE FOURTEENTH CENTURY

Year	CHURCH HISTORY	ENGLISH HISTORY	CULTURAL HISTORY
1300	Boniface VIII / The Great Jubilee	Edward I	Ramon Lull
1	Bull *Unam Sanctam*		
2	Anangi outrage		
3			
4			
1305	Clement V	Robert Bruce in Scotland	Duns Scotus
6			
7		Edward II acceded	*Book of Vices and Virtues* / *Handling of Sin*
8			
9	Papacy at Avignon		*Cursor Mundi*
1310			
11	15th Ecumenical Council	The New Ordinances	
12			
13			
14	Templars suppressed	Battle of Bannockburn	
1315			
16	John XXII		*The Divine Comedy*
17			
18		Duke of Lancaster in power	Richard Rolle: lyrics, treatises
19			
1320			d. Dante
21			
22		Hugh Despenser in power	Minot, *Political Songs*
23			
24			
1325		Edward II impeached, Edward III acceded	
26			
27	Mission to China		
28			
29			
1330		d. Earl of Mortimer	
31			
32			
33		Battle of Halidon Hill	*Ayenbite of Inwit*
34	Benedict XII		*Gesta Romanorum*
1335			
36			
37			
38			
39	Papal palace at Avignon	c. Introduction of firearms	c. birth of Chaucer, Langland, Pearl-Poet
1340			
41			
42	Clement VI		Petrarch: Poet-Laureate
43	Bull *Unigenitus*		
44		War with France	
1345	Crusade against Turks		
46	Bull defending Jews	Battle of Crecy; Black Prince	Mystic Writers: Suso, Tauler, Eckhardt, Rhysbroek
47		The Black Death	
48			
49	Flagellants condemned		Boccaccio: *De Cameron*
1350			
51		Statute of Laborers	

Vertical band labels (Church History): Inquisition at height · Babylonian Captivity · Abuses in religious orders · Religious revival in Netherlands · Waldensian Crusade

Vertical band labels (English History): Wars of Scottish Independence · Decline of wool industry · Parliament vs. taxation · Manorial system at height · Struggles of magnates vs. Crown · Start of the Hundred Years' War

Vertical band labels (Cultural History): Thomism · Religious lyrics, satires · Use of paper introduced · Sermon and story collections · High Gothic period · Dawn of Italian Renaissance · New thought in the universities · French courtly verse

(Continued)

THE FOURTEENTH CENTURY (Continued)

	CHURCH HISTORY		ENGLISH HISTORY		CULTURAL HISTORY	
52	Innocent V					
53			Statute of		William of	
54	Franciscans		Praemunire		Occham	
1355	divided					
56			Battle of Poitiers		Penitential	
57					manuals	
58	Brothers of					
59	Common Life					
1360			Treaties of		Richard de Bury,	
61			Bretigny, Calais		*Philobiblon*	
62	Urban V					
63					c. Alliterative sat-	
64					ires, romances,	
1365					chronicles	
1366					Chaucer: alle-	
67	Brief return of				gories, lyrics	
68	Pope to Rome				c. *Patience*	
69						
1370	Gregory XI				Wycliffe's Bible	
71					*Mandeville's*	
					Travels	
72	St. Catherine of				*Bk. of Knight of*	
	Siena				*Tour Landry*	
73					c. *Cleanness*	
74					John of Trevisa	
1375					*Piers Plowman*, B	
76			d. Black Prince			
77	Return to Rome		Richard II		c. *Sir Gawain and*	
78	Urban VI		John of Gaunt in		*the Green Knight*	
79	Anti-Pope:		power			
1380	Clement VII				MysticWriters:	
81	Wycliffe		Peasants' Revolt,		Hilton, Dame	
	condemned		Wat Tyler		Juliana	
82					c. *Pearl*	
83					*Cloud of*	
84					*Unknowing*	
1385					*Troilus and*	
					Criseyde	
86	Lithuania				St. *Erkenwald*	
87	converted		Lords Apellant			
88			Merciless		Chaucer:	
89	Boniface IX		Parliament		*Legend of Good*	
1390			Quarrels with		*Women*	
91			barons		*Canterbury Tales*	
92						
93						
94	Anti-Pope:					
1395	Benedict XIII					
96						
97			Richard's revenge			
98						
99	Papal states re-		Henry IV acceded		d. Chaucer	
1400	organized				Langland?	
					Pearl-Poet?	
					MS Cotton Nero	
					A.X.	

Vertical spanning labels (Church History section): Abuses of indulgences · Great Western Schism · Missions to the Far East · Conciliar Theory

Vertical spanning labels (English History section): Rapid economic and social changes · Lollardy · Anti-Semitism · Rise of Banking

Vertical spanning labels (Cultural History / far right): Alliterative Movement · Art center in Florence: Giotto, Fra Angelico · Beginning of Humanism · Flemish art: Van Eycks

PATIENCE

DIVISIONS	SERMON STRUCTURE	ACTION	THEMES, IMAGERY	BIBLICAL (SOURCES)	OTHER (SOURCES)
Part I 1	Protheme: Excellence and need of patience				
9	Dilatio: Text, the Beatitudes, emphasis on eighth	Personification of Beatitudes		Matt. V: 3–12	
29	Application, life in poverty and patience				
57	Address to listeners, presentation of story				
Part II 61		God's command		Jon. I:1–2	
75		Jonah's angry resistance (original)			
97		Flight to Tarshish		Jon. I:3	
		Embarcation (original)			
120	Homiletic exhortation: God sees all			Ps. 94	
129		The storm (amplified)		Jon. I:4	
159		The sailors lighten ship, call on their gods, wake Jonah, and cast lots. He pleads guilty, is thrown overboard. The men are saved and offer sacrifice		Jon. I:5–14	
Part III		Jonah swallowed by the whale		Jon. II:1 / Isa. V:14	
245		His experiences inside the whale (original)		Matt. XVI:4	
270					
282		His first prayer (original)		Matt. XXI:40	
289	Homiletic reflections: God is merciful				
296		The whale's discomfort (original)			
Part IV 305		Jonah's prayer		Jon. II:2–10	
336		God bids the fish cast up Jonah		Jon. II:11	
345		Conversation with God (original)			
		Jonah has learned first lesson			
351		He preaches through Nineveh; the king and people do penance		Jon. III:1–9	
405		God pardons Nineveh		Jon. III:10	
Part V 410		Jonah protests and asks to die (amplified)		Jon. IV:1–3	
430		God rebukes Jonah		" " 4	
436		Jonah builds a bower; God raises the woodbine		" " 5–6	
445		Jonah rejoices (original)			
466		A worm destroys the vine and the heat beats down		" " 7–8	
481		Jonah protests and God answers (amplified)		" " 9–10	
501		God will spare the foolish and the innocent		" " 11	
520	Peroration: Homiletic exhortation. Return to theme—excellence of patience. Last line echoes first				

Vertical labels spanning the ACTION column: **The Exemplum**; **First lesson**; **Second lesson**

THEMES, IMAGERY (vertical text): A foolish man flees from trouble; a wise man accepts it as God's will in obedience to the divine order. "The fear of the Lord is the beginning of wisdom." The Divine Hunter pursues the human soul; imagery of "tricks and traps," obedient elements. Personifications.

OTHER SOURCES (vertical text): Biographical? / Piers Plowman / Tertullian: De Jona et Nineve / Aeneid / Anglo-Saxon sea traditions / Anglo-Saxon "Wyrd" / Popular legends / Warlow, Raguel / Liturgy of Passion Week / Book of Vices and Virtues / Biblical paraphrases, sermon manuals / Exegetical commentaries / Manuals of penance

CLEANNESS

DIVISIONS	SERMON STRUCTURE	ACTION	THEMES, IMAGERY	BIBLICAL	SOURCES OTHER
Part I				Wisd. X: 1–19	
1	Protheme: Excellence and need of cleanness	Worthy priests at mass		II Pet. II: 3–13	
25	Dilatio: Text—sixth Beatitude			Rev. I, II	
29	Applications:	Rude man at a banquet (original)		Matt. V:8 / Matt. XX, 16–20	
48		Parable of the wedding feast (amplified)		Luke XIV: 7–14	
Part II					
161	Homiletic commentary: Beauty of good deeds, harm of bad deeds				
176					
Part III	Address to listeners:				
193	Punishment of impurity				
205	Minor exempla: 1	Fall of Lucifer and rebel angels		Isa. XIV: 12–16	
235	Lighter punishment 2	Fall of Adam		Gen. II	
Part IV		God wills to punish the corruption on earth; He commands Noah to build the ark		Gen. VI: 1–13	
249					
Part V	Major exemplum 1 — Noah's flood	Noah and his family enter the ark		Gen. VII: 1–11	
345					
363		The flood comes (amplified)			
435		The waters subside			Legends of Cain / Cursor Mundi / Legends of the raven
453		Noah sends out the raven and the dove (amplified)			
Part VI		The olive branch; the ark lands, Noah sacrifices; God blesses him; the animals go out (amplified)		Gen. VIII:1 / Gen. IX:1	
485					
529					
541				Ps. 94	
Part VII	Homiletic warnings: Be pure as a pearl			Rev. II:23	
556	God hates impurity				
Part VIII					
601	Minor exemplum 3	Abraham entertains God in the guise of angels; Sarah doubts His word; God shows His purpose to Abraham		Gen. XVIII: 1–22	
Part IX					
689					
696	Homiletic exhortation:	God speaks of the joys of married love (original)			
713		Abraham's prayer			
Part X					
781		Lot entertains angels		Gen. XIX: 1–27	
Part XI	Major exemplum 2 — Sodom and Gomorrah	The men of Sodom riot; angels lead Lot's family to Segor			Cursor Mundi / Mandeville's Travels, XIII
892		His disobedient wife becomes a pillar of salt, while the cities are destroyed (amplified)			
947					
1004		The Dead Sea (original insertion)			

THEMES, IMAGERY (column, running vertically):
Chivalric courtesy / Clean clothing: virtues / All sin is uncleanness / Fleshly uncleanness is a social sin; it calls for instant vengeance / Pleasant and unpleasant sense images contrasted throughout / Natural law is right order; disobedience brings disorder / Courtesy and cleanness are linked; Pearl as a symbol of purity / Value of penance / Violation of the soul is sacrilege

SOURCES OTHER (column, running vertically):
Sermon manuals / Apocryphal tales / Biblical paraphrase tradition / Knight of the Tour Landry, XVII / Legends of Cain / Cursor Mundi / Legends of the raven / Exegetical commentaries on Genesis / Tertullian: De Sodomo / Manuals of penance / Legends of the Jews / Romance of the Rose / Cursor Mundi / Mandeville's Travels, XIII

(Continued)

CLEANNESS (Continued)

Divisions	Sermon Structure	Action	Themes, Imagery	Biblical (Sources)	Other (Sources)
1049	Homiletic reflections: Be clean, please / Christ who is a pearl / Purity of Mary and of Christ / Cleanness of the pearl				Pearl lore / "Five Joys of Mary" / Townley Play / Tour Landry
1133	Warning against relapse; doctrine of penance			I Cor. III:17	
1149	Address to listeners				
Part XII					
1157	Minor exempla 5	Faithlessness of the Jews / Treachery of Zedechiah		II Chron. XXXVI:11–20	Book of vices and Virtues / Mandeville's Travels, XXIV / Patristic exegesis: Babylon
	6	Nebuchadnezzar's conquest		Jer. III:4–14	
1311		The sacred vessels are taken to Babylon / Belshazzar reigns and commits idolatry (original)		Jer. LII:17–19	Anglo-Saxon "Waissa!"
Part XIII			Sacrilege: worst uncleanness		
1357		Belshazzar plans a banquet in his magnificent palace (original)			
1392		Belshazzar's feast (amplified)		Dan. V:1–4	
1425		He profanes the sacred vessels	Evil feast is parallel to marriage feast		
1489	Homiletic comments: Evil of sacrilege:				
1528	Belshazzar's feast exemplum 3	The handwriting on the wall		Dan. V:5–20	
1588		The King sends for soothsayers / At the Queen's request / Daniel interprets the message			
1541	Minor exemplum 7	He tells the story of the repentance of Nebuchadnezzar	Pride, the worst sin, is at the root of uncleanness	Dan. IV:27–33	
1725	Major exemplum	Daniel reads the three words		Dan. V:22–28	
1741		Daniel is rewarded and the feast continues		Dan. V:29	Penitential disciplines
1753		The guests go home at nightfall and the weather darkens (original) / The Persians attack (amplified) / Belshazzar is beaten to death		Dan. V:30	Pictures of medieval life
1753		Darius reigns		Dan. V:31	
1797	Homiletic comment: The king cursed for uncleanness				
1805	Peroration: Return to theme / Prayer for the grace of cleanness; promise of heaven				

SIR GAWAIN AND THE GREEN KNIGHT

SOURCES, ANALOGUES

Troy Books
Brut
Arthuriad

Eastern vegetation myths
Celtic mythology
North-European folklore

Alliterative tradition

Bricriu's Feast
The Mabinogion

Lays and interludes
Green Knights of 14th century
Gawain ballads

THEMES, IMAGERY

Chivalric ideal of knightly perfection *vs.* amour courtois

"Rite de passage"
Testing the court, axe
Christmas revels,
Green: magic color

Eastern lore
Endless knot
Five joys of Mary

ACTION

Fall of Troy; foundation of Rome and New Troy; Arthuriad

Revelry of the Round Table; the banquet; Arthur's custom

A Green Knight challenges the king and the court

Gawain accepts the challenge and makes a pact

He beheads the Knight who departs

Interlude: the seasonal cycle

The farewell banquet

Gawain's arming

His shield and Pentangle; he rides away

The first journey: hard, cold, beset by foes

He prays and approaches a castle

He is welcomed by a Knight, his wife, and an Old Lady and is lavishly entertained

STORY STRUCTURE

Characters:
Arthur and the
    Round Table
Gwenevere
Antagonist/Hero:
    Gawain

First blow

Gryngolet

Departure

The Lady
The hag
Courtiers
Retainers

Beheading game accepted

Historic frame — Rising action

SETTING PLACE TIME

| long ago | Christmastide New Year's Day | A year passes November |
| Troy Rome Britain | Camelot | North-west country |

DIVISIONS

Part One I 1–3   4–6   15–18   19–21 Part Two II 22–23   24   25–26 III 27–28   29   30–32   33–34 IV 35–42

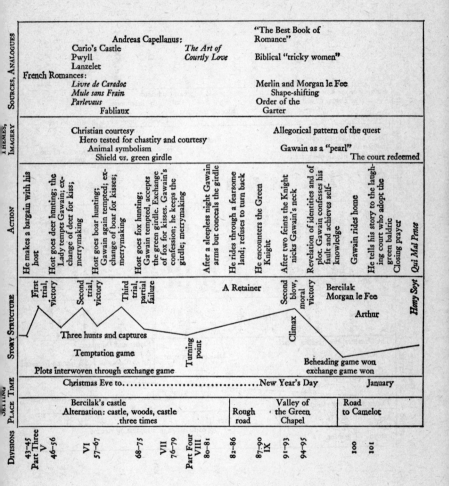

SOURCES, ANALOGUES

Andreas Capellanus: *The Art of Courtly Love*

"The Best Book of Romance"

Curio's Castle
Pwyll
Lanzelet

Biblical "tricky women"

French Romances:
Livre de Caradoc
Mule sans Frain
Parlevaus
Fabliaux

Merlin and Morgan le Fee
Shape-shifting
Order of the Garter

THEMES, IMAGERY

Christian courtesy
Hero tested for chastity and courtesy
Animal symbolism
Shield *vs.* green girdle

Allegorical pattern of the quest
Gawain as a "pearl"
The court redeemed

ACTION

- He makes a bargain with his host
- Host goes deer hunting; the Lady tempts Gawain; exchange of deer for kiss; merrymaking
- Host goes boar hunting; Gawain again tempted; exchange of boar for kisses; merrymaking
- Host goes fox hunting; Gawain tempted, accepts the green girdle. Exchange of fox for kisses. Gawain's confession; he keeps the girdle; merrymaking
- After a sleepless night Gawain arms but conceals the girdle
- He rides through a fearsome land; refuses to turn back
- He encounters the Green Knight
- After two feints the Knight nicks Gawain's neck
- Revelation of identities and of plot. Gawain confesses his fault and achieves self-knowledge
- Gawain rides home
- He tells his story to the laughing court who adopt the green baldric
- Closing prayer
- *Qui Mal Pense*

STORY STRUCTURE

First trial, victory
Second trial, victory
Third trial, partial failure
A Retainer
Second blow, moral victory
Climax
Bercilak Morgan le Fee
Arthur
Three hunts and captures
Temptation game
Turning point
Plots interwoven through exchange game
Beheading game won exchange game won
Honi Soyt

SETTING, PLACE TIME

Christmas Eve to.................................New Year's Day   January

Bercilak's castle
Alternation: castle, woods, castle three times

Rough road

Valley of the Green Chapel

Road to Camelot

DIVISIONS

43–45 Part Three V
46–56
VI 57–67
68–75
VII 76–79
Part Four VIII 80–81
82–86 IX
87–90
91–93
94–95
100
101

PEARL

Pentads	Setting	Dramatic Structure	Key Words	Action	Symbols	Themes	Other Sources	Biblical Sources
I	Act I — Earth garden	The Dreamer, the Maiden, Pearl; August feast-day; The problem, the vision	spot	A jeweler grieves for his lost pearl in a garden where he falls asleep.	flowers, spices, seed	Death and loss; struggle of the human will	Romance of the Rose	1 Cor. XV:36-38; John XII:24
II	Act II — Dream garden		adorn	His soul springs into a gleaming land where he forgets his grief.	jewels, music, Fortune	Harvest: life through death	The Divine Comedy; Olympia?	Rev. XXII:1-2
III			more and more	Trying to cross a stream through pleasure-gardens, he sees a Maiden whom he knows.	running water			Rev. XIX:1
IV	Act III — Opposite banks of a separating stream		set in pearls	She welcomes him, and he pours out his troubles.	pearls			Ps. XX:4
V			jeweler	First question: why must he suffer loss?	Wyrd			Ps. XIX
VI			judge	Accept; go by Another's way.	coffer, rose	Free grace through Christ's redemption	Elegiac tradition	John XX:1
VII		Dialogue between: Father and Daughter / A jeweler and his pearl / An earth-bound and a heaven-free soul / A Christian and grace	ground of bliss	The Dreamer yields, and is shown her status in the heavenly court.		Divine courtly love	Pearl traditions; Cult of the marguerite	Ps. L:6; Ps. XXII:14
VIII			courtesy	Second question: how can she be a Queen in heaven, so young?	Phoenix		Patristic theology, scholastic debate	I Cor. IX:24-25; XII:12-27
IX		Rising action: thought and desire are elevated	end	God is right and wise in free choices,	Mystical Body			Matt. XX:1-16
X			still more	as shown in the parable of the workers in the vineyard.	penny	Salvation of the innocent		Ps. LXII:1-12; Rom. VII:29-30
XI			great enough	Third question: how can heavenly rewards be equal?				Rev. XX, XXI; John XIX:3-; I Cor. XV:2

Pentads	Setting	Dramatic Structure	Key Words	Action	Symbols	Themes	Other	Sources Biblical
XII	into experience and solution		right, innocent	God's gifts are free; the innocent like the just are rightly saved.	gushing water	Relation of heaven to earth / Consecrated virginity	Mariology	Ps. XV, XXIV, CXLIII; Wisd. X:9-10; Gen. XXVIII:13-15
XIII			spotless pearl	The pearl on her breast is the kingdom of heaven; he should buy it.	pearl of price			Luke XVIII:1;5,7 etc.; Matt. XIII:45-46; Cant. IV:7-8
XIV			Jerusalem	The Dreamer yields. The Maiden is the Bride of the Lamb who died for man in the Old Jerusalem, and is adored in the New.				Rev. VII, XIV, XIX; Luke XXII:64; Isa. LIII, John I
XV			no less	The Dreamer now yields fully, and asks to see her home.				Rev. I, XIV, XIX, XXI; I Pet. 1:19; Heb. X:10-14; I Cor. XXIII:11-12; Heb. XII:20; Ezek. XIII:16
XVI	turning point	The Lamb saves all men	spot	He may glimpse heaven.			Four-level biblical exegesis, allegory	
XVII	Act IV New Jerusalem		John	He follows the stream; he sees the heavenly city, the stream of life.	twelve jewels			Rev. XXII; Exod. XXIII
XVIII			sun and moon	The procession of virgins and the glories of the blessed.	fruits	Man's end: obedience to the divine order		Ezek. XLVIII
XIX			great delight	The Lamb and His wounded Heart. Joy enraptures him.	light			
XX	Act V Earth garden	climax	please, Prince	He tries to cross the stream unbidden, wakes on earth, accepts God's loving will and prays for us all.	Prince / Host at mass	Peace in His will		Rev. V, XVI, XXI, XII; Matt. XIX, XXVI; John X:10

ABOUT THE TRANSLATOR

MARGARET WILLIAMS, R.S.C.J., is Professor Emeritus of English Literature at Manhattanville College in Purchase, New York, and is presently teaching at the University of the Sacred Heart in Tokyo, Japan. She received her M.A. from Oxford University and is the translator of *Word-Hoard* and *Glee-Wood* as well as the author of several biographies and a number of critical articles. Sister Williams is at work on a translation of the classic, *Piers Plowman*, which Random House will publish next year.